Accountable Systems of Behavioral Health Care

Accountable Systems of Behavioral Health Care

A Provider's Guide

Howard A. Savin
Susan Soldivera Kiesling
Foreword by Ronald P. Burd

Published in
Partnership with

Devereux

JOSSEY-BASS
A Wiley Company
San Francisco

Jossey-Bass books and products are available through most bookstores. To contact Jossey-Bass directly, call (888) 378-2537, fax to (800) 605-2665, or visit our website at www.josseybass.com.

Substantial discounts on bulk quantities of Jossey-Bass books are available to corporations, professional associations, and other organizations. For details and discount information, contact the special sales department at Jossey-Bass.

 Printed in the United States of America on acid-free, recycled stock that meets or exceeds the minimum GPO and EPA requirements for recycled paper.

Library of Congress Cataloging-in-Publication Data

Savin, Howard A., 1946-
    Accountable systems of behavioral health care : a provider's guide /
Howard A. Savin, Susan Soldivera Kiesling.
        p. cm.
    Includes bibliographical references and index.
    ISBN 0-7879-5005-X (alk. paper)
    1. Mental health services—Standards—United States. 2.. Mental health
    services—United States—Quality control. 3. Psychotherapy—Outcomes
    assessment. 4. Managed mental health care—United States. I. Kiesling,
    Susan Soldivera, 1966- II. Title.
    RA790.6 .S38 2000
    362.2'02'1873—dc21   00-008479

FIRST EDITION
PB Printing   10 9 8 7 6 5 4 3 2 1

Contents

Foreword

TWENTY-FIVE YEARS ago, I was helping then psychiatrist-in-chief of Boston's Children's Hospital and future surgeon general of the United States, Dr. Julius B. Richmond, prepare for a presentation on the future of health care in the United States. As I plotted the trend of the growth of health care expenditures as a percentage of the gross domestic product (GDP), I noted its current level at 8.3 percent. Dr. Richmond commented that once the line crossed the 10 percent barrier, we could expect a dramatic change in this country's health care industry. He correctly surmised that when one out of every ten dollars is spent on health care, corporate America would feel the pinch in health benefits that it pays for its workforce, and the federal government would bridle at the level of Medicaid and Medicare expenditures.

When that event occurred in 1982, the stage was set for the emergence and ultimate prevalence of managed care. Prospective payment schemes such as diagnosis-related groups were introduced and became the harbinger of the more formalized managed care solutions that we know today. During a good portion of the decade of the 1980s, the behavioral health care industry was able to stay out from under the glare of the public and the payers. While acute care hospitals and medical and surgical practitioners had to adapt to this strange new world, mental health providers were able to operate without the same scrutiny and to garner funds without much regulation, often dwelling in some very untidy houses.

As we fast-forward to the dawning of our new millennium, the landscape has changed for all of us in the health care arena, including those of us in behavioral health care. You may be compelled to read this book as a survival guide for navigating a behavioral health care organization in the managed care waters of the twenty-first century. But the CEO, the executive director, the clinical or medical director, or the program administrator of any behavioral health care organization today, large or small, cannot simply be content with survival. We are constantly in search of approaches, methodologies, and structures that can provide excitement, vision, and purpose to the wide array of people we depend on to make our organizations successful.

The authors assert that this book can demonstrate how healthy organizations flourish by building on the strengths of well-designed systems of quality and accountability. And in reality, Dr. Howard Savin and his dedicated team have successfully applied this comprehensive approach here at Devereux. They have demonstrated to the clinician and the administrator alike the importance of establishing quality standards and of using quantitative approaches to measure outcomes. Those responsible for paying for these measured services and the recipients of empirically effective interventions likewise have reaped the rewards of a quantifiable quality experience.

Ultimately, this book does more than extol the virtues of measurement and accountability in behavioral health care practice today. Its natural conclusion and ultimate challenge is for practitioners and managers to move from outcomes measurement to outcomes management that will permeate the entire organization. It calls on those of us in leadership roles to reassess how we organize and integrate all aspects of our administrative and delivery systems based on data and results.

This book is not just about having a house with well-ordered rooms, standards of care, practice guidelines, data gathering and utilization, professionalism of frontline staff, and so on. It compels us to build a foundation that will enable this house to stand proudly and securely on less certain and constantly shifting terrain.

Villanova University
August 2000

Ronald P. Burd
President and CEO
Devereux Foundation

Acknowledgments

AS WE REFLECT on the scope and complexity of our book project, we find that one of the most difficult tasks is now at hand: properly recognizing the many individuals whose assistance made it all happen. We were ably supported by a network of professionals from within the Devereux Foundation and across the behavioral health care field.

The work on which this book is based would never have occurred without the vision and continuous support of Devereux's board of trustees. Particular thanks and recognition is owed to Ron Burd, Devereux's CEO and president, for his vision and unswerving commitment to mission. Similarly, we are very appreciative and grateful to Jean Beard—parent, clinician, trustee, and chair of Devereux's clinical and professional committee for her consistent support and uncompromising approach to quality in behavioral health care programming.

We would like to express special gratitude to Paul LeBuffe, assistant director of Devereux's Institute of Clinical Training and Research (ICTR). Paul assisted us as a reviewer and sounding board from the outset of the project, served as a contributing coauthor (Chapter Seven), and directed ICTR's professional psychology trainees (PPTs) in conducting our provider survey and gathering vital reference data. With specific regard to ICTR's outstanding 1998–1999 class of PPTs, consisting of Amit Bernstein, Shelly Steele, Julie Alvarez, and Cleo Jacobs, we extend our warmest thanks, along with best wishes for much success in their graduate studies. The PPTs of the class of 1999–2000—Jessica Lynch, Carrie Spindel, Robin Nusslock, and Jeremy Blair—deserve recognition for their contributions as well.

A number of individuals toiled ceaselessly and tirelessly behind the scenes and contributed meaningfully to the development of this book. We are most appreciative of the resourcefulness of Devereux's operating group QI coordinators, Helene Bartlett and Glynn Fraker, for their help in accessing critical background material for a number of chapters. Pennye

Rosenfeld, our executive assistant, must be recognized for her cheerfulness throughout the many long hours devoted to this endeavor, during which she established complex communication pathways to ensure that chapters were completed and disseminated on time. We are also thankful for the steady hand of Bernice Belger, ICTR's secretary, for facilitating the flow of information between Paul LeBuffe, the PPTs, and us. We would also like to acknowledge and thank Devereux's librarians, Joyce Matheson and Rachel Resnick, for their able and abiding assistance with this project.

To complete the roster of contributing Devereux staff, we would like to thank Tom Shurer for his computer wizardry in generating graphs. The organization of regulatory and outcome data was also facilitated by the assistance of Charlee Bumgardner, Patty Hurst, and Donna Strickland in Florida and Pam Helm in Texas. In addition, Frank Carrera in Florida was generous to share the many wonderful systems and tools that he developed throughout his years at Devereux, and for that we are most appreciative.

From the outset of this project, we were committed to achieving a national, industrywide perspective in the various topical areas. To a large extent, the willingness of a select number of behavioral health care leaders to make themselves available for interviews and site visits allowed us to meet this objective. Accordingly, we are very appreciative of the time and support given by Charlotte McCullough of CWLA, Joy Midman of NAPTCC, Mike Montgomery of the Cleo Wallace Centers, Ron Milestone and Ron Scroggy of Inner Harbour, June Cairns of CYFC, Matt Mason of Pressley Ridge, Lloyd Malone of the El Paso County Department of Human Services, and Shelly Botuk of YAI. A special thanks also goes to the numerous agencies that so graciously took the time to complete our survey.

To our reviewers, Mario Hernandez, Charlotte McCullough, Michael A. Freeman, and David Liederman, we are indebted for their time and attention to our manuscript.

Last and certainly not least, we would like to recognize key individuals. First, we would like to thank Jane Brooks, who worked closely with us as editorial consultant. Jane, an accomplished author and editor, took on the role of trusted adviser. She provided a continuously friendly but firm hand in shepherding us through the rigors of writing and organizing a book of this scope. Jane helped to sensitize us to the sins of "and/or," and for that we are eternally grateful.

We also thank Jossey-Bass editors Katie Crouch and Amy Scott, whose deft skills helped polish the manuscript. Finally, we are deeply appreciative of Alan Rinzler, executive editor of the Trade and Psychology Series at Jossey-Bass, who believed in the merits of our work and guided us from concept to reality.

To my wife, Jill, and my sons, Adam and James, who continuously challenged me to establish accountability in mental health services. This work is also dedicated to the memory of my father, Sanford Savin, who would have loved to have read the book.

Howard Savin

To my husband, Michael, and my mother, Judy Bombardi, and father, Bob Soldivera, for their continual love, support, and belief in me, which made this book possible.

Susan Soldivera Kiesling

Introduction

DURING THE PAST decade, the managed care industry has grown at a staggering pace, from initially serving no more than 5 percent of America's insured population to now serving an incredible 70 percent. The meteoric growth of managed care has propelled us so speedily along its twisting, turning path that those of us who are providers can scarcely catch our collective breath. In its lightning-like ascent, managed care has exerted ever-tightening controls on traditional mental health care and substance abuse treatment providers.

The Changing Landscape of the Behavioral Health Care Industry

Responding to spiraling behavioral health care costs, funders took unprecedented action in demanding that providers demonstrate accountability with respect to the benefits of their care. What prompted this demand? Several factors were at work. As the stigma associated with mental health and chemical dependency treatment waned and more and more people sought these services, more and more providers entered the arena. And these providers reported equivocal results. It wasn't clear which treatment modalities were effective and which were not. The profusion of providers, treatment modes, and settings—along with rapidly rising costs—hastened the arrival of formal accountability in health care. An unparalleled avalanche of new funding criteria and documentation changes deluged behavioral health care providers. What had been customary for years—routine funding, with minimal inquiries from insurers—was no longer the order of the day.

Funding cuts and increased scrutiny have forced providers to do some serious soul searching. Rather than fold under the pressures of these dramatic changes, many behavioral health care and child welfare services providers, from small outpatient clinics and operators of group homes to psychiatric hospitals with many sites, have seized this opportunity to not only improve their operations but to flourish in the altered environment. As providers of care, we are now compelled to look beyond merely measuring utilization and cost containment in considering the effectiveness of our services. This is the ongoing challenge for all of us in this field.

We need not delve too deeply to discover the rationale for the intense scrutiny of the behavioral health care field. Hans Strupp (1996), a historian and renowned researcher on the effectiveness of psychological treatment, reported a paucity of scientific data over the past one hundred years to substantiate the benefits of psychotherapeutic endeavors. With little data to support treatment, providers can now expect that their practices will be questioned.

So rapidly are these changes occurring that at this writing, performance measurement requirements have been mandated by four different types of entities: (1) major behavioral health care regulatory and accrediting bodies, (2) managed care organizations, (3) statewide initiatives, and (4) provider research initiatives. For example, the Joint Commission on Accreditation of Healthcare Organizations (JCAHO) is a private, not-for-profit organization that accredits more than eighteen thousand health and behavioral health provider organizations for state licensing and for state and federal funding eligibility (Joint Commission on Accreditation of Healthcare Organizations, 1999b). To meet accreditation requirements, providers must participate in JCAHO's ORYX initiative, which is designed to integrate outcome and performance information into the accreditation process (Joint Commission on Accreditation of Healthcare Organizations, 1997). Initially, providers select from a multitude of measures—two to five clinical or perception-of-care indicators affecting at least 20 percent of their population. The Council on Accreditation (COA), a JCAHO competitor, requires measurement of client or other stakeholder satisfaction, as well as evidence that the provider has achieved operational and budgetary objectives in order to obtain accreditation (Council on Accreditation of Services for Families and Children, 1996). Although JCAHO and COA requirements overlap in some areas, such as clinical performance and patient satisfaction, there are differences between the two entities (see Figure I.1).

If you are participating in a managed care network, the requirements don't end with JCAHO or COA. You must answer to additional accrediting bodies as well. To be eligible for contract and reimbursement, for example, providers have to conform to the standards of the National Committee for

FIGURE I.1

Sample of Accreditation Requirements or Initiatives

Performance Measure	JCAHO[a]	NCQA[b]	COA[c]	HCFA[d]
Clinical performance	x	x	x	
Health or functional status	x			x
Patient satisfaction	x	x	x	x
Administrative-financial	x		x	
Accessibility of services		x		
Length of stay				
Recidivism				
Service utilization		x		

Sources: [a]*Joint Commission on Accreditation of Healthcare Organizations, 1999a.* [b]*National Committee for Quality Assurance, 1999.* [c]*Council on Accreditation of Services for Families and Children, 1996.* [d]*Health Care Financing Administration, 2000.*

Quality Assurance (NCQA). A private, not-for-profit organization, NCQA monitors managed care organization performance to ensure quality of care (National Committee for Quality Assurance, 1999). Additionally, NCQA mandates that providers self-assess performance in clinical outcome, patient satisfaction, accessibility of services, and service utilization.

Health care providers must also face the demands of the Health Care Financing Administration (HCFA)—a federal agency that administers the Medicare, Medicaid, and Children's Health Insurance programs ("HCFA at a Glance," 2000). HCFA has its own performance requirements that apply to any provider reimbursed by Medicaid or Medicare.

Many states have their own contract requirements and initiatives. If you are based in Colorado, Florida, Georgia, Kansas, Maryland, New Jersey, New York, Ohio, South Carolina, or Texas, you may be subject to a number of projects or initiatives for gathering outcome-based performance measures (see Figure I.2) (Gordon, 1999; McCullough & Schmitt, 1998). In Kansas, for example, officials are looking at recidivism rates for adjudicated juveniles and at family member satisfaction to determine effectiveness of care. And in Florida, providers are measured by performance on expected outcomes in the school and in the community as a function of the services they provide (for example, the percentage of children served who attend the minimum number of days in school, the percentage of children served who

FIGURE I.2

Sample of State Contract Requirements and Initiatives for Gathering Outcome-Based Performance Measures

Performance Measure	Colo.	Fla.	Ga.	Kans.	Md.	N.J.	N.Y.	Ohio	S.C.	Texas
Clinical performance	x	x	x							
Health or functional status	x	x	x		x	x		x		
Patient and family satisfaction		x	x	x			x	x		
Administrative and financial	x	x						x		
Accessibility of services	x					x		x		
Length of stay	x			x				x	x	x
Recidivism	x			x						x
Service utilization										
Community integration	x	x				x				
Educational functioning	x	x		x	x					
Appropriateness of care	x	x		x				x		
Family reunification										x
Family involvement				x				x		
Continuity and stability of care	x	x		x	x			x	x	x
Protection from harm	x	x		x	x			x		

Sources: *Gordon, 1999; McCullough & Schmitt, 1998* .

spend the minimum number of days in the community, and the extent that the reading scores of students served increase by a minimum of one grade level per school year).

The user defines the relevance of specific outcomes for services provided; what may be important to one consumer or constituency group may not be important to another. Most agree, however, that improved functioning at some level is a desired, if not expected, outcome of services. In other words, as a result of care provided, individuals should be able to function better in their home, family, or community. They should also be able to stay in school or hold a job and avoid trouble with the law.

Several provider organization consortiums have launched their own initiatives to gather outcome-based performance measures (see Figure I.3). One of these, the Family League of Baltimore City, is using behavioral health-related indicators such as the incidence of child abuse and neglect, the rate of children being placed outside the home, and juvenile crime and delinquency rates to assess the quality of care provided by participating organizations. The Child Welfare League of America (CWLA), a national association made up of almost nine hundred private and public nonprofit child welfare agencies (Braziel, 1996), has established physical safety, access to care, appropriateness of care, and client satisfaction, to name a few, as indicators to measure the performance of participating organizations (Gordon, 1999).

The federal government has also gotten into the act through an initiative called the Treatment Outcomes Performance Pilot Studies (TOPPS), implemented by the Substance Abuse and Mental Health Services Administration, a division of the U.S. Department of Health and Human Services ("SAMHSA Grants," 1998). The initiative offers two-year contracts to states to develop a system for monitoring and evaluating substance abuse treatment. Indicators include severity of addiction and clinical performance.

This cornucopia of requirements and initiatives is among the changes that confront today's behavioral health care provider and represents substantial and compelling challenges to the behavioral health care and welfare services industry. Compliance is particularly daunting for the provider who operates in the state of Florida, for instance, and participates in a managed care network that serves Medicaid recipients and must meet NCQA and JCAHO standards, comply with state contract performance requirements, and satisfy HCFA regulations. The picture gets even cloudier if the provider participates in a consortium initiative such as CWLA. The good news is that there is some overlap among the various organizational performance indicators. The bad news is there are some unique requirements as well.

FIGURE I.3

Sample of Provider Organization Consortium Initiatives to Gather Outcome-Based Performance Measures

Performance Measure	Child Welfare League of America	Family League of Baltimore City	Treatment Outcomes Performance Pilot Studies (TOPPS)
Clinical performance			x
Health or functional status	x	x	
Patient and family satisfaction	x		
Administrative and financial	x		
Accessibility of services	x		
Length of stay	x		
Recidivism	x		
Service utilization			
Community integration			
Educational functioning		x	
Appropriateness of care	x	x	
Family reunification			
Family involvement			
Continuity and stability of care			
Protection from harm	x	x	

Source: *Gordon, 1999; Treatment Outcomes Performance Pilot Studies (TOPPS), 1999.*

Results of Changes to the Industry

The result of all this tumult is that it is no longer sufficient to be caring, dedicated, and committed caregivers. In order to establish credibility with the payer and consumer communities, it is imperative that providers demonstrate and quantify treatment efficacy and client benefits. As we hasten to meet these new requirements, we have had to take a hard look, not only at our programs and their efficacy but at the very nature of our organizations as well. Regardless of the size or the nature of our setting—whether a single group home, a community mental health center, a child welfare service agency, or a large psychiatric chain with multiple sites—each and every one of us must be prepared to respond to these more stringent demands.

Indeed, we are operating in a professional climate that has experienced its own El Niño.

In an article on the challenges facing nonprofit organizations in the new millennium, Abelson (1998) notes the alarming pace of change: "Today's nonprofits are faced with the multiple challenges of reduced governmental support, increased competition, greater accountability, and the need for sophisticated information systems capable of tracking outcomes" (p. 1). In the same article, Abelson quotes Frazierita D. Klasen, program officer for the Pew Fund for Health and Human Services, regarding the challenges at hand. According to Klasen, "Business as usual may not be appropriate. The world is changing." Further, she admonishes that organizations must ask themselves, "How do we need to change to adapt?" (p. 1). Clearly, those of us in nonprofit or for-profit behavioral health care entities find ourselves in the same boat as we pose this question.

Responding to the Challenge

How a range of providers in a variety of settings, from a large organization with a multi-million-dollar budget to a group home operating on a shoestring, have responded to the demands and changes brought about by managed care is the substance of this book. The challenge and compelling considerations of our own organization, the Devereux Foundation, provided the impetus for writing it.

In the eighty-three years following its founding in 1912, Devereux grew from a single program to include more than two dozen discrete behavioral health care treatment programs located in thirteen states and the District of Columbia. Among the staff of talented clinicians and skilled administrators, there was a deep caring and commitment to client welfare. Despite our success, by 1995 we recognized that something critical was missing. There were few systemic benchmarks, goals, or standards to guide the operations of our organization.

When we looked around the field, we found much encouragement and lip service being given to the value of benchmarking quality indicators and conducting outcome studies. In fact, to this admittedly less than detached observer, it seemed that the major payers and regulators were trying to host a tango party for guests unfamiliar with the steps. Furthermore, the hosts were offering neither lessons nor a budget for a band. How could the guests be expected to dance?

Observing this dilemma, we set out to bridge the gap between expectations and reality, to give providers operational guidance. This is the challenge that all behavioral health care providers face today; to accomplish this calls for systems for quality and accountability. In our case, that meant systems that would encompass our entire organization—a large, national provider of residential and community-based behavioral health and child welfare services.

Our demographics defined what we perceived as our number one challenge: how to facilitate movement of a geographically and clinically diverse provider network into a coherent, quality-focused, and data-driven organization. Within this framework, we recognized that we needed systems to be applicable to a variety of clinical settings. This would not be a simple task. Nor was it our sole challenge. What Devereux and other human services organizations learned from these experiences can pave the way for fellow behavioral health care providers scrambling to meet the demands of new requirements.

In the current climate of cost containment and performance-based contracting, providers must figure out how to gauge consumer and payer interests. Recognizing this issue led our team to aggressively pursue a second challenge: how to accomplish this task of measuring dual interests, along with short- and long-term clinical objectives, and concretely track progress through treatment and beyond. Provider entities like ours are increasingly expected to address more complex and challenging behavior problems, including severe aggression, property destruction, and sexual disorders in mental health, mental retardation and developmental disabilities, and child welfare settings. Compounding the demands and difficulties of these expanded expectations is the fact that functional outcomes for such programs have never been clearly established. In addition, burdensome regulations often have an impact on the efficacy of behavior modification interventions (Spreat & Jampol, 1997).

Like other behavioral health care providers, Devereux struggled to find ways to satisfy requirements while ensuring that our programs would continue to thrive. Our action planning followed a four-pronged approach to accountability:

1. Clinical quality standards must be adopted.

2. Quantitative approaches to gathering care-relevant data, establishing benchmarks, and measuring outcomes must be developed.

3. Medical and psychiatric services must be integrated into the mainstream of clinical and administrative functioning.

4. Empirically based practice guidelines must be identified and implemented.

Most important, we realized the need to launch a meaningful, organizationwide continuous quality improvement (CQI) process. This process would have to be nurtured and sustained to enable grassroots ownership and dynamic refinement of the four initiatives we had defined. The issue of establishing a relevant and enduring CQI commitment proved to be a daunting challenge.

Large, older, decentralized organizations like Devereux tend to pride themselves on their historical survivability, uniqueness, and autonomy. Thus pervasive institutional inertia, often reinforced by a decade or more of failed initiatives in quality assurance (QA), total quality management (TQM), and CQI, stands out as the most critical and essential point of entry for effecting organizational change. We must find strategies to overcome this inertia, breathing new life into our institutions by demonstrating the value of these initiatives.

We wished to make this book more than "The Devereux Story," though. We wanted to present the experiences, both positive and negative, of providers of all shapes and sizes. To this end, we sent surveys to the CEOs, executive directors, or other executive officers of 397 organizations. The organizations are members of one or more of the following mental health associations: Pennsylvania Community Providers Association; Maryland Association of Resources for Families and Youth, the Child Welfare League members that participate in the Odyssey Project; the Children, Youth and Family Council of the Delaware Valley; and the National Association of Psychiatric Treatment Centers for Children. To increase the response rate, executive directors of the National Association of Psychiatric Treatment Centers for Children; the Children, Youth and Family Council of the Delaware Valley; the child welfare administrator of the El Paso County Department of Human Services; and the director of the Managed Care Institute of the Child Welfare League hand-selected organizations to solicit. Fifty-nine of the surveys, from organizations in twenty-one states and Canada, were completed and returned—a 15 percent return rate. These organizations serve clients of differing ages and of various presenting problems, as shown in Figure I.4.

The ten-page Organizational Survey consisted of forty-one questions relating to the following topics: QI history, current QI initiatives, QI staffing, committee structure, standards for clinical practice, information resources, ethics and client rights, culturally competent practice, medical-psychiatric leadership, professionalization of direct care staff, and measurement and performance improvement.

To facilitate the analysis and interpretability of the data, we subdivided the surveyed organizations into three categories based on their average

---

FIGURE I.4

Population Profile of Surveyed Agencies

Age of Clients Served	Number of Organizations
Preschoolers	28
Children	38
Adolescents	43
Adults	26
Geriatric adults	7
Major Presenting Problems of Clients Served	**Number of Organizations**
Juvenile delinquency	27
Abuse or neglect	42
Mental health (MH)	28
Mental retardation (MR), developmental disabilities	9
Substance abuse (SA)	13
Dual diagnoses: MH/MR MH/D&A Behavioral/SA Bipolar/MR	4

---

daily census: (1) sixteen small organizations, having an average daily census of fewer than 100, (2) eighteen medium organizations, with an average daily census of more than 100 and fewer than 375, and (3) seventeen large organizations, having an average daily census more than or equal to 375.

In addition to the written survey, we conducted extensive telephone interviews with June Cairns, executive director of the Children, Youth and Family Council; Joy Midman, executive director of the National Association of Psychiatric Treatment Centers for Children; Mike Montgomery, CEO of the Cleo Wallace Centers; and Charlotte McCullough, director of the Child Mental Health Division and the Managed Care Institute of the Child Welfare League. Follow-up interviews to the written questionnaire were conducted with eleven respondents to obtain further information about their best and worst scenarios.

• • •

In the chapters that follow, we explore findings and experiences from a variety of diverse provider organizations to illustrate how the challenges of CQI and other related initiatives have been constructively addressed. We include strategies for overcoming institutional resistance in the quest for quality and accountability in our collective organizational operations. We also include a review of the nature and methodology for adopting systemwide clinical standards in the areas of credentialing, client records, supervision, training and education of professional staff, and development of outcome-driven quality plans. Approaches to developing and implementing client-driven practice guidelines are supplied, with key elements integrated into a self-auditing process (a gap analysis and quality site visit). We also address quantification issues and the complex areas of patient rights and guidelines for ethics. Finally, we present a structured approach for designing and conducting outcome studies.

Our own organizational journey in these areas has been both challenging and rewarding. It has been an enriching adventure to share our experiences and conclusions with a cross-section of fellow providers who detail their own experiences within these chapters. Their findings are an essential and important part of this book. With this input, it is our hope that we can hasten and broaden each other's learning curve and that we can demonstrate how healthy organizations flourish by building on the strengths of well-designed systems for quality and accountability.

Above all, it is our guiding belief that the articulation of viable and integrated systems, supported by broadly shared experiences, will enhance the behavioral health care provider's capacity not only to survive but to thrive during these rapidly changing times. The challenges are the same for all of us. How we respond to them will dictate our success or failure. It is in the spirit of continuous quality improvement—which incorporates team effort, openness to the investigation of the effectiveness of treatment interventions, organized systems of care, and reliance on data to support critical treatment decisions—that we present our thoughts, experiences, and findings. And we hope this spirit will guide you as you begin the process of putting your own house in order.

## Chapter 1

Developing a Quality Improvement Infrastructure

WHEN REFLECTING on the complexities and challenges of today's operating environment, it's easy to feel lost, confused, and somewhat devoid of direction. Given the ever-escalating demands for often differing measures of accountability and performance by public payers, managed care companies, and accrediting organizations, what's a provider to do?

All too frequently, the knee-jerk reaction to these increasing demands for accountability is resentment. Each new regulator or payer demand seems like an intrusion into the legitimate mission of service delivery. This resentment, though understandable, is not so different from the reaction to policy dictates that are generated from either distant or senior management within one's own organization—that of grudging compliance. When each requirement or mandate is approached in isolation, without any attempt to constructively integrate new data or to refine the service delivery system, we're inclined to comply in the hope of getting by. Sometimes compliance serves to hold the system together, but more often than not the protection afforded by "getting by" wears off, leaving the exposed wound of resentment. A situation that occurred within Devereux's Treatment Network illustrates the point.

Some years back, the CEO of the network had mandated that all treatment centers immediately begin administering a particular behavior rating scale to assess each client's functional status at the time of admission and at the point of discharge from an episode of care. This well-intentioned directive was meant to spur systemwide movement to gather data on clients' functional outcomes as a result of the treatment and services provided. At the end of the operating year, each center's executive director was asked to present the results. One of the directors produced several cartons of completed but unscored behavior rating scales. When queried, this senior manager opted to play out his organizational poker hand by stating that the CEO's directive only mandated *administration* of the outcomes instrument and that staffing resources at his disposal did not permit the scoring and reviewing of results. Despite the protracted and rather passive-aggressive approach taken in this instance, some valuable organizational learning took place. We quickly realized the merits of a more democratic and participatory approach and took care to incorporate those values into our quality initiatives.

Apparently, Devereux's quality improvement (QI) compliance experiences are shared by many of the fifty-nine behavioral health care organizations we surveyed (the survey is discussed in depth in the Introduction and appears in Appendix A). The Organizational Survey asked respondents to rate the degree of QI adoption by their organization on a scale of 1 to 5 (1 = noncompliance, 2 = grudging compliance, 3 = compliance as an organizational duty [business as usual], 4 = willing compliance, and 5 = fully internalized and acted upon as a corporate value). Results indicate that 38 percent of small organizations, 56 percent of medium organizations, and 24 percent of large organizations rated their level of QI adoption as "compliance as an organizational duty (business as usual)." Rating their QI adoption level as "willing compliance" were 38 percent of the small organizations, 33 percent of the medium organizations, and 29 percent of the large organizations. Although 19 percent of small organizations and 6 percent of medium organizations indicated that their organization's QI adoption level was "fully internalized and acted upon as a corporate value," surprisingly, 41 percent of large organizations rated their level of QI adoption at this fully internalized level.

Going Beyond Compliance

Compliance alone (and certainly grudging compliance) is by nature self-limiting. You make some changes to meet the requirements, take a deep breath, and go back to business as usual. But there are other, far more effective and productive ways to respond to policy demands and dictates. Take, for example, the organization that opts for a more complex, soul-searching, and transformational approach to the process of doing business as a provider of human services. This approach does not come naturally. It may have a lofty ring, but the reality is that for many organizations, change is brought about by the need for compliance—the catalyst that focuses an organization's attention on self-assessment.

Regardless of the initial motivation for change, the successful organization is one that ultimately sees the increasing demands not as an encroachment but as an opportunity to retool and fine tune itself. This is the path of the strategically focused provider who embarks on a course of continuous quality improvement that is rooted in a solid QI infrastructure—the supportive environment carefully developed to meet the challenges of quality initiatives.

One of the large organizations that responded to our survey—Lutheran Child and Family Services of Illinois—provides a good example of how QI initiatives, when creatively and constructively implemented, can result in improved systems of care. The agency developed an organizationwide peer review system to review client records. Peer review committees were assembled; members included program directors, support staff, area directors, direct service workers, and senior management. During the monthly reviews, members looked at various sections of the client record—assessments, service plans, case notes, and discharge summaries—from programs other than their own.

Initially, staff did not welcome the initiative. The review committee members felt that it was intrusive and that it would be uncomfortable to review programs they knew little or nothing about. To address this, someone from the program being reviewed was present at all times, and a series of support documents were developed to help participants unfamiliar with the program review it constructively. Once the process began, the staff's attitudes began to change; as a result, the initiative has helped improve the agency enormously. For example, staffers have learned a great deal about other programs and services offered by the agency. As a result of this increase in knowledge of services available, there have been more cross-referrals in the agency. Additionally, the agency experienced an improvement in the quality of the client records. The records review has allowed the agency to identify problems that a program may be experiencing systemwide and has enabled them to report the problem to the program's director so changes can be made. They have also been able to create program reports for staff on what corrections need to be made in specific records.

CQI Defined

Quality initiatives are known by a variety of interchangeable names. *Continuous quality improvement* (CQI) is alternatively referred to as *total quality management* (TQM). Both terms describe an organizationwide approach geared to achieving better results by constantly making improvements in processes and performance. *Performance improvement* and *quality improvement* both refer to action taken to improve the quality of services. All of these terms refer to a dynamic, democratic process for establishing measurable goals and vigorously pursuing them; the effort is routinely and dispassionately reviewed and modified until targeted outcomes are achieved. Within the health care arena, authorities have fully embraced this basic methodology from theories that W. Edwards Deming (1986) and Joseph Juran (1979) developed for the manufacturing industry. Throughout this book, we use the term *QI* to refer to quality improvement methodology and processes. To pursue the path of quality improvement, the provider organization empowers leadership team(s) from within to use CQI processes to address operational and programmatic issues. By seeking nominations of team members representing a vertical and horizontal array of stakeholders, the organization's leadership ensures that the team embraces a cross-section of players.

Of the fifty-nine surveyed organizations, 78 percent have standing QI leadership committees; members include line staff, foster parents, consumers, admissions staff, board members, training director, consulting psychiatrists, program managers, nursing coordinators, clinical supervisors, directors of clinical services, medical directors, senior management, and corporate staff. Performance or QI teams address such vitally important areas as standardization of data elements for inclusion in clinical or case management records and the establishment of operational definitions for monitoring risk events within and across provider groups. Team members study the area in question and report back with a plan for correction or improvement.

When leadership is successful in launching a team-based QI culture, it provides the organization with a mechanism to objectively prioritize organizational values and goals. This culture encourages and establishes the capacity to respond to change as a normal component of workflow. Most important, it sets the stage to evaluate empirically the merits of various regulatory and reporting requirements. After all, one's approach to matters of compliance may legitimately differ from the approach to matters that represent opportunities for bona fide performance improvement.

Need for QI Infrastructure

It's nearly impossible to look at QI without a discussion of infrastructure—the components of the provider organization that enable assessment and improvement to occur. Consider a house, for instance. Its infrastructure consists of the foundation and framing, and the heating, plumbing, and electrical systems. These interdependent structural components determine the capacity of a home to be resilient to the often unpredictable elements of nature and to afford a relatively comfortable and predictable environment for its occupants.

In a similar vein, the QI infrastructure of a behavioral health provider organization is composed of broadly representative quality management teams that are authorized to study and report on key operational processes, standardize workflow, and engage in quantitative analysis and refinement of the system of care. The development of a QI infrastructure enables the provider organization to address the pressing concerns of customer satisfaction and consumerism (see Campbell, 1998) and weather the storm. Here the aims are to involve clients and family members in program development and to formally gauge their satisfaction with services rendered.

Historically, senior management teams have determined policy and procedure without having input from frontline staff or (in many cases) from geographically dispersed multidisciplinary teams. Although payers and regulators have loudly and legitimately insisted on being recognized as "customers," rank-and-file staff and such vital internal stakeholders as clients and families have traditionally been left out of the loop. We cannot allow these exclusions to continue. Of the respondents, only 20 percent directly include clients, parents, or guardians as members of their QI committee. However, clients, parents, and guardians are involved indirectly in the meetings by 80 percent of the organizations through satisfaction and outcome questionnaires and surveys. Some of the respondents have found other ways to give voice to their internal customers by creating separate QI client and parent committees, involving parents in QI committee projects, and conducting focus groups.

Listening to Input

Devereux has begun to address these concerns by creating student government-type programs that have input into the process, such as refinement of motivational systems , staff evaluation, and participation in their treatment center's QM committee. In a similar vein, parents are invited to participate in monthly QM meetings on a rotating basis, and many of our treatment centers have local advisory boards on which a client's family member may have a standing appointment. If we are truly committed to studying service outcomes as a key and critical element of mental health services, it is crucial that we legitimize and empower the internal customers of the provider organization so that each constituency has a voice.

"Ultimately, it is at the level of people communicating with each other that human values have the greatest potential for becoming incorporated into the institutions of society. Through an open architecture of knowledge, production and exchange, research and evaluation can become a value-added force in the delivery of mental health services" (Campbell, 1998,

p. 23). If you keep in mind that the underlying purpose of QI is to remain operationally competitive, then it follows that at this phase of putting your house in order, the task is to gauge openness to change by addressing issues of "managed care readiness." The QI infrastructure becomes the staging area for this endeavor.

The Four Stages of Infrastructural Development

Just how does a QI infrastructure develop? The answer is, slowly. From simple reliance on an imposed environment, the infrastructure evolves over time to finally become a viable, self-sustaining entity. In the evolution of the QI infrastructure, we can draw parallels from the unfolding of human life itself. At its inception, the QI infrastructure, much like a newborn, relies on its parent for sustained nurturing. And, like a child who looks to parents to lead the way, a newly created QI process depends on senior management to drive its evolution with a mixture of guidance and limit setting. In staying the course, often over a period of several years, the QI process encourages new skills and increases self-confidence, as the mix of influence from school, home, and peers does for the developing young person. Eventually, compliance with QI requirements transitions to buy-in. Frustration, opposition, and uncertainty give way to autonomous functioning and innovation. Just as the healthy transition from adolescence to adulthood requires some work at separation in order to achieve independence, the road to autonomy requires some effort.

Getting from here to there, that is, to independence, generally involves a willingness to address four stages of infrastructural development: (1) assessing the organization's current status, (2) identifying and refining structural elements, (3) countering resistance and promoting buy-in, and (4) acknowledging that you've arrived. Let's review each of these evolutionary stages.

Stage 1: Assessing the Organization's Current Status

In the past, most behavioral health and welfare services organizations had no proverbial "1-to-10" scales to enable objective assessment of the effectiveness and quality of their programs. It may have been common to find systems in place to track referral, census information, and basic financial data, but there was no methodology for measuring or monitoring outcomes. Rarely was there evidence of organizationwide monitoring of the outcomes of behavioral health care services. Nor were there formal means for all stakeholders to have input into shaping programs and services. This was the case at our own provider organization.

To rectify this situation, we began a needs assessment at Devereux to identify our resources. We also wanted to be able to anticipate barriers to compliance with the systemwide QI initiative, then in its embryonic stage. As part of this process, we visited each treatment center to survey programs and to interview executive directors, clinical directors, and staff responsible for overseeing QI.

One of our first meetings was with a grizzled senior manager with more than twenty years of organizational experience under his belt. This dedicated soul had recently been promoted from executive director of a single program to vice president of an entire region. He wanted us to know that most treatment centers (like his former program) were, in his opinion, already qualitatively rich. Although he was supportive of our mission, he made the point that the last three individuals charged with rolling out an organizationwide quality assurance (QA) program had failed. (For clarification, his use of *QA* refers to an organization's initial attempts at a quality initiative by setting up monitoring and evaluation systems. QA was the forerunner of the current initiatives and is now considered an initial building block for a true initiative.) His perception was that QA initiatives had become corporate witch hunts in which a significant crisis erupted and a clinically oriented QA team was dispatched. According to him, findings would invariably consist of blaming one or more staff members for problems at hand, and "guilty" staff members were usually fired. A guiding QI construct was inherent in this manager's strenuous and sincere message of encouragement—to succeed by adopting a posture of teacher, listener, and consultant.

He was saying, in effect, that for a QI project to succeed it must be perceived as democratic and instructive. In fact, the aim of moving forward with a QI initiative is to advance the average effectiveness of the organization while avoiding the trap of being perceived as serving a policing function. This is satisfying work, but it is not necessarily work for those with thin skin. Be sure to keep in mind the following guidelines:

Consider the Goals

Any organization undertaking needs assessments must consider the dual goals of reducing variability in clinical operations and improving quality of care. Begin with an assessment of "quality improvement mindedness" in the setting of care that constitutes a given behavioral health or welfare services organization. At this phase, a discussion of the importance of "managed care readiness" is often what it takes to focus attention on problems and start looking for solutions.

Initially, the assessment task is threefold: (1) to identify resources, (2) to anticipate barriers to compliance with a broad, contemporary QI initiative, and (3) to gauge the level of buy-in to prospective organizational change. The assessment survey should determine leadership support and commitment to QI. When developing the needs assessment survey, the assessor should tap opportunities for democratic input into decision-making processes, thus providing a role for clients and families in program development. The survey should review the status of current QA or QI initiatives and examine the types of information systems (IS) resources available. Additionally, the assessor looks at the extent of reliance on standardized measurement tools to quantify care indicators, customer satisfaction, and clinical or functional outcomes (see Figure 1.1). The assessor acts as both an internal consultant and an agent for change. In these dual roles, the assessor employs clinician-like active listening skills to begin to germinate the seeds for buy-in with the interviewees.

Typically, the results of needs assessments will reveal a number of assets. Many programs have developed their own satisfaction surveys. It is not uncommon to find one or more clinicians who have been gathering data on symptom reduction or discharge status among their clients. Behavioral health care centers that are accredited by the Joint Commission on Accreditation of Healthcare Organizations (JCAHO) have at least made defensive use of quality indicators: length of stay, planned versus against-medical-advice (AMA) discharges, medication errors, and so on. Further, detailed intake information on each client is usually available, although each program tends to have its own unique clinical record system. However, clinical records are usually found in handwritten form. Data compiled from the Organizational Survey indicate that 96 percent of the organizations use computerized systems to carry out their financial duties, whereas only 33 percent of these organizations use computerized clinical records.

Similarly, information systems are generally found to be primitive and have historically been used for financial and administrative tasks. In short, although potentially valuable data may have been collected, it is seldom possible to analyze the information and learn from it.

Implement a Needs Assessment

The needs assessment of an organization can proceed in a variety of ways. A needs assessor might meet with rank-and-file managers and directors from all disciplines to inventory their range of attitudes, perceptions, and beliefs, as well as to articulate assets in each targeted area. Alternatively, the assessor could meet with existing QA-QI or human resources (HR) staff in

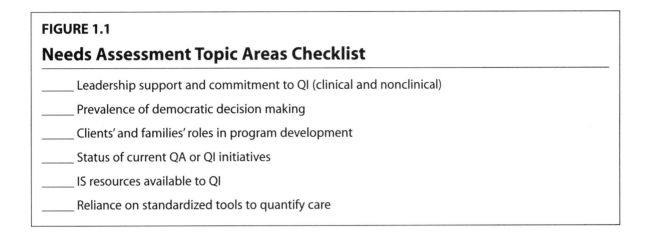

FIGURE 1.1

Needs Assessment Topic Areas Checklist

_____ Leadership support and commitment to QI (clinical and nonclinical)

_____ Prevalence of democratic decision making

_____ Clients' and families' roles in program development

_____ Status of current QA or QI initiatives

_____ IS resources available to QI

_____ Reliance on standardized tools to quantify care

medium and large organizations to instruct them in the gathering of data. Finally, a pencil-and-paper survey could be administered across multiple programs or settings of care such as medium-to-large provider organizations or provider consortiums. The survey tool that we developed for the purpose of gathering industrywide quality initiatives information is available for the reader's review in Appendix A.

Stage 2: Identifying and Refining Structural Elements

The experience of most provider organizations demonstrates that to develop and install a QI infrastructure requires from one to four years of focused effort; the amount of time needed depends on variables such as organization size, availability of resources, and current organizational structure. The roll out of the QI infrastructure includes the development of an organizational chart for quality management (QM) teams, along with standards governing the composition and functioning of the teams, agenda items, annual QM plans, and reporting requirements.

At Devereux, for instance, we spent two years cultivating our QI infrastructure, whereas The Children, Youth and Family Council of the Delaware Valley (CYFC)—a coalition of private, nonprofit agencies serving at-risk children, youth, and families—took four years to develop a sound infrastructure that would create a system involving its member agencies (personal communication, November 25, 1998). The four-year period began when the fifty-seven member agencies that formed the council decided to pursue inservice training in outcome measures. This led to a desire to explore a comprehensive range of indicators and measurement tools that could serve the needs of the broad member constituency. Due to limited internal resources, a decision was made to develop a request for proposal in conjunction with a public sector children and youth agency and to have outside vendors of outcomes research services bid for the CYFC contract. By the time the council had identified appropriate stakeholders, selected a vendor, developed an implementation plan, and initiated the first pilot, four years had elapsed.

Once the QI system is in place, its refinement remains an ongoing process. Development of the QI system doesn't exclude pursuing a variety of closely related objectives simultaneously, but the *first* order of business is to make QI a reality, as shown in the sections to follow.

Link the Organization

And what is the reward for the QI quest? The golden ring is nothing less than a team-based system of governance that links the organization from bottom to top. Figure 1.2 represents a template for a QM committee in a nonmedical model—a non-hospital-type setting. Information at the program level, with critical input from frontline staff and consumers, should drive the QI system. Even though senior management usually initiates QI endeavors, the success of their undertaking depends on buy-in from rank-and-file staff. To the extent that frontline workers and middle managers perceive that they have real input into decision making and that they share in developing the architecture of their organization's future, a QI initiative will survive and thrive. Accordingly, program design and refinement should increasingly become a bottom-up (versus a top-down) enterprise. As desirable as this approach may be, however (as indicated by our survey), the full and active participation of frontline staff and consumers in QI committees remains more the exception than the rule.

Designate QM Teams and Committees

Depending on the size of the organization, the QI infrastructure may consist of either a single QM leadership committee or multiple QM subcommittees that link into the central committee. Similarly, each subcommittee may be subdivided into a number of discrete performance improvement (PI) teams that meet independently in the course of a month and report to the full QM team (see Figure 1.3). For instance, a program may have a safety subcommittee. This subcommittee may in turn establish several PI teams to address safety-related food service and facility issues.

Ideally, a full complement of stakeholder representatives makes up the QM leadership committee. This might include senior administrators and clinicians (both medical and nonmedical), a frontline staff person, staff responsible for HR and finance, an educational or vocational staff member

FIGURE 1.2

Template for QM Committee

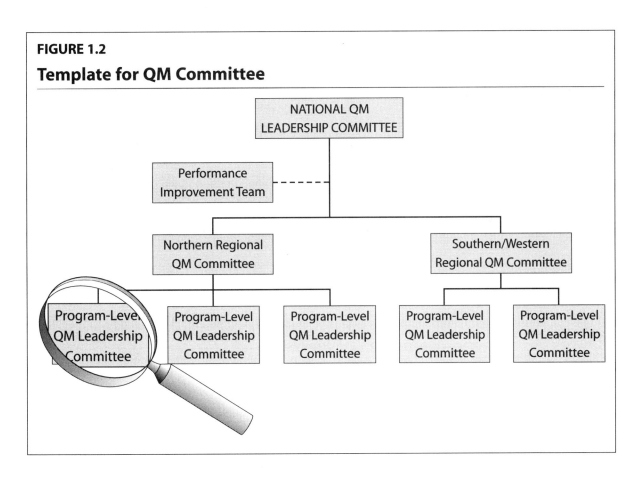

(if appropriate), and various consumer constituencies such as clients, families, community members, and payers. Consumers typically participate at the QM leadership committee level on an appointed or rotating basis or through focus groups, satisfaction surveys, and special open meetings by which staff gather feedback that is used to drive PI activities. Optimally, the senior administrator empowers a staff person to be responsible for QI functions and to serve as chairperson of the QM committee. Note that if a medical model is in use, the chair must be a physician. It is not a good idea for the senior manager to head this committee. After all, the goal is to have the team function as a relatively autonomous and self-directed group.

Individual QM subcommittees and PI teams should usually consist of people who are closest to the process, who have the greatest ability to implement the improvement in question, who have the greatest stake in implementing the improvement, and who are affected by the process. These groups should also include an individual who has decision-making authority. In some cases a staff member may participate on more than one team, depending on the nature of the project.

FIGURE 1.3

QM Subcommittees

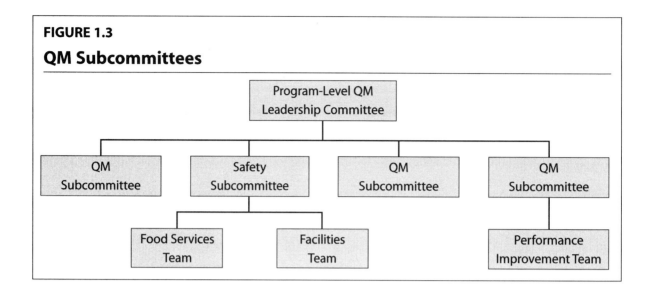

Customize for Size of Agency

Of course, the single-site agency with limited resources customarily would not have multiple QM subcommittees with individual functions. Rather, a single leadership committee would be created with individual committee members assigned to areas of responsibility. One person could have responsibility for multiple functions (for example, the person responsible for risk management could also be responsible for safety). The leadership committee would routinely review information on the various functions to identify PI opportunities. This committee would then establish a time-limited, project-specific PI team to address an identified opportunity. This team may be composed of a subgroup of the larger committee and additional frontline staff within the agency.

In essence, the QM infrastructure of the smallest organization can be conceptualized as a microcosm of a larger organization. Representatives of an individual site of a larger provider group serve as members of the parent group's QM leadership committee. The experiences and findings of the individual site feed up through the larger structure and inform the creation of policies and procedures at the parent organization level that get disseminated down. Thus the greater resources of the parent organization are being used to help the individual site consistently improve performance.

Develop a Plan

The QM leadership committee has the responsibility for developing an annual QM plan. The plan should reflect the goals and guiding philosophy of the provider organization vis-à-vis quality care and continuous improvement. Additionally, the plan should articulate specific objectives the program is committed to complete for that year. For example, one objective might be to ascertain the impact of a diversionary program, the aim of which is to enable clients to successfully receive services at less restrictive levels of care. Additionally, there should be a focus on consumer or parent satisfaction and related efforts to increase their involvement in various aspects of the process of care.

At Devereux, each of our centers designs two outcome studies per year that examine the impact of specific treatment methods and programs on outcome. One such study in progress assesses the ability of an alternative education program to successfully keep students mainstreamed in the regular classroom. To determine this, for example, we measure (among other things), the number of students who successfully complete the program who subsequently avoid expulsion from their public school and the number of students who ultimately graduate. Another study, three years in the making, examines the impact of family involvement on clinical outcome through a program developed to increase family participation in children's treatment. The children are assessed at discharge using the Devereux Scales of Mental Disorders and later at follow-up using a specific follow-up survey. Although the findings to date reveal that family involvement has little impact on symptom reduction during residential treatment, the expectation is that postdischarge follow-up will reveal something quite different. We expect that children whose families were more involved in the treatment program will have less contact with police, attend school more regularly, and generally function better than clients whose families had little to no involvement.

Establish Regular Meetings and Agendas

QM committees meet formally at least once a month and often operate from a standing agenda that includes, at a minimum, review of credentialing activities, proactive case reviews, grievances and complaints, PI team activities, and findings from outcome studies. Survey data indicate that small organizations typically hold QM meetings quarterly, whereas medium and large organizations typically meet on a monthly basis. Standing agendas are used during QM committee meetings by 59 percent of the organizations surveyed. In these meetings, the group can also complete reports or summaries of risk management issues. To review credentialing, the committee might summarize outcomes of staff applications and the global actions that were taken to complete the credentialing process.

Proactive case reviews are multidisciplinary reviews of client cases that are randomly selected to assess clinical progress and appropriateness. All identifying information is omitted or disguised to protect confidentiality. The advantage of conducting these reviews in this forum is that it gives individuals who may not necessarily participate in a treatment team the opportunity to provide valuable input that the treatment team could otherwise not access.

It's important to remember that the primary focus of the meeting, regardless of the review activity, should be to monitor and improve systems, not to assess the performance of individual employees. Any information in each of the key areas of programmatic functioning should be presented in aggregate form to identify trends and patterns. The emphasis, after all, is on identifying opportunities for improvement. A sample agenda with minutes for such a QM committee meeting are provided in Appendixes B and C.

Create QI Positions

Because of certain conditions (including size and geographical diversity), the QI infrastructure at Devereux included the development of several key QI positions—a quality improvement coordinator (QIC) at the treatment center level, regional QICs, as well as a national QIC. However, the national QIC was the only dedicated, full-time position created; the other slots were filled with volunteers from operations. The regional QIC role has since become a full-time position.

Devereux's QI staffing experiences are not unique. According to the survey respondents, most QI departments operate with one QI manager whose QI responsibilities have been added, in a secondary fashion, to their primary work duties. The amount of the manager's time devoted to QI management, expressed as an FTE (full-time equivalent), varies by size of the organization. The QI departments of 58 percent of the small organizations surveyed tend to be managed by persons who devote .25 FTEs or less to QI. Fifty percent of the medium-size organizations devote .70 FTEs or more to QI. Of the large organizations surveyed, 36 percent have at least one full-time QI management position, whereas 64 percent devote .5 FTEs or less to QI.

In addition to the QI director position, surveyed organizations reported using from none to twenty additional QI staff positions. Forty-four percent of small organizations have no such additional QI FTEs, whereas 38 percent have at least one additional FTE. Of the medium-size organizations surveyed, 61 percent have at least one additional FTE, whereas only 11 percent have no such position. Last, 76 percent of large organizations reported at least one additional FTE, whereas 23 percent reported no additional staffing. Interestingly, one large organization reported employing twenty additional QI FTEs.

Stage 3: Countering Resistance and Promoting Buy-In

Perhaps the single most important provision in the quest to develop a QI infrastructure, especially in the wake of the universal experience of less than fully successful initial attempts, is strong, unwavering support from the most senior levels of management (Townsend & Gebhardt, 1992). Senior management must recognize that success is dependent on buy-in and genuine empowerment at the grassroots level. Regardless of size, it seems that organizations whose senior leadership is committed to QI processes over the long haul are equipped to stay the course.

Paying heed to the very real phenomenon of "no pain, no gain," an organization's leadership must be prepared to support the embryonic QI culture with dedicated staff. No matter how QI support needs are met—whether by new hires, the allocation of one or more full-time staff members, or dividing up duties among existing staff—one or more individuals need to lend support in the role of outcomes-database specialist and QI champion (coordinator). Provision for training in areas such as process improvement and outcomes measurement is essential. And it's critical to minimize fear by adopting a systemwide educational and consulting model toward QI initiatives rather than a system based on finger pointing and meting out punishment.

Respondents to the Organizational Survey indicated that only 54 percent have some type of staff-mandated QI training. Of the small organizations surveyed, 44 percent have mandated training, whereas 60 percent of both the medium-size and large organizations mandate QI training.

Understand Buy-In

When we speak about buy-in, we refer to a gradual, positive shifting in mindset among key stakeholders as to the relevance and virtues of any given undertaking. In order for the organization or its stakeholders to move away from a mode of grudging compliance with a newly instituted QI initiative, it is important to supply some victories in the form of "quick wins." For example, organizing credentialing files or preparing outcome data may be perceived as ivory-tower-inspired drudgery. Yet one positive experience can be all it takes for an organization to see the merits of the QI initiative.

One New England provider had a surprise visit from a major referral agency and was lauded for its exemplary program because it had this type of data in hand. Indeed, the acclaim the provider received soundly reinforced the value of the QI initiative for this organization, which had previously complied somewhat grudgingly. Now this provider willingly embraces QI processes as the preferred way of doing business.

Introduce Standardization

For an organization to reap the benefits of QI processes, standardization must become the order of the day, despite much predictable resistance to this change. Standardization is often perceived as the veritable "bad guy," whereas variability in established provider entities is often tenaciously defended as evidence of creativity and uniqueness. But standardization replaces potentially boundless variability in the operation of programs. Accordingly, the roll-out of the QI infrastructure not only includes the development of a table of organization for QM committees and teams, it consists of standards governing the composition and functioning of the teams, agenda items, annual QM plans, and reporting requirements, as mentioned in Stage 2.

Whatever the reason for the initiative—whether driven by an intrinsic desire to standardize delivery of care and establish efficacy or to confront the performance mandates of payers and regulators—implementation of an outcomes-oriented QI initiative generally means more work. Unfortunately, more work doesn't necessarily translate to more pay, as many private, nonprofit providers have discovered. June Cairns, past executive director of the Children, Youth and Family Council of the Delaware Valley (CYFC), a broad-based organization of more than fifty-seven child welfare, mental health, substance abuse, and juvenile justice agencies in the five-county Philadelphia area, shared the agony and ecstasy of a four-year project (personal communication, November 25, 1998).

Independent of size, there was enormous variability among CYFC's members as to quality initiative and outcomes systems. The membership (the majority of whom are child welfare service providers) was interested in improving the quality of staff and of service delivery. Initially, using the training platform, Cairns systematically introduced the conceptual virtues of establishing organizationwide guidelines of care and a bona fide outcomes initiative. Stakeholders extended beyond the membership per se to include senior managers at Philadelphia's Department of Human Services (DHS) and various consumer constituencies. The group met every two weeks to read articles about outcomes and to begin to conceptualize how a project in Philadelphia could occur. After initial buy-in was achieved, DHS and CYFC committees were established to map the philosophy and goals of child welfare services and to study current versus optimal workflows. This part of the effort resulted in the development of a request for proposal (RFP) to various consulting groups for assistance with making the outcomes project a reality. A consulting group was selected, a model and framework was adopted, outcome measures were identified, workflows were revamped, and a successful pilot study was undertaken.

First, the group discovered that the improved model of care was more resource intensive and necessitated a new workflow and thus higher rates. However, reimbursement rates had been frozen by DHS for a number of years. A second political sticking point emerged. It turned out that a number of DHS workers were union employees, and changes in workflow constituted significant issues in contract discussions. Project committees went back to the drawing board to expand their group of stakeholders to include representatives from the unions. At this writing, the effort remains a positive work in progress.

Take Another Approach

At the outset of Devereux's QI initiative nearly four years ago, we approached our task at hand from a different perspective than Cairn's group did. Although staff at all levels sincerely believed in the quality of their program's services, they were not necessarily ready to subject themselves to "corporate" scrutiny. Many feared the overlay of yet another set of unwanted or seemingly irrelevant senior management requirements. Early-stage or conceptual buy-in was achieved by invoking the mantra of managed care readiness. A general consensus already existed with respect to the need to look more like one organization. Nearly everyone agreed on the need to focus more intensively on credentialing, record keeping, generating meaningful outcome studies, and the structure and function of QM committees. Indeed, the specter of managed care and its attendant needs was largely responsible for sparking this receptive attitude. The staff acknowledged what it would take for the behavioral health care programs to survive and at least remain competitive in rapidly evolving provider networks.

Further, we were able to ensure that the corporate clinical department would take an active role in minimizing any further stress to staff members at the various centers. This de facto team of internal consultants would provide technical assistance in the form of QM training and research design and statistical analysis. We issued one warning to our stakeholders: there would be some degree of pain as they struggled with the learning curve on the journey toward compliance and beyond.

Combat Resistance

Whether going about the business of implementing an outcomes-oriented QI infrastructure from the vantage point of improved workflows or managed care readiness, one thing is certain: resistance will invariably rear its ugly head. Typically, resistance from staff appears in any number of ways:

FIGURE 1.4

Sources of Resistance

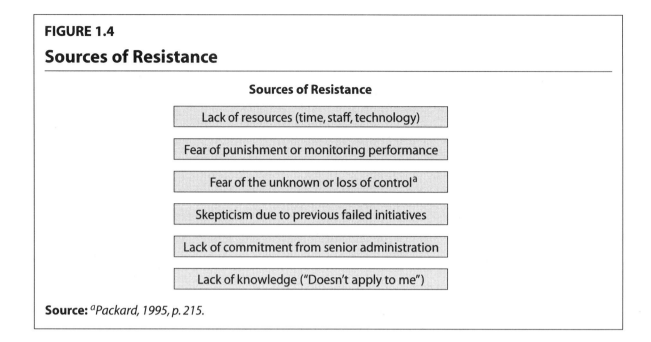

Sources of Resistance

| Lack of resources (time, staff, technology) |
| Fear of punishment or monitoring performance |
| Fear of the unknown or loss of control[a] |
| Skepticism due to previous failed initiatives |
| Lack of commitment from senior administration |
| Lack of knowledge ("Doesn't apply to me") |

Source: [a]*Packard, 1995, p. 215.*

poor data collection or data omission, procrastination, grudging compliance, destructive criticism, or avoidance. As illustrated in Figure 1.4, sources of resistance tend to emanate from a familiar list including fears, ignorance, limited resources, and suboptimum leadership style.

The experience of the previously mentioned Children, Youth and Family Council of the Delaware Valley (CYFC) speaks to the issues and remedies of such resistance (personal communication, Nov. 25, 1998). Given enormous variability in size and sophistication of the fifty-seven provider members, there was concern about the unknown, particularly in relationship to the impact of and expectations about the public sector managed care scenario that was unfolding in the greater Philadelphia area. There was a shared interest in pursuing training among the member organizations, although resources within any one provider entity were generally limited. The council's full-time executive director was able to form a steering committee from member delegates, which then developed a series of inservice training programs on the design and conduct of outcome studies. With this growing base of knowledge and experience, the steering committee was able to identify a "doable" list of QI-related goals and objectives to achieve organizational buy-in. Resource issues were addressed with the decision to go forward by outsourcing their outcomes initiative. By partnering with the public agency, the council was able to develop an outcomes system rather than a program-specific project.

FIGURE 1.5

Ways to Overcome Staff Resistance

- Provide opportunities to communicate.[a]

- Seek feedback (from surveys, focus groups, and so on).

- Increase opportunities to participate in the decision-making process.[b]

- Provide staff to support the QI culture (for example, appoint champions).[c]

- Provide training.[a]

- Eliminate the fear.[d]

- Start small and raise the bar.[a,c]

- Establish and communicate clear purpose and objectives.[a,c]

- Capitalize on internal expertise and interest.[c]

- Use systems already in place for data collection when possible. Do not reinvent the wheel.[e]

- Translate the process into meaningful information. Use the results to improve services.[c,d]

- Provide recognition.

- Demonstrate commitment from senior management.[c]

Sources: [a]*Townsend & Gebhardt, 1992, p. 115.* [b]*Packard, 1995, p. 216.* [c]*Meadowcraft & Mason, 1997, p. 132.* [d]*Deming, 1986, pp. 23–24.* [e]*Carins & Koch, 1997, pp. 103–104.*

It is important to remember that resistance is a normal, predictable organizational dynamic. To counter resistance, it must be addressed proactively. Figure 1.5 lists thirteen methods for effectively overcoming resistance that we have identified.

Keep the Doors Open

One way to ensure a viable, energetic, and positive dynamic in your organization is to be certain that you maintain an open-door policy. So often perceived as mythical and elusive, the open-door policy is real; it is up to leadership to endorse and encourage it. Both formally, through meetings, and informally by encouraging and prioritizing requests for input from all stakeholders, leadership must stimulate communication from the top and reinforce it down through the managerial pyramid. Similarly, management can solicit feedback through formal and informal surveys. This is an important action because it teaches the art and science of "listening down" (Townsend, 1990, p. 141). Listening down is the active process of senior management to hear, understand, and incorporate staff members' perspectives. Leadership that has effectively mastered listening down will be able to identify reasons and causes, then proceed to develop an appropriate action plan in response.

It makes great sense to capitalize on the interests and expertise of various staff persons to enhance positive motivation (always preferable to overcoming resistance head-on). A great QI starting point is the identification of a clinician or caregiver who has already begun to assess some aspect of service outcomes or a financial operations person with strong quantitative skills. For example, during our needs assessment phase of QI program development, we became acquainted with a highly regarded QI coordinator at Devereux's treatment center in Massachusetts. This woman proved to be creative and passionate in her approach to customer satisfaction, was interpersonally skilled, and was a dynamic trainer. She viewed fellow staff members as key internal customers and had already developed several versions of satisfaction surveys, process improvement teams, and a fairly comprehensive employee recognition program, including a staff newsletter.

Think Small

Thus in Massachusetts, the appropriate starting point for the systemwide QI initiative was to build on the expertise and positive momentum that was already there. For the rest of the organization, our task was to operationalize the Massachusetts customer service–employee recognition program and disseminate it as a "best practice." In any event, it is important to think small and build on existing strengths in launching a QI program. Target simple processes for improvement and basic outcome indicators for study during the early stages of building your QI infrastructure.

Most important, use multiple forms of recognition to consistently reward staff for accomplishments and to reinforce buy-in. Figure 1.6 offers a sampler of recognition opportunities for staff.

To facilitate buy-in, to demonstrate "walking the talk" at Devereux (behaving in a manner consistent with expressed goals), and to recognize staff efforts, we created an internal QI newsletter. The newsletter served to share ideas and systems, highlight accomplishments, and offer tips and educational advice. We also launched a recognition-celebration system. This included the dedication of a quarterly issue of Devereux's newsletter, *Networkings,* to feature laudatory QI team projects. Additionally, we introduced an annual presentation of the most outstanding team project to the organization's board of trustees, a variety of smaller quality improvement innovation awards, and the subsequent development of a QI bulletin board on our intranet.

FIGURE 1.6

Eight Ways to Celebrate and Recognize Staff

- Create and distribute newsletters.[a]
- Set up a central bulletin board to post notices.[a]
- Display storyboards throughout the workplace.
- Establish an employee- or team-of-the month program.
- Award gift certificates, monetary prizes, or memorabilia.
- Host an employee recognition event (awards ceremony, pizza party, sundae party, and so on).
- Provide employees with the opportunity to present their QI projects.
- Send a "Thank You" letter from top management.

Source: [a]*Meadowcraft & Mason, 1997, p. 133.*

Stage 4: Acknowledging That You've Arrived

You know your staff have arrived and truly embrace the philosophy and tenets of QI when you can use the following adjectives to describe them: open-minded, creative, energized by challenges, innovative, receptive to feedback, data-driven, inquisitive, responsive, flexible, enthusiastic, focused, goal-oriented, and collaborative.

We knew we were on the right track when we witnessed this kind of outcome in the staff at one of our California programs. In that endeavor, staff were faced with the task of reviewing a behavioral incident that had occurred in their program. The clinical director had to facilitate the process. Anticipating resistance, frustration, anger, and hostility, she was greatly surprised to find staff eager, alert, motivated, and determined. The process of reviewing the incident led them to meet well into the night. To the clinical director's delight, everyone was more than willing to put in the extra hours to learn what could be done better or differently. The results were enlightening for all. Not only did they emerge with new perspectives, they learned that the process can work; all were convinced of the benefits of the QI process.

As a QI initiative takes root, it becomes apparent when the staff are constructively engaged in learning QI techniques. They have started to adaptively implement standards and are beginning to take risks and innovate. Now there is a staging area from which it becomes possible to witness growing independence and expansion of QI processes into all programming levels. And finally, the crown jewel of buy-in and staff involvement is evidenced by the seamless integration of QI processes into the fabric of daily operations.

With the establishment of a viable QI infrastructure, provider organizations have the adaptive mindset and tools to begin addressing content areas in their delivery system. An excellent place to turn next is to the development or refinement of standards of care.

Reading Suggestions

Gummer, B., & McCallion, P. (Eds.). (1995). *Total quality management in the social services: Theory and practice.* Albany: Rockefeller College, University at Albany, State University of New York.

Scholtes, P. R. (1998). *The team handbook: How to use teams to improve quality.* Madison, WI: Joiner.

Townsend, P. L. (1990). *Commit to quality.* New York: Wiley.

Townsend, P. L., & Gebhardt, J. E. (1992). *Quality in action: 93 lessons in leadership, participation, and measurement.* New York: Wiley.

Townsend, P. L., & Gebhardt, J. E. (1997). *Recognition, gratitude and celebration.* Menlo Park, CA: Crisp.

Chapter 2
Establishing Standards for Care

> Not everything that can be counted counts, and not everything
> that counts can be counted.
>
> ALBERT EINSTEIN (1879–1955)

ONCE YOU'VE STARTED to address QI issues, consider yourself well on the way to putting your house in order. But however exhilarating that thought may be, take heed—it's too early to start thinking about replacing the furniture. Instead, this is the time for a rigorous review of all aspects of delivering care, with particular emphasis on reducing the variability in your services and maximizing client welfare.

No task is more critical for the provider than to ensure that its clients are well served. Historically, there have been few objective safeguards to guide the interface of behavioral health and child welfare consumers with the provider community. At minimum, however, there is clear provider consensus around the old maxim for physicians, "First, do no harm."

It is not farfetched to speculate that, until recently, the owner of an automobile seeking "genuine factory service" might enjoy more satisfactory service from a qualified technician than a consumer of behavioral health care services would from a provider. Without established standards of care, the consumer has no way to gauge quality. In fact, the pairing of clients with providers often occurs by word of mouth, the phone book, the locale of a particular provider or agency, and referrals based on friendship or contracts. In short, clients choose their providers based on very little information. It's rare that the behavioral health or child welfare consumer is able to make an objective, results-based choice of provider. In contrast, the automobile owner who receives "factory service" gets a guarantee of satisfaction based on established standards. Should the service be less than satisfactory, the owner can keep returning the car to the shop until the problem is corrected.

Unlike in the auto repair industry, standards of care in the behavioral health care arena have not been adequately defined. Several factors have determined local or organization-specific provider patterns. Chief among these is the consumer demand for differing types of services provided by various clinicians such as social workers, marriage and family therapists, psychologists, and psychiatrists. Additionally, provider patterns have been influenced by the availability of some or all of the components of a full continuum of care in both child welfare and mental health settings. Another influence has been the varying state laws. The laws that regulate the requirements for providing behavioral health care services to private and commercial clients are different from those regulating public sector consumers.

Why set standards? In essence, standards of care make good business sense. Adherence to specific standards of care can provide safeguards for our clients. Further, there is increasing congruence among major accrediting bodies such as the Joint Commission on Accreditation of Healthcare Organizations (JCAHO), the National Committee for Quality Assurance (NCQA), and the Council on Accreditation (COA), as to acceptable standards of care (Council on Accreditation of Services for Families and Children, 1996; Joint Commission on Accreditation of Healthcare Organizations, 1999; National Committee for Quality Assurance, 1999b). Thus provider organizations that set and follow certain standards can move forward more confidently in delivering behavioral health and child welfare services; they will be in compliance with the regulatory standards of today's marketplace.

Standards also help guide organizations through licensure and accreditation. Many provider organizations must adopt standards that are aligned with accreditation requirements by JCAHO, NCQA, and COA for the credentialing of clinicians and case managers. Also, providers often embrace system components that may represent the organization's greatest areas of exposure—comprehensiveness of documentation, for example—as standards.

Positively stated, standards promote performance consistency, optimize value, provide accountability, and ensure that services are driven by clinical appropriateness criteria (Strickland, 1997). Standards also establish the gauge by which the quality of care is measured. They ensure that minimum criteria for performance are achieved and that the provider uses the most effective strategies or best practices. Standards of care facilitate collaboration and the coordination of continuums of care. They offer the potential to provide a common language for dialogue and bring everyone onto the same page (Shaffer, cited in Voelker, 1997).

This chapter speaks to four basic standards of quality care: (1) the credentialing of professional staff, (2) the supervision of clinical staff, (3) client records, and (4) the continuing training and education of professional staff. A fifth closely related component—the structure and functioning of quality management (QM) teams—was detailed in Chapter One.

Credentialing of Professional Staff

At Devereux and at the other provider agencies surveyed, a number of tenured clinical staff members were found who were hired on the basis of their reputation—their personal contact with existing staff. Degrees, licenses, malpractice insurance policies, DEA certificates, and references attesting to professionalism were neither consistently nor vigorously verified. Also, it is common to find, from an earlier time, overstuffed file folders containing every type of document, starting with an employee's date of hire. These file folders can usually be found in storage crates, cartons, or filing cabinets as combination HR-credentialing files.

But times have changed. A good reputation in the community, positive relationships with referral sources, and periodic reviews of clinicians' credentials—all this is no longer enough. Payers and regulators alike expect compliance with longstanding, albeit loosely enforced, QA requirements for the credentialing of clinicians. Comprehensive and up-to-date credentialing files are now a minimum prerequisite for membership in provider networks and continued accreditation. In fact, if a provider organization had to choose one area that is essential to its continued existence, that area would be credentialing.

Credentialing addresses the issue of who is qualified, by formal education and training, to provide specific professional services such as psychotherapy, counseling, case management, and the prescription of medication. In the quest to ensure competency in the largest number of cases, the creativity and artistry of both lay and degreed clinicians should initially be set aside. Instead, what takes precedence is the belief that educational attainment and prescribed amounts of supervised clinical experience set the bar at a level sufficient to ensure good "factory service." (Fortunately, "softer" qualitative issues are not forsaken as processes of privileging and recredentialing seek to capture effectiveness of care and consumer satisfaction.) It is desirable and a lot less confusing to keep credentialing files separate from HR files.

Technically, *credentialing* refers to the process of validating specified levels of education, training, licensure, malpractice insurance coverage, and demonstrated competencies of professional staff. Flanagan (1998) states that the purpose of credentialing and peer review activities is to (1) protect clients by exercising reasonable care in the selection of the organization's staff, (2) establish standards of professionalism, (3) ensure operational efficiency, (4) comply with legal and regulatory requirements, (5) meet accreditation standards, and (6) address liability concerns.

Credentialing activities have been traditionally directed toward clinicians—medical and allied health care providers. In behavioral health care and child welfare settings, the universe of clinicians typically encompasses physicians, psychiatrists, dentists, nurses, psychologists, social workers, marriage and family therapists, and interns, along with other health care professionals such as those listed in Figure 2.1.

Depending on the operating climate in a particular location, the state law, or a particular service contract, credentialing standards may vary with regard to the use of licensed versus unlicensed clinicians, or interns, as providers of care. The aim for every provider organization should be to ensure that all of its clinicians, either employed or contracted, meet the minimum standard of expertise by being properly credentialed.

We are all acutely aware that staff competence is one of the greatest areas of risk for both the consumer and the organizational provider of behavioral health care and child welfare services. The skills and ethics of an individual clinician will have significant impact on the satisfaction and outcome of care for a given consumer or family. Because organizations are liable for the care its staff provide, they are at the mercy of staff competence in supplying the contracted services with skill. Clearly, it is prudent to thoroughly investigate and verify the credentials of the individuals they hire—before those individuals deliver services. Failure to do so can lead to devastating consequences.

Stages of Credentialing

Credentialing activity typically occurs in three stages. *Temporary credentialing* is successfully completed prior to a clinician's first day of employment. *Permanent credentialing* is usually completed within ninety days of employment and can involve peer review in the case of physicians. *Recredentialing or decredentialing* involves the formal updating of clinicians' credentials and is typically undertaken every one to two years, based on organizational preferences or regulatory mandates.

In comparison to initial credentialing and privileging, information sources for reappointment (recredentialing) may come from direct skill observation, absence of negative outcomes, quality and appropriateness reviews, client and family satisfaction, productivity, ongoing training or continuing education, and results of supervision or peer review activities. This information is used to establish a professional's current level of competence, identify patterns and trends in an individual's performance, determine staff's learning needs, and develop staff training.

In the quest to operationalize essential elements of quality behavioral health care services and then to gauge compliance across a broad array of settings, we developed a set of guidelines at Devereux. These were designed to incorporate basic clinical standards, gleaned from widely recommended

FIGURE 2.1

Other Health Care Professionals

Addiction counselor	Movement therapist	Pharmacist
Art therapist	Music therapist	Physical therapist
Dance therapist	Nurse	Recreational therapist
Dietician	Occupational therapist	Speech and language therapist

best practices within the behavioral health care industry, with the requirements of major accrediting agencies such as JCAHO, COA, HCFA, and NCQA. Accordingly, standards for implementing and quantifying Devereux's approach to credentialing, supervising care, maintaining client records, and continuing the training and education of professional staff were established, based on a variety of accreditation standards (Council on Accreditation of Services for Families and Children, 1996; Joint Commission on Accreditation of Healthcare Organizations, 1999; National Committee for Quality Assurance, 1999b). The basic clinical standards incorporated into Devereux's guidelines are generic to most, if not all, provider organizations and are represented in the remainder of this chapter.

Suggested Guidelines for Credentialing and Recredentialing Standards

Both employed and contracted health care professionals should demonstrate the minimum standard of expertise by being properly credentialed. This includes, but is not limited to, validation of academic degrees, prior professional work and formal training experiences, licensure (if applicable), malpractice insurance (if applicable), history of sanctions and legal judgments, and professional references attesting to clinical expertise and ethical practices.

Temporary Credentialing

Prior to the first day of employment or contract, each provider covered by this procedure must provide a copy of the applicable license or certificate, Drug Enforcement Agency (DEA) registration (if applicable), and evidence of malpractice coverage (if applicable). Upon receipt of these documents, the chairperson of the credential and privilege committee or the director of human resources must forward notification of new employment to the appropriate senior manager. The balance of the credential requirements must be completed and the Credentialing Checklist (see Figure 2.2) forwarded within ninety days of employment or contract to the appropriate senior manager or medical or clinical director for approval.

Permanent Credentialing

Each element must be verified and reviewed according to the structure established in the provider organization's professional staff bylaws and include, at a minimum, (1) licensure, (2) sanctions or limitations on license, (3) liability insurance, (4) education, (5) recommendations, (6) disclosure form, and (7) work history.

1. *Licensure (where applicable):* The applicant must be licensed or certified according to the state and specialty as established by primary source verification. If there is no state licensing or certification program, the applicant must have acquired the certification from the appropriate national organization. At the time of the initial review, the applicant must provide a letter of certification, or a phone verification must be completed from the applicable state licensure board that indicates that the person is in good standing. At the time of hiring or contracting and every two years thereafter, the organization shall query the National Practitioner Data Bank (when applicable), which provides information as to pending or settled litigation related to malpractice or ethical infractions. Every physician who practices specialty medicine must meet the criteria for board eligibility or certification as defined by their national organization. Primary source verification must be submitted documenting the certification and stating that the applicant is in good standing. When recertification is a requirement, evidence of current standing must be provided.

Verification from a primary source must be obtained for DEA registration when possible and applicable. Letters or other acceptable methods of primary source verification from all facilities where the candidate holds privileges must be submitted indicating that the person is in good standing.

Acceptable forms of primary source verification include written letters of inquiry or oral confirmation. If the confirmation is oral, a form must be completed that includes the printed name and signature of the person completing the phone inquiry, the name of the organization, the person (including title) contacted, and the date the inquiry was completed.

2. *Sanctions or limitations on license (where applicable):* Documentation from the State Board of Medical Examiners or Federation of State Medical Boards providing information about sanctions or limitations on license must be obtained (National Committee for Quality Assurance, 1998). Documented inquiry of the Federation of State Medical Boards or reports issued by HCFA (Health Care Financing Administration) or the state regarding previous Medicare and Medicaid sanctioning is required.

FIGURE 2.2

Credentialing Checklist

Organization/Program: _____

The following individuals are submitted for appointment:

Name				
Profession				

I. Items necessary for temporary credentialing:

	Date Sent	Date Received	Date Sent	Date Received
Copy of License (Expires:) _____				
Copy of Malpractice Insurance ($1 million/$3 million) (Expires:) _____				
Copy of DEA Certificate				
II. Additional items necessary for permanent credentialing:				
National Practitioner Data Bank				
Verification of Educational Degree: (Must include year graduated) 1) 2)				
Primary Source Verification/Residency				
Primary Source Verification/Internship				
Primary Source Verification/Licensure				
Specialty Board Certification				
Primary Source Verification/DEA				
Primary Source Verification/Malpractice				
Curriculum Vitae				
Annual Disclosure Form				
Letters of Recommendation 1) 2 3)	1) 2) 3)		1) 2)) 3)	
Previous Employers: 1) 2)	1) 2)		1) 2)	
Memberships: (Other hospitals, medical societies, etc.) 1) 2)	1) 2)		1) 2)	

Appointment Approved:

Signature (Program Credentialing Specialist) _____   Date _____

Signature (Appropriate Senior Manager or Medical/Clinical Director) _____   Date _____

Signature (Board of Trustees Member) _____   Date _____

3. *Liability insurance (where applicable):* Each applicant must provide proof of liability insurance, with minimum limits of $1 million each wrongful act or $3 million aggregate, or other limits as required by state law or regulation.

4. *Education:* Each applicant must provide a letter or transcript from the primary source verifying successful completion of her professional education and training.

5. *Recommendations:* Each application must be supported by a minimum of three letters of recommendation from the appropriate professional sources. A recommendation should attest to the professional's clinical competency and good standing at previous facilities. Appropriate sources may include supervisors, partners, or colleagues in the professional community. Recommendations may be gathered verbally or in writing. A verbal recommendation requires the procedure outlined for primary source verification. A written recommendation must be on official stationary. Verification of dates of employment by itself is insufficient.

6. *Disclosure Form (see Appendix D):* Each applicant must complete a form that asks the following questions:

Has your license to practice ever been revoked, suspended, or denied?

Have your privileges at any facility ever been revoked, suspended, denied, or restricted?

Has your DEA certificate ever been revoked, suspended, or denied?

Since the last renewal of your license, have you been convicted of a felony?

Are you unable to perform the duties of your position, with or without accommodations, as outlined in your job description or as defined in your independent contract?

In the past year, have you been the subject of a malpractice suit? If yes, please explain circumstances.

In the past year, have you been subject to any disciplinary hearings or proceedings?

7. *Work history:* The past five years must be stated on the application, curriculum vitae (CV), or other documents.

Per state law, provider organizations commonly use two types of clinicians who are unlicensed. These clinicians are supervised in the provision of individual, family, group, and couples therapy and case management services. The first category, or type, is the clinician who possesses a master's or a doctoral degree in a mental health discipline such as psychology, social work, counseling, or marriage and family therapy. Although many degreed clinicians accumulate supervised hours of care with the aim of meeting licensure requirements, a number of states, such as Florida, New Jersey, and Pennsylvania, permit degreed clinicians to practice without the requirement of ever becoming licensed (Necessity for Licensure, 1999; Practicing Psychology Licensing Act, 1999; Regulation of Professions and Occupations, 1999). Regrettably, some states require neither supervision nor continuing education for certain kinds of clinicians who are permanently unqualified for licensing.

The second type of unlicensed clinician includes interns, who often represent an important segment of a clinical staff. These aspiring clinicians are in the process of obtaining master's or doctoral degrees in the various behavioral health care disciplines and, by definition, are not yet degreed or licensed.

Each treatment program must follow its state's requirements for the use of interns and unlicensed clinicians in providing direct services. The credentialing of nonlicensed bachelor's (in social work), master's, and doctoral degreed clinicians includes primary verification of education, letters of recommendation attesting to clinical competency, completion of a disclosure form, and a work history (résumé).

To credential an intern, there should be a review of graduate transcripts and appropriate course work. Additionally, the provider should request letters of reference attesting to the intern's proficiency and adherence to ethical standards in previous supervised practicum settings.

Recredentialing and Decredentialing

For internal recredentialing, renewal occurs annually or biannually (see Figure 2.3). In addition, primary source verification of renewal documents are required (as applicable). These include a valid license if it is due to expire, adequate malpractice coverage if it is due to expire, a DEA certificate (for physicians) if it is due to expire, and board certification (for physicians) if recertified or initially certified since the last credentialing-recredentialing cycle (National Committee for Quality Assurance, 1998). An original, signed, and completed disclosure form must also be renewed, and a query of the National Practitioner Data Bank must be completed every other year as required by federal law (not all practitioners are subject to this law).

Documentation of renewal information must be forwarded to the appropriate senior manager or medical or clinical director.

Methods of Credentialing

The credentialing process can be carried out in several different ways, either internally or by outsourcing the job to a credentialing service. Credentialing activities are crucial as well as time-intensive and costly for any provider organization. It's not unusual to spend six to ten hours of administrative time obtaining primary source verification of all pertinent information for a licensed clinician.

FIGURE 2.3

Recredentialing Notification Form

The following individuals are submitted for reappointment:

Dept	Name	Position	Degree	License Type	License Exp. Date	Cert.Type (DEA/ Board)	Cert. Exp. Date	NPDB Query- Date	Liability Insur. Date	Disclosure Completed

Approved for reappointment:

Signature (Credentialing Specialist)   Date

Signature (Executive Director or Appropriate Medical/Clinical Director)   Date

Outsourcing Credentialing Services

Given the generally recognized importance of and mandates for first-rate credentialing files, a rapidly growing number of vendors have emerged to service provider organizations. At this writing, NCQA lists on its Web site over thirty vendors that it has accredited to provide outsourced credentialing services (National Committee for Quality Assurance, 1999a). Based on an internal review of the total costs of credentialing and recredentialing, it is possible to determine the value of contracting with an outsource vendor to compile all or part of a provider organization's credentialing files, including the periodic updating of files. In a number of situations, particularly when there are sizeable numbers of providers to be credentialed, outsourcing can offer a better and cheaper solution.

However, one caveat exists with regard to outsourcing: because it's important for the provider organization's credentialing specialist to review the information on a timely basis, the vendor must respond quickly. Although you can't expect the vendor to advise you about whether or not to hire someone, you can insist on a timely response that will enable you to move ahead with the credentialing process. The vendor provides documentation that may occasionally contain negative and discrepant information but does not pronounce fitness to provide care. That is the job of the provider organization. Thus the provider's ability to complete the process hinges on how quickly the vendor can provide the necessary information.

Conducting Peer Review

The process of credentialing a provider typically occurs under peer review. Peer review has a dual purpose. It is both a credentialing and a supervisory function designed to investigate and compare the clinician's credentials, capabilities, and performance to defined standards and to ensure that all are appropriate. Peer review is used to establish staff competence, with *competence* defined as the demonstration of clinical performance or the application of knowledge and skill. Competence must be assessed, maintained, demonstrated, and improved and is integral to initial privileging and to reappointment activities. Competence is specific to age, disability, and the presenting problem of the population being served.

For instance, is a particular clinician actually performing the job he's supposed to be doing? If he's credentialed to work with juvenile sex offenders, is he indeed treating these clients rather than adults with posttraumatic stress disorder? Although the nurse with temporary credentialing has performed her job adequately, she may be ineligible for permanent credentialing when a peer review reveals that she is not licensed to dispense medication, which her job requires.

Frequently, physicians represent a component of a clinical staff. When physicians are part of a staff, most states and accreditation standards mandate medical staff participation on the credentialing and peer review committee (Flanagan, 1998). Other members of the committee must be qualified to evaluate credentials, clinical competency, and past performance (peer to peer). Peer review is done under the supervision of a governing body, and the committee must have bylaws or procedures governing the process.

Supervising Clinical Staff

Taking great pains to credential clinicians does not sufficiently safeguard against a lack of professionalism or substandard service. Without clinical and administrative guidance, peer-to-peer feedback, and formal performance review, the quality of services cannot be assured. Unfortunately, it takes only one proverbial "loose cannon" or questionable practice to undermine the reputation of a provider organization or trigger a malpractice lawsuit.

To ensure the quality of clinical and case management services, it is important to establish a comprehensive system of clinical supervision. With this system in place, all clinical staff who provide direct care and related consultative services for a given provider organization will participate in routine scheduled supervision or peer review. The system of supervision should be organized in a hierarchical, or pyramidal fashion, under the direction of a medical or clinical director.

Ideally, supervisors should be trained and experienced in the process of clinical supervision. They are the keepers of clinical best practices and the key quality control agents for the interns and clinical staff they supervise. Using both individual and group supervisory formats, supervisors must establish a tactically congruent and systematic method to ensure that each supervisee's cases get reviewed. Beyond issues of clinician-client relationship development and proper ethical conduct, the supervisor would be expected to model and teach a particular system of care, such as cognitive-behavioral therapy, or operate from the context of specific treatment, or care, guidelines for a targeted client population. (Practice guidelines are discussed in depth in Chapter Five.)

Supervision and peer review are actually parallel processes—both review the delivery of services by a given provider. In the medical world, the term *supervision* has an established connotation that speaks to the training of interns and fellows and may carry the same medico-legal responsibilities as the actual provider of care. Conversely, peer review has been established as a quality assurance activity and is nondiscoverable in a legal proceeding. Hence, psychiatrists participate in "peer review," whereas all other clinicians engage in "supervision." Individual, group, and provider profiling are customary methods of providing supervision and peer review. (Provider profiling is a quantitative approach to evaluating clinicians that takes outcomes of care, client satisfaction, and frequency of grievances or complaints into account. This method can also serve a dual role in the recredentialing process.)

The goal of supervision of care is for all mental health clinicians who provide direct care and related consultative services to participate in routine, scheduled supervision or peer review. Clinician supervision is organized under the direction of the organization's medical or clinical director.

Implementing Supervision of Care

Licensed, nonphysician clinicians on full- or part-time status will participate in a weekly group supervisory session of at least one hour's duration or on a pro rata basis. On a rotating basis, participants will present clinical cases for supervisory review. The clinical director, or designee, at each program will be responsible for organizing and conducting weekly group supervision meetings.

Nonlicensed, degreed clinicians, in accordance with respective state laws, will receive individual supervision from a licensed staff clinician that equals or exceeds state requirements. The clinical director from each program is responsible for the organization and oversight of individual supervision of nonlicensed clinicians.

Interns typically require a minimum of one to two hours of individual supervision per week to be in compliance with their university requirements and to maintain eligibility for subsequent licensure. Additionally, field supervisors should be available for impromptu supervision as needed, to provide written feedback on treatment plans and progress notes, for periodic group supervision, and to provide a list of suggested readings or training seminars.

Psychiatrists will participate in monthly peer review with the senior or lead agency psychiatrist. At least three cases will be presented and reviewed at each supervisory session. The agency's medical director will be responsible for the organization and oversight of routine administrative supervision and peer review of psychiatrists.

Recording Supervision of Care

First, clinical directors at each program should ensure that a supervisory log noting the date, type (individual or group), and clinical supervisee in each supervisory event is maintained. Each line entry should be duly signed by the supervising clinician. Then the clinical records should receive an entry in the "Progress Notes" section, indicating that supervisory review occurred on the given date. Any modifications or recommendations to the ongoing course of care should be reflected on the treatment plan. The supervising clinician will sign each entry.

Maintaining Client Records

When there is uniform documentation, the potential for fragmentation of client information, not to mention psychobabble, is reduced. Uniformity facilitates communication from one program or agency to the next (Lefkovitz, 1997). Regardless, the structure of a treatment plan will influence the way therapists and case managers think about the care they provide. For instance, if you require that clinicians identify strengths in their treatment planning and that they link those strengths to objectives, there is greater likelihood that the nature of treatment will be oriented toward skill acquisition and strengths.

Aside from the impact that the organization and content of client records have on treatment planning and subsequent outcome, integrated records support the concept of a service continuum and wraparound services (Lefkovitz, 1997). In other words, clinical records should support the process of care across different settings of care, between and within providers, and from the time of admission to postdischarge in a consistent and focused manner.

Regrettably, our surveys found significant variability in approaches to client records (both across and within provider organizations). With regard to across-provider variability, although 92 percent of the respondents to our Organizational Survey indicated that they use a uniform or standardized client record, nearly all (fifty-four out of fifty-six) of these organizations developed their own client record; only two adopted a commercial product. Therefore, although there may be uniformity within a provider organization, there is considerable variability across organizations. For instance, only 82 percent of respondents indicated that client strengths and functional assessments are areas included in their client records. Even worse, only 71 percent of the organizations included discharge criteria and permanency goals.

The various specialty programs within a single provider organization, such as adolescent chemical dependency treatment, adolescent residential care, and out-patient services, may have different client record systems. As record systems commonly vary from provider organization to provider organization, as well as across traditional service lines such as mental health and child welfare, the stage is set for a dysfunctional dialogue to ensue.

Just as we noted earlier in the chapter in our discussion of credentialing, the world has changed and the stakes are high. The same can be said with regard to client records. While the failure to properly credential clinicians can impede a provider organization's participation in a network or thwart agency referrals, substandard client records are probably the most common cause of denied payment and loss of future referrals. In today's world, many payers consistently audit client records at the time claims for payment are submitted or as part of formal periodic field audits.

To ensure effective continuity of care, a client record system can be acquired that will systematically capture essential background and history and inventory high-risk behaviors such as lethality, substance abuse, and physical and sexual abuse. The system can also identify presenting problems and strengths. Staff must then be trained to use the client record system to ensure that they correctly and consistently gather needed information. The majority of the respondents to our survey reported that training of staff in the use of clinical records was done during the orientation of new hires, with ongoing training throughout the year. Other organizations make use of inservices led by a member of the clinical team, one-to-one supervision, or self-study techniques to train the staff in their client record system.

Several years ago at Devereux, a client record development process was undertaken to address the needs of all mental health and mentally retarded–developmentally disabled (MR–DD) client constituencies and programs with "core records." The core record concept is predicated on an unambiguous functional assessment that feeds directly into a multidisciplinary treatment and discharge (transition) plan. Key elements of the Mental Health Core Record are provided in Appendix E for the reader's review.

Multidisciplinary staff providing direct care and related consultative services should document all relevant client information. Ideally, documentation consists of standardized client records incorporating medical history, strengths, and needs-based assessments, collateral contacts, treatment and discharge plans, and treatment plan summaries. Treatment plans and progress notes, across disciplines, will reflect measurable objectives and be linked to specific remedial interventions.

Implementing Standards for Client Records

Clinical directors, medical directors, and lead educators will continue to oversee the manual process of clinical records management until online systems are available. Following policy and procedure developed by the clinical director, timely and legible records will be generated for each client. All essential data elements will be captured and represented in the client record. At the rolling out of on-line client records, each entry will be accompanied by a valid coding and encryption program constituting an electronic signature of the care provider.

Keeping Standards High

Client records should be reviewed on an ongoing basis in every program as part of routine treatment planning, formal supervisory activities, QM committee meetings, and discharge planning. Additionally, the clinical director of each program should conduct a systematic review of 10 percent of the records on an annual or biannual basis to ascertain compliance—a "gap analysis." Significant gaps, or deviations, from client record standards should trigger the development and implementation of an appropriate corrective action plan.

Continuing Training and Education of Professional Staff

It is widely assumed that allied health care providers, including behavioral health care and child welfare professionals, participate in ongoing educational activities. This is generally, but not always, the case. For instance, a majority of states mandate a minimum number of continuing education (CE) units in order for a provider to get licensure renewal. In theory, proper credentialing and recredentialing of licensed clinicians in those states with CE requirements ensure that appropriate continuing education has occurred.

So what's wrong with this picture? For starters, a number of states, such as New York, have no continuing education requirements for allied health care professionals. Several states require thirty hours within a two-year renewal period for licensed clinical social workers, but the range varies from no hours to sixty hours (American Association of State Social Work Boards, 1998). Specifically, Colorado, Connecticut, Hawaii, Indiana, Missouri, New York, Vermont, Virginia, Washington, and Wisconsin require no continuing education for licensed social workers to renew their license. Continuing medical education requirements for physicians vary as well by number of hours per year and by required content (American Medical Association, 1998). Three states require twenty hours per year, whereas two other states require physicians to complete sixty hours over a three-year period. Other states require from 12 hours per year to 150 hours every three years. Eight states specify specific training topics that must be covered, including HIV-AIDS, infection control, ethics, and domestic violence.

Additionally, unlike university-directed requirements for interns, most states permit unlicensed, degreed clinicians to work either autonomously or under the supervision of a licensed clinician of the same discipline (American Association of State Social Work Boards, 1998). Ironically then, nonlicensed practitioners and those who cannot be licensed have lower continuing education and training requirements than their licensed brethren in those states with CE mandates. It is frequently observed that nonlicensed therapists and case managers are more frequently employed in public-serving systems of care than in the private sector. Thus vagaries in CE and credentialing standards from state to state and between publicly funded and private providers of behavioral health care may be contributing to disparities in systems of care. In other words, the poorest and neediest populations are often treated by clinicians with the least professional training.

Determining Value of Training

To proceed creatively and constructively with staff training, one must look at the array of opportunities for training and education, their relative virtues, and organizational points of leverage. It's essential that the provider organization first review the importance of professional training and education as an organizational value. The most important considerations in this determination are the mission of the provider organization and the nature of its services. For instance, an organization that provides long-term custodial care to a heterogeneous group of clients may have little internal need for ongoing professional education. In contrast, the organization that strives to provide cutting-edge services, especially to a more narrowly defined population, will need to keep abreast of the latest research and service models. Public organizations with long-term funding for services may value professional education less than private organizations competing for short-term managed care or private insurance dollars.

Other considerations in determining the organizational value of professional education include the need for market distinction in a highly competitive field and the necessity to gear up for a new program or clientele. Human resources issues also influence the value placed on professional training and continuing education. Where an out-patient provider using contract therapists may view continuing education as the responsibility of the contractor to maintain his or her license, the organization that provides continuing professional development to its employees may enjoy an advantage in both recruitment and retention.

If training and education are adopted as organizational values, the provider can incorporate certain types of participation into employment contracts. Both full- and part-time clinicians can be contractually obligated to participate in a specified amount of inservice training, to attend a certain number of professional meetings and conferences, and participate in supervisory and other QI activities.

Ensuring Quality of Training

The goal of professional training and education initiatives should be quality, not quantity. (It should be noted that a number of states mandate a minimum number of hours for inservice training for all staff.) When an organization can subsidize some portion of costs for clinical staff to attend meetings and training, the relevance of the proposed meeting to the programmatic needs of clients should be a criterion for funding. For example, you might wonder about the value of a conference on minimizing federal taxes for the private-practice clinician that is held at a Caribbean golf resort. This is one conference that would probably fail to yield any incremental gain in the quality of services to your clients.

Alternatively, your organization may periodically contract with outside experts to conduct seminars and clinical skills training on either a one-time or ongoing basis for topics such as chemical dependency, assessment and treatment of sexual offenders, management of challenging behaviors, or positive approaches in mental retardation–developmental disabilities (MR–DD) programming. Some provider organizations like Cleo Wallace in Denver, Inner Harbor in Atlanta, Pressley Ridge in Pittsburgh, and Devereux have committed to practice guidelines or a specific model of care, a topic covered in Chapters Five and Six. In these situations, targeted education and training begins at the time of employment. The education is integrated into the ongoing supervisory and training regimen and serves as a defining attribute of the provider organization.

Organizations may also want to consider obtaining approved continuing education provider status from professional groups such as the American Psychological Association or the National Board for Certified Counselors. Although such approvals entail additional expense and effort, the in-house provision of continuing education credits that meet state requirements for licensure renewal obviates the need to send staff to off-campus programs, typically incurring costly registration fees and transportation expenses. An approved provider has the additional benefits of ensuring that the CE program offerings meet the specific needs of the agency's staff, enhancing the organization's stature as a quality-conscious provider and perhaps generating revenue for the organization by enabling it to provide continuing education to external agencies.

It is the goal of the behavioral health care provider organization to ensure that all clinical and paraprofessional staff (frontline staff, direct care staff, psych techs, recreation counselors, mental health technicians, for example) providing treatment or case management services participate in ongoing professional training and education. Further, the value and relevancy of such training should lend itself to reflection in measurable improvement in client care.

Implementing Standards for Continuing Education

Licensed mental health clinicians will earn annual CE hours that equal or exceed state requirements for license renewal (with a minimum of fifteen hours per year for states with no CE requirements).

Nonlicensed mental health clinicians will earn annual CE hours equivalent to state licensure renewal requirements for licensed clinicians (with a minimum of fifteen hours per year for states with no CE requirements).

Full-time direct care providers (other professional, unlicensed staff functioning in a direct treatment capacity such as behavior analyst, mental health technician, or therapist—not to be confused with direct care staff or residential counselor) not otherwise covered by CE hours referenced earlier will participate in either a minimum of twenty-four hours of annual inservice training or sufficient annual inservice training to equal or exceed the requirements of various regulatory agencies.

Funding will continue to be made available, by request and approval, for specific external training and education (optional).

Keeping Standards High

Copies of current state CE requirements for each category of licensed health care professionals are to be kept on file at each program site.

A training and education log will be compiled annually at each program by the director of training or a designated individual. Training modules and CEs will be validated by the director of training.

At least one outcome study will be completed to assess the impact of training and education programs on the enhancement of care. This outcome study will be conducted under the direction of the clinical director.

Minimum standards are not always readily accepted. It is essential to reinforce the commitment to them through organizational procedure. Devereux developed a needs assessment survey or "gap" for each of the standards to help programs assess where they are and where they need to be and to develop corrective action plans based on those gaps (see Appendix F). In addition, Devereux initiated a site visit process that brings an independent team of reviewers together to provide an objective assessment of the program on the same dimensions of the needs assessment survey. This serves as both a check on perspective and an opportunity to forge consulting and collaborative relationships across the organization. This process is discussed in greater depth in Chapter Seven.

Once the QI infrastructure is in place and basic standards have been established to reduce variability and improve the quality of care for the typical client, the foundation of a provider's "house" has been adequately laid. We turn now to issues that ensure and protect the rights of the client.

Chapter 3
Ethics and Client Rights

DR. C, AN ENTERPRISING young practitioner, was new to the area and had been practicing at the local clinic for just over a month when she had a brilliant idea. Why not host a clinic social for her single-women's group, whose members were working on developing their social skills? Dr. C decided to invite some of her male friends to meet the members of her group and offered to include clients of some of the other therapists as well. She made it clear to her women's group that everyone was required to attend or there would be no party. The staff at the clinic thought the social was a superb idea, as did the majority of Dr. C's group. In fact, some of the women were so excited about the event that they volunteered to help with the planning.

Dr. C hired one of the women, who owned a catering service, to cater the affair. Another group member, who tended bar at a local club, agreed to work the event in exchange for a free session. Even the clinic staff got involved. One therapist took charge of decorating the offices while another provided the music. One by one, things fell into place.

When Dr. C realized that this event could be great publicity for her and could help promote her private practice and launch her career, she convinced the local newspaper to write a feature story about it. The clinic regarded the media coverage as an opportunity to obtain free advertising.

All of Dr. C's clients showed up for the party. A local newspaper reporter and a photographer attended as well, but Dr. C asked them to keep a low profile so that her clients would not feel inhibited. Dr. C spared no expense—the food was lavish and the drinks flowed. And just to be certain that everyone had a good time, she brought along a few adult party games. One of these required the participant to reveal deep, dark secrets. The other players determined whether or not the secrets were real. The clients really enjoyed this game. Not surprisingly, the party was an overwhelming success.

The next evening before the start of Dr. C's group, the women chatted enthusiastically among themselves about the party, each sharing "her story." One woman had made a date with a male friend of Dr. C's. The caterer had been hired for two additional parties.

Then Dr. C arrived with newspaper in hand. She placed it on the table face up and announced "You're famous." To the group's horror, a photo of the women was splashed on the front page with the caption, "Mental Patients Are People Too." Under the caption, the article chronicled the secrets the clients had revealed during the game. We leave the group's reaction to the reader's imagination.

To be sure, none of us would ever expect to have to deal with the aftermath of such flagrant abuses of clients' rights. However, the types of abuses described are not entirely unknown to the field of behavioral health care. Therapists contract with clients for personal business. Clinicians engage in sexual relationships with their clients, with or without their consent. Confidential client information is released to the public domain. One needs to look no further than the evening news to observe such outrageous infractions of the doctor-patient relationship.

Regardless, consumers of behavioral health care services have every reason to believe that their confidences, rights, and overall well-being will be respected. In fact, as providers of behavioral health care, we are morally and legally obligated to ensure and protect the rights of our clients. Accordingly, our clients are entitled to receive appropriate and effective care that is provided in a safe and nurturing environment, free from physical, psychological, and emotional harm.

The advent of managed care has compounded matters by generating ethical dilemmas never before faced by provider organizations. Now that providers are expected to serve individuals with more severe problems with fewer reimbursable services and in less time, the opportunities to neglect the best interest of the client for personal or institutional gain are great. What's a provider to do?

Basic Policies and Procedures

It is essential that providers establish some mechanism by which to address their obligation to ensure the rights and safety of consumers. The approach taken may depend on the provider's size and available resources. The action may range from the creation of sound basic policies and procedures to the implementation of a client advocate program or the establishment of a fully functioning ethics committee.

A good place to start is to establish basic policies and procedures that are consistent with fundamental professional ethics. Each major behavioral health care discipline (American Psychiatric Association, 1998; American Psychological Association, 1992; National Association of Social Workers, 1996) publishes "ethical guidelines" that can be used as a resource in developing customized guidelines for a particular facility. But these published guidelines are not laws; they provide standards for professional conduct to ensure ethical practice and promote client rights. Provider organizations can assess potential clinicians' and employees' knowledge and understanding of the standards by subjecting them to a simple written test (see Figure 3.1). Needless to say, you may want to continue your search if a potential clinician scores less than 100 percent.

Respecting Confidentiality

The ethical guidelines compel psychiatrists, psychologists, and social workers to abstain from a litany of potentially harmful and unprofessional interactions with clients. Paramount to ethical behavior, of course, is the duty to maintain confidentiality. Kagle and Kopels (1994) point out that there are limits to such confidentiality, namely the duty to report child abuse and neglect and, in a limited number of cases, the duty to warn or protect potential victims from threatened physical harm (Anfang & Applebaum, 1996; Bersoff, 1976).

Policies and procedures outlining for the provider the conditions and method for maintaining and sharing information help to eliminate uncertainty regarding expected and appropriate action. Policies should include specific directions for "creating, storing, accessing, transferring and disposing of records" under a provider's control in order to maintain confidentiality (American Psychological Association, 1992, p. 1606). They should also specify what information to document and how to document it, as well as when, with whom, and how to share the information.

For example, the American Psychological Association (1992) stipulates in its ethical guidelines that a provider should minimize intrusions by "providing only information germane to the purpose" of the communication (p. 1607). The guidelines also instruct the provider to delete or obscure confidential information whenever possible so that clients cannot be identified. In addition, given the complexities presented by electronic formats relative to information security, it behooves a provider storing records electronically to establish policies and procedures for information systems.

Maintaining Professional Boundaries and Behavior

The ethical guidelines provide clear parameters for professional practice and behavior. All guidelines forbid sexual activity with a current client and advise avoiding involvement with former clients at a minimum for a spec-

---

FIGURE 3.1

The Risk Management Quiz

True or False?

1.   T   F   The clinician-client privilege ceases upon the death of the patient.

2.   T   F   Sexual activity with a former client is not necessarily unethical.

3.   T   F   An altered client record destroys a clinician's credibility.

4.   T   F   Once a clinician begins treating a client, the clinician is legally obligated to continue providing treatment until the relationship is properly terminated.

5.   T   F   In order to qualify for involuntary commitment in most states, a client must be mentally ill and a danger to himself and others.

6.   T   F   Clinicians have a legal duty to report current, known child abuse.

7.   T   F   A clinician is required to keep patient records only until the statute of limitations for malpractice in his state has run out.

Source: *Professional Risk Management Services, Inc., 1998. The Risk Management Quiz. (Available from Professional Risk Management Services, Inc., manager of the APA-sponsored Professional Liability Insurance Program, 1000 Wilson Blvd., Suite 2500, Arlington, VA 22209, 1-800-245-3333 Ext. 347.) Reprinted with permission.*

---

ified period of time following the end of treatment (American Psychiatric Association, 1998; American Psychological Association, 1992; National Association of Social Workers, 1996). In addition, a clinician is expected to offer services strictly within the boundaries of his or her bona fide competencies. Thus the social worker trained to work with children and adolescents should not be treating an adult with schizophrenia. Establishing human resource and credentialing policies and procedures that delineate expected behavior and process, as well as cause for termination (for example, inappropriate interaction with a client), helps ensure compliance with these standards. Credentialing procedures such as those outlined in Chapter Two encourage provider monitoring of the appropriateness of staff qualifications for various positions and responsibilities.

Informed Consent

Another crucial aspect of ethical practice is to make certain that the client and the client's family understand the provider's obligations to the client and the measures being taken to enforce them. Therefore, the policies and procedures developed should include informed consent to treatment at admission. Also to be spelled out are the contractual responsibilities between provider and client, client rights (including mechanisms for reviewing grievances and complaints), and an appeals process. Even these measures, however, may not be enough to ensure ethical practice.

At admission, the clinician or provider organization should explain rights and entitlements to the client and obtain the client's informed consent for treatment (see Figure 3.2). It is important to remember that ethical practice begins with obtaining clear assurance that the prospective client is fully informed and aware of all rights and responsibilities such as the limits of confidentiality, scheduling and cancellation policies, financial responsibilities, releases of information to and from other treatment providers (past and present) or schools, and so on. This last point should not be overlooked.

FIGURE 3.2

Consent to Treatment

I/We, _____, the parent(s) of _____, a minor, and intending to be legally bound, hereby consent and authorize Devereux Center its successors and assigns and any other person or corporation duly authorized by Devereux Center the right and permission to place _____ in Devereux Center for:

(Please Initial)

_____ 1. Providing mental health treatment to include psychiatric or psychological evaluations and individual and group therapies, as well as the prescribing, adjusting, and administering of psychotropic medication under medical supervision if clinically indicated as part of treatment. To ensure the safety and well-being of the above named or of other persons, and under medical supervision, it may be necessary to use more restrictive interventions such as seclusion, restraint, and/or therapeutic holds where licensing regulations permit.

_____ 2. Providing to the client such hospital, medical, nursing, X-ray, laboratory, routine immunizations and TB tests, diagnostic and therapeutic care, services, treatment, medications, tests, and procedures as may be therapeutically necessary or admissible for the preservation of the health, safety, and welfare of the client as appropriate in accordance with reasonable treatment standards, practices, and procedures.

_____ 3. Providing to the client an appropriate educational service. To provide home school contact to assist the client in continued support of his/her academics while a client at Devereux Center.

_____ 4. Applying for and collecting payment for services rendered from the source(s) of payment identified, including but not limited to Title XIX or private insurance, at a rate established by Devereux Center in accordance with its usual charges for such.

_____ 5. Providing to the client specialized programs to enhance the total functioning of the client. These specialized programs can include speech therapy, therapeutic recreation, sex education, psychological evaluation, individual, and group or family therapy.

_____ 6. Transporting the client on local area trips planned by the Devereux Center staff.

_____ 7. Photographs (still or motion) to be taken as part of the program's activities. A photo release will be necessary to authorize any release of these photographs.

Just as the client should be fully informed, so should the provider be informed of all services the client is receiving. After all, care must be coordinated among all providers who are treating the client.

Although it may seem that getting a signature on a piece of paper demonstrates the giving of informed consent, a signature alone may not be sufficient. A provider may be liable if certain actions are not taken to ensure *true* informed consent. Legally, informed consent requires three conditions: (1) the decision must be informed, meaning that the individual understands the risks and benefits of the chosen and alternative options of treatment, (2) the individual must make the decision voluntarily, and (3) the individual

---

_____ 8. Providing for involvement and participation in therapeutic recreational programming which may include, but is not limited to, arts and crafts activities, swimming, skating and other physically strenuous activities.

| The following procedures are understood and agreed to by the undersigned: |

(Please Initial)

_____ 1. Devereux Center prefers that the client's personal money, jewelry, and other valuables remain at home. Devereux Center does not accept responsibility for loss, breakage, or theft of personal possessions. Recommendation is made that personal property be included in a homeowner's insurance policy.

_____ 2. Objects that the client will need for personal hygiene will be made available on a selected basis with appropriate supervision.

_____ 3. Devereux Center may dispose of personal property or valuables not claimed from Devereux Center within 30 days of discharge.

_____ 4. Clients are to be discharged by the mutual consent of Devereux Center, parents or guardians, and the funding agency. Should the client leave the program without this mutual agreement, he or she may or may not be readmitted at a later date.

_____ 5. Devereux Center may contact the client, client's parent or guardian after discharge to review satisfaction with and evaluate effectiveness of services.

| The Devereux Center Placement Agreement has been explained to me. I understand and agree to abide by each part of the agreement I have initialed. |

_____   _____
Client Signature   Date

_____   _____
Parent/Guardian   Date

_____   _____
Witness Signature   Date

making the decision must be competent (American Psychological Association, 1992; McCabe, 1996). Taking these conditions into account, it becomes apparent why a signature on an informed consent form is insufficient.

Involving Children and Adolescents in Decision Making

It's difficult enough to establish what constitutes informed consent when the individual is an adult, given all the required conditions. However, the matter becomes even more complicated when the decision involves a child or adolescent (for example, when the client is an emancipated minor). A number of situations exist for which states allow minors to give consent, such as treatment for alcoholism or drug dependency, or for a pregnancy (Kaplan, 1988). Given the industry's movement toward achieving greater client participation in treatment, it is incumbent on the provider to determine the client's appropriate level of involvement based on his or her ability to give informed consent.

A number of factors need to be considered with respect to informed consent for the child or adolescent client. These include the child's cognitive and social development, emotional state (for example, anxious or depressed), physical state (level of physical discomfort), family factors (cultural or religious beliefs), and the difficulty of the decision to be made (McCabe, 1996). (For further considerations in this area, see McCabe, 1996.)

When the client arrives at the program or facility, staff (either administrative or line staff) meet with the client to review rights and responsibilities point by point and to answer any questions in order to be certain that the client understands. In the case of children and adolescents, this meeting may involve parents or guardians as well. Quite often, the client and family are anxious about treatment and, at least initially, are highly vulnerable. Any actions the staff can take to ease their anxiety and make them feel comfortable and safe will facilitate the transition to treatment. Some providers have responded to this need by creating client and family handbooks with visually inviting pictures and characters. Keep in mind that informed consent is a legal form and is often filled with jargon and language that is difficult for the family and client to understand. Handbooks and face-to-face meetings help translate the informed consent into understandable terms.

Providing an Overview of the Program

Typically, the staff member will begin the meeting with the client or the family by providing an overview of the program—what to expect from treatment and what is expected of them. For an inpatient program, the overview may cover several areas, including (1) the type of care the client will receive (medical or clinical), (2) behavior rules, (3) a description of how the family will be involved in treatment, (4) an explanation of policies for visitation, passes, mail, and use of the telephone, and (5) information about meals and nutrition. Additionally, the provider will apprise the client of his responsibilities, which include giving information that the provider needs in order to care for him, to follow agreed-on care plans (National Committee for Quality Assurance, 1998), and to take care of his clothes, room, and personal belongings. Older clients and their families are notified of their fiduciary responsibilities.

In an outpatient program, the provider may review behavioral expectations with the client with respect to keeping appointments, arriving on time, and making appropriate payment for services. During the initial meeting, the client learns about his rights—specifically, the right to privacy, the right to be treated with respect and dignity, the right to be safe from harm, the right to make a complaint, and the right to participate in treatment planning. The client also has the right to information about the provider organization's services and practitioners (National Committee for Quality Assurance, 1998).

Once this information is reviewed with the client or with the family, it is important that the provider document two items: (1) that the client and family were thoroughly informed and (2) that the client and family understand the content of the information they were given. Programs often establish policies and procedures that outline the specific steps that staff must follow to educate the client and family and to be certain that they obtain informed consent. Some programs have created special client rights signature forms for children and adolescents (see Figure 3.3).

The procedure in these programs is to include the signed document as evidence that the client was informed. Similar forms are used for families and guardians. This type of form states that the family or guardian has received a copy of the handbook, reviewed it with staff, and understands its contents.

Conducting a survey is another effective way to be certain that the client has been oriented to the program and all rights and information have been reviewed. A survey to assess satisfaction and comprehensiveness of the admissions process allows the provider to identify potential gaps in the admissions process. A survey can also determine any additional needs the client and family may have; this will allow them to use the services most effectively (see Figure 3.4).

FIGURE 3.3

Children's Rights

YOU HAVE THE FOLLOWING RIGHTS AND NO ONE CAN TAKE THEM AWAY FROM YOU.

You have the right to be treated kindly and courteously as an important person.

You will always be told of any consequences, which could happen because of your behavior and what you will be expected to do the next time.

You will not be mistreated in the way you are spoken to or in the way you are touched. As a human being you have the right to have your feelings respected and protected from harm.

You will not have to do work which Devereux staff is supposed to do, like mowing the yard. But you will be expected to do chores in the Center, like clean your room.

Even though you are at Devereux, you and your family will still be able to handle your personal business.

UNLESS YOUR DOCTOR THINKS IT IS NOT THE BEST THING FOR YOU, YOU HAVE THE FOLLOWING RIGHTS.

You can have a nice, private place to visit with people who come to see you.

You can believe in and practice any religion you want to.

You can talk with or write to people outside of Devereux.

You can talk on the phone with family and friends in private.

You can write letters and receive letters without having them opened or showing them to staff.

You can wear your own clothes.

You can look at and get copies of your records.

If your doctor doesn't think the things listed above are best for you, he or she can write in your record which ones you cannot do and why. Once a week, the doctor has to decide to change it or not. Your Clinical Coordinator will talk about the list with you every week.

Your rights are important to you. Any time you believe any of your rights are being violated, be sure to talk to your Clinical Coordinator about the way you are being treated.

_____   _____
Client Signature   Date

Ensuring Implementation of Policies and Procedures

As a provider, you can establish additional policies and procedures to be certain that the rights and responsibilities, as they are explained to the client and family, are implemented in the program on a daily basis. For instance, you can outline a procedure for staff to obtain a client's signature on his treatment plan as a way to document that the client's right to participate in treatment planning is executed. Although a signature does not guarantee that the client was actually involved in the treatment planning process, it is a way to provide evidence that you have enforced the client's rights.

FIGURE 3.4

Client Admissions Survey

Name: _____ Program: _____

1. Have staff shown you around the program?	Yes	No
2. Have the program rules been explained to you?	Yes	No
3. Have you seen a list of your rights?	Yes	No
4. If you did not bring enough clothes, did staff	Yes	No
get you the clothes you need?	Yes	No
5. Were you told the name of your therapist?	Yes	No
Psychiatrist?	Yes	No
Roommate?	Yes	No
6. Has the nurse explained what to do if you get sick?	Yes	No
7. Have staff explained the program to you?	Yes	No
8. Do you think your room/unit is clean and comfortable?	Yes	No
9. Have you been able to call family/caseworker?	Yes	No
10. Are staff available when you need them?	Yes	No
11. Do you know what the goals are on your treatment plan?	Yes	No

If there is anything else you would like us to know, please write it on the back of this form. Thank you!

An effective way to demonstrate client involvement in treatment planning is to ask clients to fill out a progress report that allows them to share their perception of treatment and to summarize the report in the treatment plan. This ensures that client feedback is considered in the treatment plan review process (see Figure 3.5).

Continuing Informed Consent After Admission

Informed consent does not stop at admission. The client should also grant informed consent to initial medication prescriptions and subsequent changes in classes of medication throughout treatment. The consent form should outline potential side effects, risks, and contraindications (see Figure 3.6).

Ideally, the provider should obtain informed consent in person. Obviously, some circumstances require the provider to obtain informed consent by mail, for example, when parental consent is required and the parents aren't accessible. Other cases may require a court order for consent. For instance, a client who exhibits psychotic behaviors or is suicidal needs to be hospitalized or otherwise removed from a residential program, and staff are unable to reach the parents. In this situation, consent can be obtained from the courts directly in the temporary absence of the parents' consent.

FIGURE 3.5

My Progress Report

Name: _____ Date: _____ Time: _____

Since my last Treatment Team I worked on behaviors including:

_____

_____

This month I'm going to work on problem behaviors including:

_____

_____

I'm keeping in touch with my family by:

Telephone   Letters   Cards   Visits   Passes

In school I'm working in Language Arts on: _____

In Math on: _____

In Social Studies on: _____

In Science on: _____

In Voc I'm attending 1 _____ 2 _____ 3 _____

and learning how to:

1. _____

2. _____

3. _____

In Individual and Group Therapy I'm talking about:

_____

_____

Off-campus outings to:	Has a pass to:	Met a contract for:
_____	_____	_____

Circle any of the following you attended:

Basketball	Football	Softball	Volleyball	Dodgeball
Kickball	Swimming	Aerobics	Capture the Flag	Board Games
Fishing	Fitness	Go-Carts	Puzzles	Paddle Boating
Church On-Campus	Horseback Riding	Arts & Crafts	Boating	
Double Dutch Jump Rope		Cards	Visited "Guys and Dolls" Salon	

FIGURE 3.6

Consent Form—Antidepressant

Dear Parent/Guardian:

I would like to take some time to explain the benefits as well as some side effects associated with the usage of the antidepressant Zoloft, Prozac, and Paxil so that your consent to treatment is an informed consent.

Zoloft, Prozac, and Paxil may be used in the treatment of depression as well as in the management of obsessive-compulsive behaviors, self-injurious and ritualistic behaviors. If Zoloft, Prozac, or Paxil works for _____(client), these obsessive-compulsive, self-injurious, and ritualistic behaviors may begin to subside and reach a point of manageability.

The most commonly observed adverse effects associated with the use of these medications include insomnia, restlessness, headache, and stomach upset.

Usual doses of Zoloft range from 50 mg to 200 mg a day.

Usual doses of Prozac range from 20 mg to 80 mg a day.

Usual doses of Paxil range from 20 mg to 50 mg a day.

Effectiveness of these medications may not be seen until after four weeks of treatment or longer.

Before initiating therapy, the client's medical history is reviewed. Blood work and a physical exam may be indicated if not completed within the last six months prior to initiating therapy.

As you can see, we monitor the individual client on an antidepressant very carefully to make sure that the medication works safely and effectively.

Sincerely,

_____

I, _____on this day of_____
            (parent/guardian)   (date)

give my permission for _____to be treated with
                                                    (client's name)

_____
            (Zoloft, Prozac, Paxil)

I understand the benefits and risks explained in this form:

_____   _____
            (parent/guardian signature)   (date)

Grievance Policy and Procedures

Once the client is in care, the grievance and appeals processes provide the client with mechanisms to exercise her rights. Based on the results of our survey of providers, a grievance policy and procedure is by far the most common mechanism for protecting client rights. Nearly all of the respondents had a client grievance procedure. A grievance can cover a range of areas, from dissatisfaction with a residential facility's food, to objection to the consequences for behavioral incidents, to concerns of staff's discussion of a client's personal information in the presence of others.

A case we had at one of our programs illustrates how the grievance procedure can operate successfully. A single mother of a client complained about the staff's cultural insensitivity to her needs. Initially, staff had interpreted the mother's failure or unavailability to attend sessions as a lack of concern and interest. They insisted that the mother would faithfully participate if she were vested in the process. The mother, in turn, interpreted the staff's inflexibility with the schedule as indifference to her needs. Unhappy with the staff, the mother formally filed a complaint with the program's administration. Her action initiated a dialogue with the staff. Once the staff sat down and truly listened to the mother's concerns, they learned that she was indeed invested in the process but that the scheduled Sunday morning sessions interfered with her ability to worship. The staff and the mother worked together in a joint meeting to achieve a resolution. The program sent formal apologies to the mother, counseled staff to be more culturally sensitive, and rescheduled family therapy at a time more amenable to everyone.

A grievance procedure typically consists of several components, including the following (National Committee for Quality Assurance, 1998):

1. A definition of a grievance

2. Standards for acceptable response time to the grievance

3. The process for documenting the nature of the grievance and the actions taken

4. The process of investigating the substance of the grievance

5. The process of notifying the individual of the status of the grievance and the right to appeal

Managing Grievances

Pressley Ridge Schools—an organization based in Pittsburgh that provides treatment foster care, as well as educational, community-based mental health and residential services to children and families—faced the problem of managing grievances from multiple sites that spanned several states

(Matthew Mason, personal communication, March 1999). Grievances are managed first at the program level, following a standard policy. Unresolved grievances at this level are taken to the next management level until resolution. All reviews and resolutions are then documented in the consumer's file. As part of their quality assurance programs, state and agencywide management teams discuss grievances and possible resolutions in their regularly scheduled meetings and document the discussions in their minutes.

More than a decade ago, Pressley Ridge formed a Child Protective Services Task Force to provide oversight regarding critical incidents. Designed as a proactive model, the task force is composed of senior direct care staff members who represent each program or service site. Each member of the task force is responsible for reviewing a program site other than his or her own. The task force collects information on critical incidents and complaints, which are entered into a central database. The chair of the task force manages these data and keeps the executive management apprised of relevant issues. The task force also proactively seeks the opinions of children and families who are currently receiving services; this is done through child and caregiver interviews. These interviews are held quarterly and are anonymous; the information is passed on through local leadership and the executive team. These interviews may glean levels of dissatisfaction that have not or may not ever reach the level of formal grievance. The task force also meets quarterly to review critical incidents and ensure that issues are being resolved in an appropriate and timely manner. Although the task force does not replace a grievance committee, it functions as an information-gathering and monitoring body. Today the task force is regarded as a positive adversarial body in its advocacy of protection for children under Pressley Ridge's care.

Devereux established a performance improvement team, with representatives from the corporate office and various programs, to create a procedure that could be implemented across the organization. This team defines a grievance as any expression of dissatisfaction about any aspect of the facility's operation. The grievance may be submitted orally or in writing. Grievances include but are not limited to (1) dissatisfaction with program administration, (2) the denial, reduction, or termination of a service, (3) the manner in which a service is provided, and (4) discharge or dismissal decisions.

The task force further clarified that a grievance can be submitted by a client, family member, guardian, community member, outside agency representative, or staff member. For this procedure, we chose to exclude human-resource-related and interclient issues. The procedure itself provides explicit, step-by-step instructions for documenting and responding to the grievance (see Figure 3.7).

FIGURE 3.7

Devereux's Grievance/Compliment Procedure

Any Center staff person who receives a grievance or a compliment addressed to them shall complete the following steps:

1. Complete the Center's **Grievance/Compliment Form** within twenty-four hours upon receipt of the grievance or compliment. When reporting a compliment, please request the individual put his or her statement in writing if time and circumstances permit. Documentation on the **Grievance/Compliment Form** should include the following minimum components: time, date of grievance, person contacted, concern or issue, actions taken (initiated discussion), outcome, and name and signature of person reporting.

2. Turn the form into the Program Manager or Administrator or to a member of the Center Management Team or their designee within the twenty-four-hour time frame.

Any member of the Management Team who receives a **Grievance/Compliment Form** completed by a Center staff member shall complete the following steps:

1. Give the form to the management person most appropriate to ensure thorough investigation and follow-up (when needed). This is to be completed within the twenty-four-hour time frame.

2. After evaluating the nature of the grievance, an action plan responding to the grievance should be developed. This is to be done within three (3) working days.

3. The action plan shall be shared with the originator of the grievance within the three (3) day time period.

4. If the three (3) day time frame cannot be adhered to, the grievance shall be turned over to the next person in the chain of command.

5. If the grievance cannot be resolved at the Management Team level, the Executive Director will intervene. If the grievance cannot be resolved at the Center level, it will be submitted to the Regional Vice President for resolution.

6. After the grievance has been resolved, the **Grievance/Compliment Form** shall be forwarded to the Director of Quality Management for reporting at the Quality Management Meeting.

7. If the completed **Grievance/Compliment Form** involves a compliment, it should be distributed, ensuring that, if appropriate, the responsible staff are notified and honored.

You may note that the same form that is used to capture grievances can be (and is) used to gather compliments as well. Knowing what you are already doing well and should continue to do well is just as important as knowing what you can do better.

Key to the effectiveness of any policy or procedure is educating clients on how to use it. Obviously, a policy or procedure that is not used is meaningless. The provider should inform the client and family during the initial admissions process about how to submit a grievance and access the grievance review process.

Some clients may not feel comfortable submitting grievances directly. Pressley Ridge creatively resolved this potential problem by conducting consumer satisfaction questionnaires or focus groups (Matthew Mason, personal communication, March 1999). Most programs gather consumer satisfaction information that is specific to their own programs (and thus is maximally useful for program improvement). Although this type of information is not a formal grievance, it provides information that may help programs prevent consumer grievances. The information gathered from satisfaction questionnaires or focus groups does not identify individual consumers; summaries are housed in the program offices and become part of an annual program or area performance summary.

Finally, a postdischarge outcome interview provides yet another opportunity for children and families to voice their concerns about services they have received. This information is distributed throughout the agency as part of the annual agencywide performance evaluation. The director of research and evaluation maintains these results.

One Devereux center implemented a similar process in their program by creating a client survey process in which clients interview other clients to obtain feedback about the program. The process evolved from feedback provided by discharged clients, who suggested that getting ideas and feedback from the clients while they are still in the program enables them to effect a change in their living environment. The point was well taken, and Devereux Georgia created a satisfaction survey for existing clients. The clients were asked to generate the questions. Clinicians taught them how to interview other clients and then allowed the clients to implement the survey.

The process eventually developed into a Teen Advisory Board, established "to give clients a voice in shaping policies and procedures which affect their daily lives in the residential treatment program" (Cherri Villines, personal communication, March 1999). Members are selected through an interview and approval process and participate on a voluntary basis. Board members are nominated by their peers and sworn in by the center's advisory board member judge. The board affords clients the opportunity to have an impact on their own program. Clients learn interview skills, Robert's Rules for parliamentary procedure, and how to record the minutes of the meeting. The board's primary responsibility is to identify areas of concerns and suggestions for improvements to present to the Quality Management Council. Clients like the program so much that they are exploring the creation of an alumni group to enable continued participation.

Developing an Appeals Process

In most cases, clients are satisfied with the way their grievances are resolved. However, in some instances clients may exercise their right to appeal a decision. The provider should offer a thoughtfully developed mechanism for registering and responding to appeals. However this is accomplished, the process must be fully accessible to clients.

The National Committee for Quality Assurance (1998) offers a general guide to the basic elements of an appeals process. It stipulates an appeals process that has two levels of appeals. Procedures for first-level appeals specify steps for the timely notification to clients of the appeal process, timely response to the appeal, documentation and investigation of the appeal, resolution of the appeal, and notification to the client of the outcome of the appeal and their right to appeal further. NCQA notes that the person who makes the appeal decision should not have been involved in the initial grievance decision. Those appeals involving clinical decisions should involve at least one practitioner in the same or similar clinical discipline that typically manages the disorder, procedure, or treatment.

Procedures for second-level appeals include the same elements as those for first-level appeals, with the exceptions that second-level appeals are reviewed by an independent panel and the client is allowed to appear before the panel (National Committee for Quality Assurance, 1998). If a member cannot appear in person at the panel, he or she is provided the opportunity to communicate with the panel by conference call or other appropriate technology.

Establishing a Client Advocate

Although client rights can be addressed in the context of the QM committee forum, some providers may choose to establish a distinct role of client advocate to oversee the process. The advocate may be full- or part-time; the person may be a staff member or a volunteer who is specially trained and is answerable only to clients and outside agencies and authorities. By far the most prevalent approach is to appoint a staff member as a client advocate or to have client advocacy as part of the job description for the case manager or therapist. Of those organizations responding to our survey, 55 percent used staff as client advocates. Other common approaches to client advocacy included having clients serve on advisory councils or boards of directors (12 percent), providing clients with information about consumer groups such as the National Alliance for the Mentally Ill (12 percent), or using client advocates provided by the funding or referral agency (18 percent).

The Joint Commission on Accreditation of Healthcare Organizations (JCAHO) has been a leader in client or patient advocacy. As part of its accreditation requirements, JCAHO mandated the establishment of a mechanism to address ethical issues (Thompson, 1996). The patient advocate has a dual responsibility: to ensure that patients are aware of their rights and to report or defend any infraction against patients' rights. Known as an ombudsman in a hospital setting, the patient advocate needs to possess the same characteristics that Anderson (cited in Spratlen, 1997) applies to an academic ombudsman: to be independent, impartial, accessible, a good listener, and empowered to make recommendations.

Inner Harbour, a behavioral health care provider in Georgia, created a patient advocacy program to provide clients with a mechanism to assert their rights and register requests or complaints (Ron Milestone, personal communication, February 1999). The patient advocate serves as an agent of a human rights committee that has the larger responsibility of facilitating and enhancing "the establishment and implementation of effective mechanisms to preserve and protect the civil rights of all patients treated" at their facility. The members of the human rights committee have no affiliation with Inner Harbour other than their work with the committee.

The patient advocate receives and investigates all client requests, allegations, or complaints. This may entail interviewing the client, staff, or other clients, or reviewing the charts. A summary of conclusions is provided to the particular staff, client, or parent, and a final report of the investigation is prepared. The patient advocate may also meet with the client's unit team to educate them on specific needs or changes to the treatment strategy and objectives and to ensure that the client receives appropriate clinical services. Additionally, the patient advocate sees that all personnel receive training in this procedure.

The human rights committee receives and reviews a quarterly report of all requests and complaints that were investigated by the patient advocate and determines whether additional investigation is necessary. Any recommendations generated from this process are submitted to the board of trustees for action.

Forming an Ethics Committee

The ethics committee is the most formalized and, according to our survey, the least used mechanism that an organization can establish to address ethical issues and client rights. Only 36 percent of respondents reported having an ethics committee. Interestingly, the presence of an ethics committee did not seem to be related to the size of the organization. According to Ross, Glaser, Rasinski-Gregory, Gibson, and Bayley (1993), the first steps of an ethics committee are self-education and the education of others. In their view, the committee's initial job is to keep track of new developments in the field of behavioral health care and of their implications for clinical practice. The function expands to assessing the ethical atmosphere of the entire organization—not solely how clients are treated but how their families and visitors are treated as well.

An ethics committee can be a force for change at the systemic level. This involves going beyond individual client issues to broader thinking. Committee functions may include offering advice in cases involving life-threatening situations, ongoing education of board members, and review of organizational policies and guidelines concerning withdrawal or withholding of treatment (Thompson, 1996).

Indeed, in several published surveys of human rights or ethics committees, the function of such committees varied. Examples of functions are reviewing behavior management programs; investigating grievances, complaints, and alleged rights violations; advocating for or protecting resident rights; reviewing research programs; reviewing and developing rights policies; investigating abuse and neglect allegations; and reviewing client care (Kemp, 1983).

In order for ethics committees to be effective, Ross and colleagues (1993) argue that it needs both moral and practical institutional authority. Typically, committee membership includes a physician, a registered nurse, a social worker, a CEO (or authorized representative), a clergyman, a lawyer, and a community member (Thompson, 1996; Backlar & McFarland, 1993). Respondents to our survey also included direct care professionals, parents, QI staff, referral and funding agency staff, and finance officers on their committees. It is wise to have multiple disciplines represented on the committee to be certain that ethical practice is considered from diverse perspectives. And it is equally important to include community or consumer representation to protect the interests of the client.

What kinds of ethical conflicts might arise in a community mental health setting? Let's look at an individual who refuses treatment. How valid is the refusal? It might be difficult for the provider to assess whether the client's mental status is affected by a mood disorder or perhaps by drugs. Thus the provider faces a dilemma in determining the appropriateness of treatment. The practitioner who interferes with a person's right to self-determination or autonomy regarding his treatment on the grounds that he is acting in the best interest of the client (who has been coerced into treatment) demonstrates psychiatric paternalism (Christensen, 1997). We see examples of this in involuntary commitment, forced medication (particularly with psychotic patients), or coerced outpatient treatment. Providers may need additional consultation to determine the ethical appropriateness of such actions in certain cases.

Compounding this issue is the fact that community mental health is often faced with the problem of scarce resources; subsequently, the provider may have to allocate according to need and availability. As Christensen (1997) notes, "Allocating an emergency unit inpatient bed, assigning a case manager, or even referring to the outpatient clinic of many organizations, involves elements of triage and rationing" (p. 9).

Although an ethics committee is resource intensive and can be a costly undertaking for the individual community mental health provider, larger treatment networks can justify the cost in relation to the per capita incremental expense. The National Ethics Committee at Devereux started out in 1992 as an in-house body for dealing with new HIV laws and issues of confidentiality. In 1993, a trained medical ethicist joined the committee and expanded its function to respond to the needs of some of our local programs working with populations with special geriatric and medical concerns. Subsequently, "do not resuscitate" orders and advanced directives became key issues. The committee has since broadened its scope to serve as a national forum to provide consultation on specific cases and to advise the revision of old policies and the creation of new policies and procedures for the entire organization.

Given the multitude of ethical dilemmas a provider can face and the increasing complexity of the mental health care field, it behooves a provider to establish a system to help it navigate through the myriad regulations, standards, and issues of care. Regardless of how a provider addresses these issues, instituting basic safeguards in the form of policies and procedures, patient advocacy, or an ethics committee can greatly enhance a provider's ability to ensure that the rights and safety of consumers are protected.

Chapter 4

The Role of Psychiatry in Behavioral Health Care Settings Today

EVERYONE familiar with the operational realities in contemporary mental health and child welfare organizations knows that most clinical and case management services are not provided by psychiatrists. Rather, due to such considerations as availability, affordability, and an ever-widening base of skills competencies, the lion's share of frontline care is delivered by master's-prepared and Ph.D.-level clinicians.

Professional turf issues aside, the various mental health disciplines do overlap to some degree. However, there are a number of significant differences in training, expertise, and accountability, particularly with regard to psychiatry. Not insignificantly, the consuming public has come of age with the belief or expectation that behavioral health care provider entities are psychiatrically oriented. Let us turn, for the moment, to the hypothetical tale of Mr. and Mrs. John Q. Public.

Once upon a time (not so very long ago), Mr. and Mrs. John Q. Public sought treatment for their troubled adolescent son, John Jr. It appeared that John Jr., now thirteen years old, had been experiencing long-standing difficulties with academic and conduct issues in school and had recently begun destroying property and making violent threats involving himself and others. When the family physician referred the family to a nearby mental health services agency, Mr. and Mrs. Public assumed that the first person to see their offspring would be a psychiatrist (someone, the Publics imagined, who would be akin to Sigmund Freud himself). To the Publics, the term *mental health provider* invoked the image of a psychiatrically directed service organization. After all, reasoned the Publics, who else but a psychiatrist would be responsible for planning and assessing John Jr.'s treatment, especially since he was already receiving several medications?

To Mr. and Mrs. Public's surprise, the family's initial meeting was with a licensed social worker. That was when the Publics discovered that their beliefs about the psychiatrist's role in behavioral health care were quite different from the reality. In truth, as our survey results showed, psychiatrists have far less involvement in terms of psychotherapeutic treatment, administration of care, program development, and team leadership at behavioral health care provider organizations than the public would guess. Even more surprising is that psychiatrists play a limited role in many of these settings. With the exception of inpatient psychiatric hospital settings, psychiatric services in the treatment milieu have been far outweighed by services from nonmedical clinicians such as social workers, marriage and family therapists, and psychologists (Starr, 1982).

Why the Psychiatrist's Role Has Changed

Many economic and clinical factors are responsible for the change in psychiatrists' role. Certainly, the historically low fee schedules for providers of Medicaid and Medicare services have been a stimulus for change in delivering care to the poor, handicapped, and elderly. Perhaps, as is true with other systems issues, the most significant of these change factors is the advent of managed care. In seeking the most cost-efficient means of treatment, managed care companies have shaped the way behavioral health care is provided today.

It is not hard to imagine what happened as demand for services escalated while reimbursement levels were held in check or reduced. As caseloads increased and time constraints were imposed, few providers retained the luxury of using a team approach. Thus we commonly see what is referred to as "parallel treatment" in which nonmedical therapists conduct psychotherapy while the psychiatrist prescribes and monitors medication (Kelly, 1992). The result looks something like John Jr.'s experience (he resides in a group home setting and although he takes medication, his interaction with a medical or psychiatric staff person is minimal).

Historically, psychiatrists have had more clearly defined clinical roles in hospital-based mental health settings than in clinical settings with no specific hospital or medical affiliation (Starr, 1982). In the last decade, fee decreases or a lack of fee increases have changed the way health care systems use physicians' services. Psychiatric services are provided primarily to patients whose disorders are considered life threatening, severe, or persistent. Thus clients who are perceived as having less severe problems often have less active participation from a psychiatrist regarding their treatment plan. The psychiatrist's role is often limited to prescribing medication. To that end, both the American Psychiatric Association (1999) and JCAHO (1999b) have set standards and requirements for medical staff members in nonmedical settings, in the attempt to ensure that the psychiatrist retains ultimate responsibility for the medical and psychiatric care. But who monitors this situation and how?

The increase of the dual treatment of patients by psychotherapists and psychiatrists has the potential to be cost-efficient and successful, as long as there is open and continuous communication between the two clinicians. In fact, from the perspective of managed care organizations, the collaborative relationship between the nonmedical therapist and psychiatrist is deemed "critical in determining the quality of mental health services" (Lazarus, 1995, p. 344). Above and beyond issues of parallel treatment, there appears to be a need as well as a responsibility to increase psychiatric services and bona fide multidisciplinary input to all clients who could benefit from such services. Regardless of treatment setting, this is a need that can be pursued in a cost-efficient and successful way.

It is simply not acceptable for community-based psychiatrists to be signing off on medication approvals for patients they've never met. Nor is it acceptable to potentially shortchange those patients whose treatment plan should include medication or consideration for placement in a hospital-type setting. These patients are entitled to the personal care and expertise of a medical clinician. Furthermore, and quite critically in the world of child and adolescent behavioral health care services, there may be a tendency to overlook symptoms of underlying medical illness (Bockar, 1976; Raney, 1994) and to ascribe all behaviors and complaints to the psychological realm.

The psychiatrist, from the time of admission through completion of an episode of care, is often the only treatment team member who can appropriately monitor a client's physical health care needs. Perhaps we should be asking, as Joy Midman, director of the National Association of Psychiatric Treatment Centers for Children, has, "What's the necessary role for medical intervention in a program? Is it for medication management, physical health needs, or medical health needs?"(personal communication, December 1998).

We have written this chapter in the belief that the role of psychiatry has swung too far toward minimization and insufficiency in many care settings. Given this state of affairs, it may behoove the resolute provider organization to establish standards as to the appropriate role of psychiatry, or best practices, within their particular setting of care. Once standards of best practices are identified, it becomes possible to attack implementation issues from the cost-quality perspective.

To help identify and optimize the role of psychiatry in today's cost-contained environment, we offer a summary of the formally prescribed role of psychiatry in a number of care settings. "Strategies for Success"—a how-to section—follows the summaries.

Recommended Role for Psychiatrists in Residential and Community Care Settings

Logically, there are two ways to identify guidelines with respect to the appropriate role of psychiatry across the continuum of prevalent behavioral health care settings. The first approach involves a review of standards adopted by the dominant regulatory and accrediting organizations. Additionally, one can examine the prescriptive recommendations of the American Psychiatric Association (APA) and related psychiatric literature as to the desired role of psychiatrists.

The key regulatory or accrediting bodies are the Council on Accreditation (COA), the Joint Commission on Accreditation of Healthcare Organizations (JCAHO), and the Health Care Financing Administration (HCFA). Per state licensing laws, most behavioral health care organizations that provide inpatient or residential services must be accredited by, and therefore compliant with, either JCAHO or COA. HCFA is the governmental agency that regulates standards for providers of Medicaid and Medicare services. Whereas COA and JCAHO standards may not be applicable to ambulatory services, HFCA regulations underlie most states' licensure requirements for community mental health centers and related outpatient clinics.

Standards of Regulatory and Accrediting Agencies

With regard to the mandated functions of psychiatrists in acute care hospital and residential care settings, there is a fair degree of overlap between JCAHO and COA. Figures 4.1, 4.2, and 4.3 serve to illustrate that a provider's accreditation is contingent on a number of physician-related policies and professional activities. For example, psychiatrists in these settings need to operate in accordance with clearly established medical staff bylaws (Joint Commission on Accreditation of Healthcare Organizations, 1999b). They retain overall responsibility for credentialing and privileging, as well as for the overall management of patient care. Although various members of an interdisciplinary team may render mental health and substance abuse services, there must be "appropriate" physician involvement and sign-off on all treatment plans. Additionally, behavioral health care organizations are required to ensure that there is physician input in the development of their medical services plan. Medical staff must have a leadership role in quality improvement processes and oversee seclusion and restraint activities. They should ensure that medical and mental status exams are properly

FIGURE 4.1

The Role of Psychiatrists in Health Care Organizations

1. The medical staff has overall responsibility for credentialing and privileging, as well as responsibility for recredentialing every two years.

2. Physicians' work function is under the framework of medical staff bylaws.

3. In terms of patient care, the physician is responsible for gathering the medical history of a patient and the medical examination (for example, a psychiatrist would do a mental health assessment).

4. Overall management of patient care is the responsibility of a physician.

5. If psychiatric or substance abuse services are provided, the treatment plan will be developed in a multidisciplinary manner that includes physician involvement and approval of the plan.

6. Medical staff must have a leadership role in performance improvement.

7. Multidisciplinary professionals such as direct care staff and nurses are engaged in pieces of patient assessment; however, a physician is ultimately responsible.

8. Multidisciplinary professionals are engaged in pieces of patient treatment; however, a physician is ultimately responsible (a psychiatrist).

Source: *Adapted from* Comprehensive Accreditation Manuals for Hospitals: The Official Handbook. *Oakbrook Terrace, IL: Joint Commission on Accreditation of Healthcare Organizations, 1999b. Reprinted with permission.*

FIGURE 4.2

JCAHO Standards for Psychiatric Involvement in Behavioral Health Care Agencies

- Each discipline's scope of assessment is defined in writing, in the policy and procedure of the given behavioral health organization; that is, it indicates that a "competent licensed independent practitioner" is responsible for the degree of assessment and care for each individual treated in Emergency Care area. However, as defined by JCAHO's CAMBHC Glossary, a licensed independent practitioner is an individual permitted by law and by the organization to provide care and services without direction or supervision. (In behavioral health care this could be a physician, psychologist, or social worker.)

- In terms of assessment, each individual will have a physical and psychological status and social function assessment; however, there is no indication that a physician must do or oversee this process.

- In terms of care and treatment, qualified and competent individuals plan and provide care and services specific to the individual's need and in a collaborative and interdisciplinary manner.

- "Systems and processes are implemented for the safe and effective use of medication" (p. 183) that are appropriate to state law and regulation (physician, psychiatrist).

- Appropriate clinical staff members approve the restraint and seclusion practices. (Does not indicate who is appropriate, thus organization can define appropriateness of clinical staff relative to the existing laws and regulation.)

- An organization's leadership must ensure physician input in planning for the provision of medical services.

Source: *Adapted from* 1999-2000 Comprehensive Accreditation Manual for Behavioral Health Care. *Oakbrook Terrace, IL: Joint Commission on Accreditation of Healthcare Organizations, 1999a. Reprinted with permission.*

FIGURE 4.3

Council on Accreditation 1997 Standards for Psychiatric Involvement in Residential Treatment Settings

- A clinical team of medical, psychiatric, psychological, and social service representatives, and other disciplines as needed, make admission decisions based on referral information and the organization's own studies.

- A medical assessment is included in the initial assessment, which consists of a physician's exam within thirty days prior to admission or a physical exam performed within twenty-four hours after admission.

- With the participation of the organization's psychiatrist, clinical personnel conduct a mental health evaluation or incorporate findings of a recent psychiatric evaluation conducted elsewhere that includes a psychiatric history, mental status examination, assessment of substance abuse, and a behavioral appraisal.

- Locked seclusion exceeding two hours requires a physician's approval.

- With the participation of a licensed physician, a clinical team makes decisions about admission, additional physical and mental status examinations, level of care, treatment planning, and termination of care.

- A licensed physician, who assumes responsibility for medical care, prescribes and supervises necessary medications or procedures and makes referrals for laboratory tests and toxicology screens as needed.

- A board-certified psychiatrist with experience in the assessment and treatment of children, adolescents, or adults, as appropriate, must be on staff. This individual assumes psychiatric responsibility for the treatment program and for those in care, providing full-time coverage on an on-call basis.

- One or more physicians assume twenty-four-hour, on-call medical responsibility.

Source: *Adapted from* The Council on Accreditation 1997 Standards for Behavioral Health Care Services and Community Support and Education Services. *Used with permission.*

performed and that there is full-time coverage on at least an on-call basis by a well-credentialed psychiatrist, preferably board certified.

COA does have regulations, as well as an accreditation process for day treatment, child care, and early childhood service settings, for serving children with emotional or behavioral problems (Council on Accreditation of Services for Families and Children, 1996). For day treatment settings, a "formal" consultation arrangement is required, with at least one psychiatrist for program development, routine care reviews, and some provision of direct treatment services, along with established procedures for emergency medical services. This latter stipulation means that either a licensed physician must be on-call during all hours of operation or there are formal arrangements for emergency services at a nearby primary health care facility. In child care and early childhood education programs, there must be a consultative arrangement with a physician and a nurse to review client health needs and organizational safety practices. These services are either provided directly by the organization or through an arrangement with nearby health services. Additionally, for settings in which it is appropriate, the approval of a physician is required for any period of locked supervision that exceeds two hours.

In the attempt to capture the essence of regulations derived from HCFA pertaining to public-serving outpatient clinics, we have reviewed and illustrated the regulations in Pennsylvania (see Figure 4.4). We found that most states have parallel requirements for providing Medicaid and Medicare reimbursable services in a clinic versus private practice setting. In Pennsylvania, licensing requirements stipulate a minimum of sixteen on-site psychiatric hours per week, encompassing the supervision of all clinical staff, formal oversight of all treatment plans, and responsibilities for prescribing and dispensing of all medications.

FIGURE 4.4

Pennsylvania Code. Psychiatric Outpatient Clinics. Title 55. Public Welfare. Department of Public Welfare Chapter 5200. Psychiatric Outpatient Clinics.

- Stipulations of chapter are to apply to psychiatric outpatient clinical services for mentally ill and emotionally disturbed patients, and are not intended to regulate psychiatric or psychological services in a solo or group practice.

- A psychiatric clinic must have at least 16 psychiatric hours/week so that minimally, adequate care and supervision is provided to patients. This 16-hour stipulation will change when a treatment staff exceeds eight full-time equivalents (FTEs). The ratio is two hours per week for each FTE treatment staff member.

- Minimally, all clinical staff needs to be supervised by the psychiatrist with responsibility for diagnosis and treatment of the patient as defined in 5200.31 (relating to treatment planning).

- The psychiatric supervision of a psychiatric clinic must be provided by a psychiatrist who monitors all treatment plans on a regular basis. In addition, psychiatric supervision can be expanded based on the needs of the patient population and the services provided.

- A qualified mental health professional or treatment team creates an individual comprehensive treatment plan for every patient, which is then reviewed for approval by a psychiatrist. This plan will be reviewed and updated, for voluntary patients, every 120 days or 15 patient visits (whichever is first) by the mental health professional or the psychiatrist. An involuntary patient's plan is to be reviewed every 30 days.

- A physician must write all prescriptions and give all orders to dispense.

Source: *Commonwealth of Pennsylvania, 1990, chap. 5200.*

As we turn our attention to the body of relevant psychiatric literature, it seems appropriate to begin with a review of a model job description and treatment role, as developed by the American Psychiatric Association (1994). As can be seen in Figures 4.5 and 4.6, the psychiatrist working in inpatient and intensive residential settings is expected to provide a comprehensive and timely array of professional services based on patient need rather than on administrative or fiscal considerations. It is also expected that the psychiatrist will make final decisions on admission and discharge of patients, provide "psychoeducation" to staff, consumers, and community professionals, and take an active leadership role on the facility's interdisciplinary teams.

Psychiatrists are also directed to ensure that there is appropriate medical screening and history taking for each patient so that medical and surgical

---

FIGURE 4.5

Guidelines for Psychiatric Practice in Public Sector Psychiatric Inpatient Facilities

A staff psychiatrist (full- or part-time) must be board certified or board qualified.

Responsibilities:

- Provide direct psychiatric services through the comprehensive evaluation, diagnosis, treatment planning, and treatment of patients assigned to him or her.

- Make final decisions regarding admissions and discharges of patients in accordance with medical standards.

- Assure the appropriate psychoeducation for patients, families, staff, and community professionals and lay people.

- Ensure the involvement of families whenever possible, with the patient's consent, in treatment planning.

- Ensure that clinicians in services assigned receive appropriate clinical supervision on a regular basis.

- Participate in administrative duties as assigned, which could include, for example, being a member of or chairing the quality assurance or utilization review committees.

- Provide psychiatric leadership to interdisciplinary teams. The staff psychiatrist's responsibility on a multidisciplinary in-patient team includes treatment team planning and regular reviews, which comprehensively address the patient's bio-psychosocial needs.

- Provide psychiatric inservice training to other clinical staff.

- Serve as psychiatric liaison with community care providers, particularly with regard to continuity of patient care.

- Identify and advocate for needed resources, including staff, to the medical director.

Source: *Adapted from "Guidelines," 1994, p. 798. Used with permission.*

FIGURE 4.6

Guidelines for Proper Psychiatric and Other Medical Evaluation and Treatment of Patients

- Each patient should receive timely, comprehensive psychiatric evaluation, diagnosis, and treatment planning in the biological, psychological, and social spheres.

- Each patient should be medically screened and the history reviewed to ensure that the full range of medical and surgical considerations is taken into account in determining the diagnosis and appropriate treatment; medical-surgical consultation should be ensured when indicated.

- A psychiatrist may prescribe or adjust psychotropic medication only after direct evaluation of the patient, except in times of emergency, with timely direct evaluation to follow.

- A patient receiving medications should have his or her medications reevaluated by a psychiatrist as clinically appropriate and at least monthly, though preferably more frequently. Patients not receiving medications should be reevaluated by a psychiatrist at timely, clinically appropriate intervals.

- The frequency, process, content, and duration of any psychiatric evaluation or intervention should be based on patient need and not on administrative or fiscal considerations.

- Quality assurance and a utilization review of patients should include appropriate medical-psychiatric participation.

Source: *Adapted from "Guidelines," 1994, p. 798. Used with permission.*

---

needs are not overlooked. Prescribed medications are to be reviewed at least monthly, based on direct, face-to face evaluation of the patient. Similar to regulatory standards reviewed in the previous discussion, APA guidelines call for psychiatric participation in both quality improvement and utilization management activities.

A Look at the Treatment Literature

Within the treatment literature, discussions about the recommended role for psychiatrists in acute and residential care settings range from conservative to progressive. On one hand, authors such as Menninger (1995) and Husain (1995) stake out the old turf, calling for psychiatrists to head multidisciplinary teams and to retain exclusive oversight of all care-related activities, from the initial admissions evaluation through discharge planning.

An alternative and far more enlightened view of the role of psychiatry is shared by Pardes (1995). This author believes that in the future, "psychiatry will more closely parallel developments in the rest of medicine, especially because psychiatry has become more biological and medical in character" (p. 2802). This, in turn, would result in psychiatry becoming more mainstream in terms of its role in "medicine at universities, hospitals, and research centers" and engender "cross-disciplinary collaboration, the sharing of innovations, and the setting of rigorous standards for treatment and research" (p. 2803). Given that the mainstreaming of psychiatry "fosters a more broadly databased approach and a stronger rationale for programs of diagnosis, treatment, and prevention" (p. 2904), the result will be better service to patients.

Considering the impinging market forces and current operating parameters of acute inpatient treatment programs (brief, tightly monitored episodes of care based on the assessment of a patient's lethality or dangerousness), it seems clear that these behavioral health care settings require strong medical and psychiatric leadership. Residential care, however, presents a broader and more complex set of issues with regard to client needs and appropriate professional staffing. Decreases in the use of inpatient, psychiatric hospitalization have been accompanied by increased admissions to residential treatment centers (RTCs). Logically then, today's RTC clients present more complex and challenging presenting problems and are more tenuously adjusted than in the past.

Given these circumstances, Lewis, Summerville, and Graffagnino (1996) speak to the demands on the residential treatment center psychiatrist to manage "the increasingly complex psychopharmacological regimens the referring hospital may have initiated for many of the incoming young people" (p. 899). In this context of care, psychiatrists are uniquely credentialed to respond to an elevated need "to use referral to the short-term inpatient psychiatric hospital for emergency situations affecting the patient's safety or for severe regressive episodes that the RTC is not able to handle" (p. 899).

As with other members of the multidisciplinary team, psychiatrists must be integrated into the fabric of an organization "to help provide the unique understanding of the complexities of the individual child and to help in the ongoing and often changing need for balance in the many approaches concurrently being used to help that child" (p. 899). This cannot occur in situations where the psychiatrist's role is limited, by time and administrative expectations, to prescribing and managing medication.

We agree with many of the sources we referenced, with respect to the need to develop a job description that clarifies the duties and responsibilities of staff psychiatrists in residential treatment centers. The ten prescriptive recommendations offered by Lewis, Summerville, and Graffagnino (1996) and illustrated in Figure 4.7, serve as a model for psychiatrists working in residential treatment centers settings.

Moving out into community settings of care such as group homes, youth shelters, foster care, and Big Brothers/Big Sisters programs, the role

---

FIGURE 4.7

Prescriptive Recommendations for Psychiatrists in Residential Treatment Centers

1. Psychiatrist should meet for thirty to forty-five minutes per week with each clinician individually, addressing issues of the clinician's caseload.

2. Psychiatrist should be involved in one to two hours per week of case conference with the team, addressing all issues (treatment problems, milieu dilemmas, and so on).

3. Psychiatrist must be available to evaluate a given child for multiple purposes, that is, intake evaluation, psychopharmacological treatment, or psychiatric emergencies, to explore clinical issues as per staff clinician's request.

4. Case conference should be led by a psychiatrist, one hour per week, for clinical staff, in which one of the clinicians presents a case.

5. Psychiatrist should provide talks, seminars, and so on.

6. Psychiatrist should be engaged in "informal visits to classrooms, living units, and other residential activities" (p. 899).

7. As needed, psychiatrist should be available to participate in agency committees and working groups.

8. Psychiatrist should be involved in administrative consultation.

9. Psychiatrist should directly monitor psychotropic medication, that is, be responsible for prescription but also for regular follow-up.

10. Weekly, psychiatrist should conduct "systematic review of charts" with "appropriate documentation of findings and recommendations" (p. 899), with nurse and staff input.

Source: *Lewis, Summerville, and Graffagnino, 1996. Reprinted with permission.*

---

of the psychiatrist is less easily differentiated from that of other behavioral health care professionals. Here, there are references in the literature to an educative and consulting role, as well as to the need for the psychiatrist in these settings to adopt not only a medical approach per se but "a naturalistic or ethnographic intervention" so they can better understand the client's perspective (Grigsby, 1996, p. 911). With regard to school consultation, the psychiatrist's role is portrayed as similar to other consultative mental health professionals in helping to meet the needs of children, school staff, and parents (Schwab-Stone & Henrich, 1996).

For the purpose of a summary discussion of the appropriate role of psychiatry, it seems reasonable to bypass these considerations in acute, inpatient hospital settings due to the prevailing medical model. In hospital programs, physician leadership is mandated, responsibilities are clearly defined, and the use of these services by payers is driven by criteria for medical necessity. At the other extreme, community care and school programs look to psychiatrists to provide consulting and psychoeducational services that are not clearly differentiated from those of other behavioral health care professionals. Here too, discussion of an ideal role for psychiatrists seems not to be warranted.

Instead, let's narrow our focus to desirable levels of psychiatric service in residential treatment centers (RTCs) and outpatient mental health clinics. Demand for care continues to escalate in these settings, with clients presenting more complex and serious behavioral health needs. As one of the intended results of managed care, in tandem with strident consumer advocacy, costs have been contained and the intensity of care has been "successfully" unhinged from the setting of care. Again, this means that clients requiring more comprehensive and intensive care are increasingly seen in less restrictive settings. Given the inherent value of accessing sufficient psychiatric hours for participation in multidisciplinary assessments (including review of medical and neurological considerations, proper coordination of psychopharmacological interventions, regular staffings, peer review, staff training, program development, and quality improvement activities), the conscientious provider faces a true dilemma.

The section that follows offers a number of strategies and examples for creatively and constructively integrating psychiatry into a multidisciplinary mix.

Strategies for Success

Operational realities in many provider organizations were found to vary to some degree from both the formal regulatory requirements and suggested guidelines regarding the role of psychiatrists. For instance, of the provider organizations that responded to our survey, 58 percent had a full- or part-time medical director, and just four of these organizations (7 percent) reported having a medical-psychiatric leadership committee. The survey found an increased likelihood of medical directorship and related leadership committees in moving from small to large organizations.

Although a few provider organizations were found to reject psychiatric leadership or the medical model in general, most have endeavored to involve psychiatric staff in case consultations and team meetings and to support some level of peer review. A number of respondents indicated that they have outsourced their psychiatric service needs; it was unclear whether or not there was sufficient communication from the psychiatrist contractors back to the treatment team. In many instances, it seems that specific decisions regarding the incorporation of psychiatrists into a provider organization have been based on either the relatively high cost of psychiatric services or the desire to comply, albeit suboptimally, with regulatory standards. Alternatively, it is suggested that a provider group's senior team begin by identifying and defining the optimal role for medical and psychiatric staff in their organization. Then the task is to creatively address contracting, efficiency of workflows, and infrastructure development to make the targeted outcomes a reality.

Development of Job Descriptions and Employment Contracts for Physicians

To paraphrase a familiar quotation, a thousand-mile march begins with the first step. We recommend that a first step be to define the desired or optimal range of services and interactions that physicians should provide. The identified objectives should then be translated into one or more formal job descriptions, which in turn set the stage for contracting.

A copy of Devereux's "Position Description" for psychiatric and medical service directors is illustrated in Figure 4.8. Although Devereux is a large provider organization and the setting of care is often intensive residential treatment, many elements of the position description can be generalized to a wide range of settings and employment circumstances. Figure 4.8 reflects a full range of direct services, related professional interactions, and responsibilities for regulatory compliance; it also speaks to required involvement in a spectrum of quality improvement initiatives. An agreement at the end of Figure 4.8 addresses key considerations for physicians who serve part-time as independent contractors (a familiar situation in our field). It is increasingly common and reasonable to define the specific duties and services that physicians will provide to a program and to include in their compensation requirements for involvement in such quality improvement activities as QM meetings, peer review, and outcomes research. It may be more difficult, however, to superimpose these requirements after the fact.

Workflow and Development of a Physician-Friendly Infrastructure

For small behavioral health care providers, there may be no more than one full- or part-time psychiatrist available. Given a well-crafted job description and employment contract, it should be reasonable for the psychiatrist to participate in monthly QM meetings (see Chapter One), weekly multidisciplinary staffings, and periodic credentialing activities, and to provide or oversee specified direct treatment services.

In medium-to-large provider organizations, it is possible to appoint a senior psychiatrist to be a productive medical director. This individual can

---

FIGURE 4.8

Position Description

POSITION TITLE: Psychiatric and Medical Services Director

SUMMARY OF POSITION: Coordinates, monitors, and provides psychiatric and medical services. Serves as liaison to outside providers or agencies on matters requiring psychiatric and medical expertise. Provides advice and assistance to the Executive Director and all clinicians on clinical issues. Long, irregular hours and exposure to stressful situations. Expected to provide on-call services on scheduled weekends, overnights, and holidays. Handles detailed, complex concepts and problems and makes rapid decisions. Plans and meets deadlines.

REPORTS TO: Executive Director

MAJOR ACCOUNTABILITIES

Items 1–9 are essential accountabilities.

1. Provide and/or supervise psychiatric evaluation of all admissions and discharges.

2. Manage all aspects of client medications. Serve as active member of the Pharmacy and Therapeutics Committee.

3. Consult with Center treatment team, the various disciplines such as the education and educational programs, and provide staff education and training. Also, participate with Executive Director and Center Administration in program development, strategic planning, and continuous quality improvement.

4. Support the research and outcome studies efforts of Devereux.

5. Communicate as a representative of Devereux with parents, agencies, and guardians.

6. Monitor Center's compliance in related areas with regulatory standards and practices.

7. Cooperate with and participate in Center quality assurance programs and initiatives.

8. Demonstrate attainment of continuing education units that equal or exceed requirements for licensure.

9. Act as liaison for Center with community physicians, hospital staff, and other professionals and agencies with regard to psychiatric services.

10. Monitor department budget and adhere to Center financial guidelines.

11. Collaborate on human resource management procedures or practices to improve the delivery of clinical services, as needed.

12. All other duties as assigned.

---

organize medical staff and conduct a variety of medical-quality and risk-management activities. Based on the size and staffing level of the organization, effective peer reviews may occur on schedules ranging from monthly to quarterly. This type of scheduling would also be true of risk and safety committee meetings such as those specified by JCAHO and reflected in Figure 4.9.

FIGURE 4.9

Medical Staff Representation on Committees as Recommended by JCAHO Standards

Level of Recommendation	Typical Committee Name
Mandated	Governing Body (unless prohibited by law)
	Medical Executive Committee
Critical/Key to meeting the intent of the Standard	Budget Committee
	Strategic Planning Committee
	Performance Improvement Committee/Quality Council
	Ethics
	Pharmacy and Therapeutics
	Utilization Management/ Patient Care Monitoring Committee
	Infection Control
	Health Information Management
Desirable	Safety Committee

Source: *Joint Commission on Accreditation of Healthcare Organizations, 1999b.*

Note: *"Medical staff" refers to psychiatrists in mental health facilities or settings.*

The medical director may also participate in monthly meetings for all clinical supervisors, monthly case reviews, weekly treatment team meetings, and daily rounds. As the icing on the proverbial cake, the medical director is able to institute quarterly grand rounds meetings that feature presentations from local or national speakers with recognized expertise. (The institution of grand rounds also addresses training and education considerations, as discussed in Chapter Two.)

We can see how the medical infrastructure pieces can fit together by looking at one of Devereux's larger community services treatment networks—one that provides the full gamut of children's services (both mental health and child welfare). Services are geographically dispersed across several large counties, and treatment settings include group homes, therapeutic and regular foster homes, outpatient clinics, and partial hospital programs, as well as in-home and in-school services. A staff of six part-time psychiatrists and more than one hundred clinicians and case managers serve several thousand clients in the course of a month.

A senior psychiatrist serving this program on a nearly full-time basis was appointed medical director. He spent more than a year exploring options to meet corporate quality standards for integrating physician services. Simultaneously, he addressed the pressing operational challenges of managing a geographically dispersed, part-time medical staff. As it has evolved, medical staff meetings are scheduled six times per year. Each physician is required to present a minimum of two cases per year and to attend at least three meetings (50 percent) each year to maintain appointment to the medical staff.

Documentation of peer review activities is generated through the minutes of medical staff meetings; documentation is further reviewed at the program's clinical practice team meeting and is then forwarded in summary to the QM team, on which the medical director participates. Best of all, the medical director was able to secure financial support for the medical staff meetings from various pharmaceutical companies. Pharmaceutical representatives arrange for meeting sites and guest speakers who provide information on current and forthcoming treatment modalities. Generally, these reps succeed in making continuing medical education credits available for the medical staff in attendance.

Another creative example of physician integration and related quality infrastructure can be gleaned from activities at one of Devereux's RTCs that serves approximately 125 clients per day in a centralized location. One full-time psychiatrist, two part-time psychiatrists, and a part-time pediatrician service this client population. Under the auspices of their medical director, a comprehensive and team-based approach to medical quality management and risk management has been developed and implemented. The form, included in Appendix G, lists these activities along with responsible staff. Specific protocols have been developed for peer review requirements and the conduct of peer reviews for psychiatrists and pediatricians, multidisciplinary case reviews, professional staff profiling, and monitoring of performance improvement activities. The forms and underlying protocols in Appendixes H through S can serve as a basis for further specification of physician roles and responsibilities for a given provider entity and aid in the targeted integration of medical services into an organizational structure.

Finally, large, geographically dispersed behavioral health care organizations can achieve coordinated input from their medical staff by creating an advisory committee. At Devereux, a National Medical Advisory Committee (NMAC) was created to address best practice issues, share key programmatic concerns, review serious risk events, and develop practice guidelines of a medical-psychiatric nature. Operating vice presidents were asked to nominate a psychiatrist from each major geographical area for membership on the committee. Further, we sought members with specialization in each client constituency, such as mental health and mental retardation–developmental disabilities. There is also a representative from nursing and a primary health care physician. The NMAC meets via conference call for thirty minutes each month and has at least one full-day, face-to-face meeting each year. The chairperson of the NMAC is a member of Devereux's National Quality Management Committee, and the other members participate on their respective regional QM committees. Physicians are eager to participate in this group and have input into national program development. Accordingly, the part-time physicians on the NMAC have not requested additional compensation for meeting time, and the various executive directors heading up operations have been willing to fund the costs of their salaried medical staffs' participation on the NMAC. To date, the development and continuing refinement of the NMAC have proved to be a win-win for Devereux's clients and staff and offers a valuable tie-in to organizational QI initiatives.

With a physician staff present and accounted for, it becomes possible to direct efforts more productively to consistency of care across disciplines. In the effort to continuously put a provider organization's house in order, we now move to the topic of practice guidelines.

## Chapter 5

Developing Practice Guidelines

Strange how much you've got to know before you know how little you know.

ANONYMOUS

REMEMBER that automobile owner—the one who was seeking good, honest, quality service for his car? Regardless of whether he owned a Cadillac or a Ford, he knew one thing for certain: "genuine factory service" could keep his car running. After all, it was presumed that the mechanics at the dealership knew how to properly service the dealer's own products. The Ford mechanics, for example, were trained to assess and remediate mechanical problems in all Ford vehicles. And if they didn't correct the problem, the owner had some recourse. Not so for behavioral health care consumers of the past. Clients rarely had a clue about the treatment they were getting and when and how they could expect it to end. Thus the picture in behavioral health care was far murkier than in automobile servicing.

Historically, clinicians and their provider-entity employers have held the belief that "one size fits all" and subsequently have embraced a particular theoretical model such as the psychoanalytic, therapeutic milieu, behavioral, or client-centered model. Each tends to view the human condition differently; clients have had no idea which model was being used. That may have been just as well, because many of the techniques, or interventions, spawned by a particular model of care were not evidence-based. Often, no underlying scientific research supported the efficacy of a provider's chosen brand of care for any particular presenting problem or client type. Instead, theoretical belief, intellectual appeal, and anecdotal evidence are offered as explanations for why a given provider has "kept on keeping on."

Movement Toward Practice Guidelines

Few topics have generated more interest and controversy in the health care industry over the last few years than the development and implementation of clinical practice guidelines (CPGs). Indeed, many managed care groups, professional organizations, and government entities have created sets of guidelines and dutifully attempted to achieve full implementation. Of the proliferation of guidelines, Greengold and Weingarten (1996) write, "Clinical practice guidelines have become fruitful and have multiplied. You can find them on just about every corner: in journals, newsletters, conference symposia, and so on" (p. 391).

Sins of the not-too-distant past helped stimulate this change. Because organizations often demonstrated little consistency in their approach to diagnosing and treating patients, their practices led to varying client outcomes and little accountability among practitioners. Consumers, of course, had little basis for assessing which services might best meet their needs and little opportunity for active involvement in treatment planning.

The trend toward overcorrection was the antidote for the years of extreme practitioner variability—a trend heralded by the advent of treatment algorithms and other highly restrictive approaches such as clinical pathways. In this new order of behavioral health care, the "art" of psychotherapy is reduced to a series of decision trees—one finding leads the practitioner through a certain set of actions. This model is subject to criticism on the grounds that it represents linear thinking and practice and does not readily allow for consideration of multiple variables in a given case. Not too surprisingly, many practitioners have reacted quite negatively to these narrowly focused equations.

Driving the Trend Toward Practice Guidelines

Independent of the controversy surrounding clinical pathways, there is enormous and understandable stakeholder interest in provider accountability. Stakeholders are focused on the capability of behavioral health care providers to deliver quality interventions that result in positive outcomes. Consumers of care have become increasingly assertive in questioning the overall quality and effectiveness of therapeutic services, which puts them in opposition to the current focus on the bottom line, increased out-of-pocket costs, and, all too often, reductions in benefits. In our new era of accountability, consumers as well as payers are striving to engage in data-driven decision making.

For example, consumers are requesting more information before choosing health plans and individual practitioners. In response, accrediting bodies such as JCAHO are requiring each accredited organization to submit facility-based outcomes for comparison against national benchmarks. Health plans have increased the specificity and frequency of reporting information about their own practitioners and those of contracted organizations.

And for the first time provider utilization data are being funneled into "report cards" to compare outcomes across practitioners, settings, and treatment interventions (Kramer, 1997). With demands for real-time data increasing, how can a quality-focused provider organization proceed?

The immediate reaction may be to do nothing or merely to complain loudly regarding incursions into the "art" of clinical practice. Certainly, some practitioners have taken the position that the art of psychotherapy and child welfare services cannot be quantified or that existing scientific evidence is equivocal as to the "best" treatments for most clinical conditions.

A constructive alternative to restrictive treatment algorithms or anachronistic chanting about the artistry of care is a move in the direction of adopting practice guidelines. The field of behavioral health care has grown tremendously in the last fifty years, both in its ability to empirically validate various clinical treatments and in its robust efforts to document treatment outcomes (Nathan, 1998). (Yes, there are a number of treatment interventions we do well, so we succeed in generating the desired outcomes.) Provider organizations seeking to improve consistency of care and achieve targeted outcomes via a practice guidelines approach will find themselves in favor with quality managers and health care administrators. And that is why we have devoted the balance of this chapter to the development of practice guidelines. Our goal is to assist provider groups in this quality quest.

Finding the Right Approach

Any behavioral health care organization desiring to implement practice guidelines must first take its particular operating context into account. This includes, but is not limited to, identification of the unique client constituencies being served, expectations or mandates of major referral sources, and a realistic appraisal of staff receptivity and available resources for successfully launching a practice guidelines initiative. As we shall see in subsequent sections of this chapter, practice guidelines may be "home-baked," theoretically derived, or adapted from guideline sets that have been promulgated by professional associations.

CPGs have been defined in varying ways during their rapid profusion over the last ten years. Lewis (1995) writes that CPGs "constitute a branch of scientific review, summation and prescription refracted through the prism of healthcare practice. CPG production generally pursues or claims to pursue a classic scientific model: accumulation of evidence, transparency of method and replicability" (p. 1073).

According to McIntyre (1997), the American Psychiatric Association espouses the Institute of Medicine's definition that clinical guidelines are "systematically developed statements to assist practitioner and patient decisions about appropriate health care for specific clinical circumstances. Practice parameters are strategies for patient management developed to assist physicians in clinical decision-making" (p. 232). Similarly, the American Psychological Association (1995) describes practice guidelines as "a set of statements that will guide practitioner and patient decisions about appropriate treatment interventions for cognitive, emotional, and behavioral disorders and dysfunctions and psychosocial aspects of physical disorders" (p. 190).

What these definitions share is the fundamental aim of increasing the quality of service and ensuring that clients will be provided with the best possible care for the conditions that bring them to treatment. Embedded within these definitions, of course, is the implicit assumption that practice guidelines will produce the most cost-effective result. In addition, the interventions chosen are presumably based on clinical evidence. Greengold and Weingarten (1996) define "evidenced-based" guideline development as a "systematic and up-to-date review of the medical literature, as well as an assessment of the quality of that evidence as employed in the formulation of practice guidelines" (p. 391).

Choosing Effective Clinical Guidelines

The guidelines reported in the literature may roughly be categorized into one of two kinds: evidence-based or practice-based guidelines (Retsinas, 1998). Evidence-based guidelines are based on a scientific exploration of the research literature on a disorder, which seeks to answer the basic question, What works? This type of pursuit can be problematic for any number of reasons. Large-scale, scientifically controlled studies are expensive to conduct, and it is unlikely that the government or any one professional entity could provide the financial support to examine each diagnosis or condition.

Similarly, psychotherapy as a treatment regimen is difficult to evaluate because of the variance that the relationship with the therapist brings to the equation. Retsinas (1998) also points out that the "pure" cases studied in controlled research studies do not mirror the everyday realities of actual clients who present with a hodge-podge of problems and conditions. Finally, there is the very real problem of delay in publication and presentation of research findings, as compared to the rapid inclusion of new treatments into everyday practice.

The second type—practice-based guidelines—also has strengths and weaknesses. When pursuing guidelines development with this technique, a basic assumption is that clinicians truly know their clients and have strong ideas about what works and what does not. However, given the variations in clinicians' opinions, two work groups could generate two very different sets of guidelines, even when given the same direction. Additionally, although a particular treatment protocol may be popular at any point in time, it may not be the most effective solution for any given condition (Retsinas, 1998).

Given the very real problems associated with the use of either approach in isolation, Retsinas (1998) supports the use of a combined approach called *expert consensus guidelines*. This approach combines the review of scientific research, the consideration of preferred treatments by practicing clinicians, and the inclusion of an expert panel to coordinate both sets of data. The Practice Guidelines Coalition emerged in 1996 to support this combined approach in their pursuit of one disorder, one guideline. The aim of this approach is to construct user-friendly guidelines that will guide interventions with clients who present with complex combinations of issues (Practice Guidelines Coalition, 1997).

Addressing the Key Issues

Three major sets of CPGs and the enabling bureaucratic context at the time of their development highlight both the controversies and the opportunities at hand. The Agency of Health Care Policy and Research (AHCPR) was established by an act of Congress in 1989, with the dual mission of controlling Medicare spending by developing and distributing clinical practice guidelines (Brown, Shye, & McFarland, 1997). In a separate action, the Institute of Medicine (1992) was funded to study methods for establishing and using guidelines to influence the dynamics of the practitioners' behavior. These efforts were designed to have sweeping effects on the health care field by setting quality review criteria, guiding health care benefits decisions, and setting information and decision-support agendas.

Three Examples of Developing Guidelines

By 1994 the Agency of Health Care Policy and Research had completed ten clinical practice guidelines, and nine more were in the planning stages (Brown et al., 1997). For example, in 1993 AHCPR had begun work on Clinical Practice Guidelines for Depression (U.S. Agency for Health Care Policy and Research, 1993). The guidelines panel commissioned literature reviews and evidence tables for twenty-one diagnostic topics related to depression. The resulting 1,220-page Depression Guideline Report cited more than 3,500 publications. The effort resulted in three publications: a two-volume *Clinical Practice Guideline,* a twenty-one-page *Quick Reference Guide for Clinicians,* and a pamphlet-style *Patient's Guide.*

Clearly, these guidelines had a heavy research orientation, were very lengthy, and appeared to have the most direct applicability to psychiatric practice rather than to treatment of depression in the primary care setting (Brown et al., 1997). Therefore, their direct relevance and transportability to the primary care setting are in question. In addition, some in the field (Karon & Teixeria, 1995) felt that biomedical interventions were favored, whereas the equal or superior effectiveness of psychotherapy was ignored. Psychologists were critical because the guidelines had not been developed solely on the basis of empirical findings. Rather, they seemed to favor clinical experience in according higher precedence to medical interventions (Nathan, 1998).

Another set of CPGs has been in development by the American Psychiatric Association since 1993. Emphasizing the importance of clinical flexibility in meeting clients' individual needs, the APA has specifically decried a prescriptive stance in their use. To date, guidelines have been developed for the treatment of major depressive disorder in adults, bipolar disorder, alcohol, cocaine and opiate abuse and dependence, nicotine dependence, and schizophrenia (Nathan, 1998). All APA guidelines share a similar format, and all are quite lengthy. Using categories of endorsement, the guidelines place each recommendation into a category indicative of the levels of clinical confidence of the treatment efficacy (American Psychiatric Association, 1993). One of these categories includes options that may be recommended on the basis of individual circumstances (McIntyre, 1997). Thus clinical flexibility is permitted to enter the equation, both strengthening and weakening the potential for the best therapeutic choice to be made in that particular circumstance. For example, the exhaustive number of potential interventions permit targeted treatment that can meet the unique needs of almost any client. However, the guidelines are long and complex and do not lend themselves to ready application by frontline clinicians. Although the APA guidelines were generally well received, they were criticized for underrepresenting the contribution of the various cognitive and behavioral therapies (Crits-Christoph, 1996).

The American Psychological Association (1995) began an effort to develop CPGs by convening a task force in 1995. A condensed set of empirically supported treatments and an initial set of practice guidelines were published, with proposals for three categories of treatment outcomes: well-established, probably efficacious, and experimental. The vast majority of efficacious treatments listed were behavioral in nature (Nathan, 1998). The guidelines were updated in 1996, with a noted lack of completeness in the area of children's problems. Garfield (1996) voiced significant concerns over the set, suggesting that emphasizing specific mechanisms for specific problems implies a more perfect knowledge of the exact operative factors than currently exists in the literature. In addition, he suggested that these APA guidelines did not give appropriate weight to factors such as therapist variance. Similarly, therapies that are difficult to quantify and whose outcomes are thus more difficult to measure are underrepresented in the how-to and when-to approach represented in the APA's efforts.

As we have seen, the noble intent of three major efforts in establishing CPGs has resulted in three somewhat different outcomes. The disparity fuels the controversy surrounding guidelines development. Many practitioners and clinical researchers continue to cite important concerns about the adequacy of the database and about the effectiveness of various treatments for identified clinical issues.

The Rationale Behind Developing Guidelines

Despite these objections, solid rationales remain for the development and implementation of CPGs. First and foremost, it is believed that CPGs limit variations in practice that might signal problems in the quality of service (Lewis, 1995). In addition, limiting variations in practice is anticipated to reduce or to eliminate unnecessary costs associated with that variation. To illustrate, let's consider the circumstances of a client with major depression. Given a correct diagnosis, evidence-based guidelines tell us that antidepressant medication in conjunction with cognitive psychotherapy is the preferred intervention. A different treatment regimen could lead to a protracted course of care, "refractory" symptoms, and possibly hospitalization. At the same time, active practitioner participation is necessary in the refinement of clinically useful guidelines and the movement of health care practice in a scientific direction.

Additionally, CPGs provide a much-needed basis for educating the consumers of service and the general public on the risk-reward ratio of various treatments and related therapeutic benefits. For instance, guidelines can also help improve quality review techniques and reduce professional liability costs. Finally, guidelines are intended to be helpful to the critical end user (the clinician) by providing up-to-date summaries of empirically based practices in a user-friendly format.

On December 15, 1998, toward this latter overarching objective, the National Guideline Clearinghouse (NGC) launched a free Web-based resource for evidence-based CPGs (www.guideline.gov/index.asp). The

NGC was developed by the Agency for Health Care Policy and Research in partnership with the American Medical Association and the American Association of Health Plans. The Web site (National Guideline Clearinghouse, 2000) offers twenty-four-hour access and includes these features:

- Standardized abstracts containing information about each guideline and how it was developed

- Comparison of guidelines covering similar topic areas, and listing major interventions addressed, recommendations made, and areas of agreement and disagreement

- Full text of guidelines (when available) or links to full text (when not)

- Topic-related e-mail groups where registered users can exchange information about aspects of guideline development, content, and implementation

The ability to compare, contrast, adopt, or adapt established CPGs is now literally at our fingertips. Today's options for providing sound, standardized behavioral health care protocols are more varied, more client specific, and more scientifically grounded than ever before. With this in mind, we shift to a review of the status of the CPGs used by our surveyed cohort of provider organizations.

The Nature and Prevalence of Clinical Guidelines Use in Surveyed Provider Organizations

Data gleaned from our survey of behavioral health care provider organizations are illustrated in Figure 5.1. It is noteworthy that more than half of the responding organizations (53 percent) affirmed that they are either using practice guidelines per se or are using manualized treatment approaches. Our impression is that this finding reflects a steadily growing trend. The use of practice guidelines is somewhat more common in small (56 percent) than in large (47 percent) organizations. Further, it seems that larger organizations using guidelines, including Devereux, have been slightly more inclined to develop their own guidelines (62.0 percent as opposed to 45.0 percent), with a smaller percentage of provider groups opting to customize existing guidelines (25.8 percent) or to adopt existing practice guidelines "as is" (22.6 percent).

Currently, behavioral health care provider organizations may have differing ideas as to what constitutes a bona fide approach to the implementation of practice guidelines. For instance, one respondent might be referencing their organization's commitment to a particular set of QA stan-

FIGURE 5.1

Standards for Clinical Practice

	All Organizations (n = 59)	Small Organizations (n = 16)	Medium Organizations (n = 18)	Large Organizations (n = 17)
Do organizations use practice guidelines or manualized treatment approaches?	53% Yes 37% No 10% no data	56% Yes 38% No 6% no data	50% Yes 39% No 11% no data	47% Yes 41% No 12% no data
If yes to above:				
Organizations that develop their own guidelines	51.6%	45%	45%	62%
Organizations that adopt published documents	22.6%	22%	33%	13%
Organizations that both develop and adopt published guidelines	25.8%	33%	22%	25%

dards, whereas a peer from a different surveyed group has shared information about adoption of a uniform approach to providing clinical care. The varied and transitional nature of provider organizations' status regarding the use of guidelines is suggested by the summary of related survey findings found in Figure 5.2.

A review of responses in Figure 5.2 is encouraging in that movement toward the selection of standardized systems of care by providers is suggested. However, practice guidelines per se are not clearly differentiated from allegiance to a particular theoretical model, compliance with regulatory requirements, or adherence to basic clinical standards such as credentialing and documentation. What's more, one is left to wonder about varying concepts and approaches to guidelines adoption. For instance, one provider organization might intensively train and continuously supervise their clinicians from a set of evidence-based practice guidelines, whereas another might use an orientation manual on cognitive-behavioral therapy as their adaptation of practice guidelines. Based on extensive interviews with organizational leaders and visits to a number of provider sites, a sampling of approaches to the use of practice guidelines is provided.

FIGURE 5.2

Adoption of Published Practice Guidelines Documents: Survey Responses

- National treatment standards for sex offending and substance abuse
- Common Sense Parenting (Boys Town), Strategic Family Therapy
- State, Federal, and License guidelines
- National Association of Social Work (NASW) guidelines
- Reality Therapy/Choice Theory treatment modalities
- Council on Accreditation (COA)
- Brief Solution-Focused Therapy
- Province of Ontario Risk Assessment model
- Department of Human Services (DHS) practice standards
- American Psychiatric Association (APA) Practice Guidelines (adopted and modified)
- Guidelines addressed in Family Service Licensing requirements
- Department of Human Services and Community Behavioral Health regulations
- Clinical Practice Guidelines developed by Medical Director Association for long-term care
- COA, Family Focus and Treatment Association (FFTA), and Child Welfare League of America (CWLA) standards

---

A Trio of Practice Guidelines Initiatives

Cleo Wallace Centers—a child and adolescent behavioral health care organization—is headquartered in Denver and recently affiliated with Devereux. The facility has been providing care for more than fifty years and operates residential, acute care, and partial hospitalization programs in both Denver and Colorado Springs (Mike Montgomery, personal communication, February 1999). Cleo Wallace also manages day treatment services in some of Denver's public schools.

In 1997 Cleo Wallace adopted the solution-focused treatment approach developed by Insoo Kim Berg and Steve de Shazer as its clinical practice model (Cleo Wallace Centers, 1998). The approach is described this way in the clinician's manual:

> *Solution-Oriented Treatment is one of the three technologies that constitute the Biopsychosocial Model of Treatment used by Cleo Wallace Centers. The "bio" or biology part of Biopsychosocial represents the use of psychopharmacology by psychiatrists in the treatment of patients. Solution-Oriented Treatment used by clinicians makes up the "psycho" or*

FIGURE 5.3

Assumptions of a Solution Orientation

1. Change is a constant and is inevitable.

2. Patients have resources and strengths to resolve complaints.

3. The clinician's job is to identify and amplify positive change.

4. It is usually unnecessary to know the cause or function of the complaint in order to resolve it.

5. A small change is sometimes all that is necessary. A change in one part of the client system can effect changes in the rest of the system.

6. The client system collaborates in defining the goal.

7. Treatment should focus on what is possible and changeable rather than on what is impossible and intractable.

Source: *O'Hanlon & Weiner-Davis (cited in Cleo Wallace Centers, 1998, p. 12).*

---

psychology part of our model. Finally, "social" is the technology of Social Learning used by direct care staff as part of our overall treatment strategy. (p. 3)

To implement this practice model, Cleo Wallace developed and distributed a manual titled *The Basics of Solution-Oriented Treatment and the Role of the Clinician* (Cleo Wallace Centers, 1998). This model offers periodic inservice training sessions on the topic and incorporates assumptions and principles of solution-focused treatment into the process of clinical supervision. It is a broad, humanistic, and inclusive model of care that derives from the work of O'Hanlon and Weiner-Davis; it is illustrated in Figure 5.3.

Although principles of care are articulated and clinical tactics are reviewed, Cleo Wallace Centers have embraced a transitional model and philosophy of care consistent with its mission rather than an evidence-based or disorder-specific approach to practice guidelines. There is much merit in beginning with such a coherent model and a philosophy of care, but still the question remains: What are desirable, systemwide approaches for intervening in such areas as substance abuse, posttraumatic stress disorder, and sexual offending? If an organization's goal is to provide targeted, focused behavioral health care services that will have a measurable, positive impact on clients' daily lives, then one size doesn't necessarily fit all when it comes to practice guidelines.

In the world of child welfare services, the structured decision making (SDM) model developed by the Children's Research Center (CRC)—a division of the National Council on Crime and Delinquency—is particularly noteworthy. The SDM model is described in a pamphlet published by the CRC (1994). It is both an expandable and flexible child protective service model that enables service systems to make judicious use of actuarially derived risk-assessment tools. By accurately gauging levels of neglect and abuse at the time of referral and periodically thereafter, SDM supports a "case management system that integrates agency decision making from the bottom to the top and provides each agency with the ability to assess its clients, plan its service interventions, and evaluate case outcomes more effectively" (p. 13).

A three-year study compared two widely used consensus-based systems for assessing risk of child abuse and neglect with the actuarial-based SDM model (Baird, 1997). Results confirmed that inter-rater reliability for the SDM system was far higher than risk estimates made by raters using other systems. In speaking to the need to move toward empirically grounded and systematic approaches to child protective services, the researchers commented that "actions taken often are inappropriate and sometimes completely indefensible. In far too many agencies, child protection can best be described as a loosely affiliated group of workers asked to make extremely difficult decisions with very little guidance or training. Their actions are rarely monitored, data related to program effectiveness are not available, and their access to computer technology is virtually nonexistent. As a result, case decisions are based on the expertise, education, intuition, and biases of individual workers" (p. 13). The comprehensive case management model derived from SDM is currently being used in at least thirteen states and is under consideration for adoption by at least five other jurisdictions (Janice Ereth, personal communication, April 1999).

In a similar vein, YAI, a large New York City–based provider agency, has recently undertaken the development of their own unique model of care: the YAI Clinical Care Assessment Model (CCAM) (Shelly Botuck, personal communication, May 1999). YAI mainly serves mentally retarded and developmentally delayed clients of all ages. Although clinicians and direct care staff are trained to intervene as case managers and to apply principles of applied behavior analysis, the CCAM is intended to provide an integrated framework for conceptualizing cases across treatment areas.

YAI is developing its model for practice guidelines in collaboration with Donald Meichenbaum, drawing heavily on Meichenbaum's Case Conceptualization Model (Meichenbaum, in press). Beginning with intake assessment, the Clinical Care Assessment Model "provides a standardized framework for collecting and organizing demographic, clinical, medical, developmental, familial, ecological, and cultural information about each patient/consumer" (Shelly Botuck, personal correspondence, May 1999). YAI is building its model by starting with this uniform, multidimensional approach to intake and assessment. To date, staff have "bought in" on a conceptual level, but the model has not yet been fully implemented.

We have drawn on our own organizational experience at Devereux to illustrate the process and mechanics of practice guidelines development. The final section of this chapter highlights various phases of a practice guidelines initiative, from philosophical conception to implementation and periodic revision.

Development and Implementation of Practice Guidelines at Devereux: A Case Study

The development of practice guidelines at Devereux was undertaken as part of the QI initiative. We built from an organizational commitment to become data-driven, to hold minimum standards of care, and to implement a training curriculum to professionalize frontline staff.

Identifying the Needs of the Organization

The corporate QM team began with an understanding that the clients referred to Devereux present complex symptoms or challenging behaviors that have not been effectively treated in less restrictive settings of care; reported clinical outcomes of treatment for these behaviors have been historically weak and inconclusive. Philosophically, the QM team was committed to using a two-stage, best practices approach to devise or adapt a consistent set of behavioral health care interventions to effectively meet the needs of Devereux's clients. The two stages were (1) review and summarize the treatment literature to glean empirically grounded interventions and (2) identify senior clinicians from various disciplines within the organization with demonstrated expertise in serving a specific client constituency. (The second stage can be described as an "internal panelist best practices" approach.)

Through surveying the administrative and clinical leadership of the organization, four dominant client subpopulations were identified: (1) disruptive behavior disorders, (2) sexual disorders, (3) mental retardation-developmental disabilities and pervasive developmental disorders, and (4) major depressive disorders.

Additionally, we recognized a need to develop a training curriculum for all levels of staff across programs on the topic "suicide prevention, detection, and postvention." The various cross-organizational, multidisciplinary guidelines workgroups were charged with reviewing the respective outcomes summary review of the literature, which was sent to them in advance, and to bring pertinent literature with them to their face-to-face work group meeting; most groups met only one or two times. In each case, a chairperson was appointed, homework was assigned, and routine conference calls were used to sustain the guidelines development process until completion. Each set of CPGs was completed within six months, and the parameters for formal review and revision of guidelines were set for two years. Thus an almost continuous cycle of guidelines development and revision was set in motion.

To provide a more in-depth perspective on Devereux's approach to guidelines development, the basic structure and content of guidelines documents will be illustrated with examples from our *Guidelines for Support of Children and Adolescents with Disruptive Behavior Disorders* (Devereux, 1998). (It is noteworthy that approximately 80 percent of Devereux's clients are youth with referral problems related to the diagnosis of disruptive behavior disorders. This finding appears common to many behavioral health care provider organizations serving adolescents and preadolescents and is particularly so in the more restrictive settings of care.)

Structuring the Guidelines

Devereux clinical practice guidelines begin with a "Statement of Philosophy." For example, the *Guidelines* document states:

> *The guidelines for support of children and adolescents with disruptive behavior disorders are derived from the basic philosophy that disruptive behavior disorders are severe and complex forms of psychopathology, presenting with multiple deficits in a wide range of domains of functioning. Thus psychiatric and psychological interventions can only be successful if they are carefully coordinated, aimed at multiple domains of dysfunction, and are delivered over an extensive period of time. (Devereux, 1998, p. 1)*

Following the statement of philosophy, the "Population Profile" encompasses all relevant clinical features and considerations for the targeted client population. This consists of a range of applicable diagnoses (for example, oppositional defiant disorder and conduct disorder), degree of impairment, and comorbidity. The "Risk and Resiliency Factors" section follows, which is an attempt to catalogue characteristics, events, or processes that either increase or mitigate the likelihood of problem onset. The section called "Prevailing Philosophies Guiding Treatment" deals with trends and political realities in providing behavioral health care services to specific consumers. For instance, for disruptive, behaviorally disordered youth, care should be child-focused, family-centered, ecologically minded, and provided in the least restrictive setting, preferably in the home or community.

Action-oriented practice guidelines components include "Best Practices in Assessment," "Best Practices in Intervention," "Best Practices in Staff Development," and "Best Practices in Outcomes." Keeping disruptive behavior disorders as our frame of reference, assessment should use a combination of "multiple methods, multiple informants and data collected over a period of time" (Devereux, 1998, p. 5). Sholevar and Sholevar (cited in Devereux, 1998) suggest that to make the appropriate differential diagnosis of disruptive behavior disorders, one needs specific instruments that contain subscales related to behavior disorders, skill deficits associated with behavior disorders, or those that identify comorbid conditions.

Components of an intervention with disruptive behavior disordered clients include Structured Environment, Operant Conditioning Strategies, Social Skills Training, Cognitive Approaches, Family-Based Treatment, Academic and Vocational Skills Training, Intervention for Comorbid Conditions, and Psychopharmacology. Key considerations in staff development are addressed in Chapter Six and relate to acquisition of essential therapeutic type skills by means of training and supervision. The outcomes section of each Devereux practice guideline reviews key issues in demonstrating program accountability and treatment effectiveness. (We expand on this topic in Chapters Seven and Eight.)

All guidelines conclude with a concise articulation of program components titled "Elements of a Devereux Program." Essential elements are translated into a Quality Site Visit Review and Gap Analysis Checklist, which is represented in Figure 5.4 (see Chapters Two and Seven for more discussion on gap analysis and the site visit process). Finally, each guideline concludes with a reference section to permit a primary source review of pertinent literature.

Implementation of Practice Guidelines

Upon completion, each CPG was distributed to operating vice presidents, executive directors, clinical directors, and medical directors at all Devereux treatment centers. Additionally, guidelines were placed on Devereux's intranet so all staff could easily access it. Each treatment center was asked to read and review the appropriate guideline and complete a gap survey (see Figure 5.4) to assess level of compliance.

Each member of a guidelines work group was considered a consultant on his or her particular topic. Because work groups were both professionally and geographically diverse, an "expert" consultant was nearby or was

FIGURE 5.4

Site Visit Checklist for Disruptive Behavior Disorder Guidelines

QUALITY SITE VISIT REVIEW CHECKLIST AND GAP ANALYSIS

Compliance with Devereux's established quality standards should be rated on the following scale:

Complete Compliance 1	Substantial Compliance 2	Partial Compliance 3	Marginal Compliance 4	Non-Compliance 5

Where a rating is not applicable, this should be indicated by recording N/A. The threshold for immediate action planning is any score of 3, 4, or 5. Please describe and comment upon all minimum standards that are found to be below threshold.

STANDARDS

IV. DISRUPTIVE BEHAVIOR DISORDERS PROGRAMS

A. Admissions

    1. Inclusionary and exclusionary criteria are identified by program.   1 2 3 4 5   N/A

    2. There is evidence that less restrictive forms of treatment have been attempted and have not been effective.   1 2 3 4 5   N/A

    3. There is evidence that discharge planning is initiated at admission with the goal of returning the individual to a less restrictive environment (family- and community-focused environment) as soon as possible.   1 2 3 4 5   N/A

    4. There is evidence that admission and discharge planning is conducted in cooperation with the family and agency involved with the child/adolescent.   1 2 3 4 5   N/A

CRITERIA: Admission is based on appropriateness of care and placement in least restrictive setting. Treatment planning emphasizes goals for successful discharge to lesser level of care.

* * * * *

present at every Devereux location to assist in gap surveying and guidelines implementation. As the various guidelines were rolled out, they became incorporated into the formal, biannual, quality site survey conducted by corporate management.

Once CPGs are in hand, a blueprint for care is in place. To energize and fully activate the caregiving process, it is critical to train, and thereby professionalize, the frontline staff. Chapter Six is designed to help you meet that challenge.

B. Assessment

1. A comprehensive assessment is conducted by one or more members of the multidisciplinary team within 30 days of admission and, at minimum, annually thereafter.	1	2	3	4	5		N/A
2. There is evidence of appropriate diagnosis, including the identification of any and all comorbid conditions (indicate "none" if there are no comorbid conditions).	1	2	3	4	5		N/A
3. Multiple methods (such as rating scales, direct observation, parent/guardian reports, functional assessment) are used to complete the assessment.	1	2	3	4	5		N/A
4. Identified strengths and needs from the assessment are targeted in the resulting, individualized program plan.	1	2	3	4	5		N/A

CRITERIA: Assessments are comprehensive and utilized to guide the development of treatment plans that meet the individual's needs and capitalize on his or her strengths.

* * * * *

C. Program Plan Development

1. Goals developed are linked to (address) expectations in the postdischarge environment.	1	2	3	4	5		N/A
2. There is evidence of family involvement in developing the individualized program plan.	1	2	3	4	5		N/A
3. There is evidence that the child/adolescent participates in plan development.	1	2	3	4	5		N/A
4. All deceleration goals include a corresponding acceleration goal (for example, teaching prosocial skills to reduce target behaviors, teaching other adaptive alternative behaviors to reduce target behaviors).	1	2	3	4	5		N/A
5. Goal mastery is determined by objective criteria (for example, zero incidents of aggression).	1	2	3	4	5		N/A
6. There is evidence that individualized plans are reviewed on a quarterly basis and that areas of insufficient progress are addressed (for example, there is a change of intervention to achieve goal).	1	2	3	4	5		N/A

CRITERIA: The program plans for generalization to the discharge environment and decision making is data-driven. Treatment focuses on skill acquisition as well as deceleration of challenging behaviors.

* * * * *

(Continued)

FIGURE 5.4

Site Visit Checklist for Disruptive Behavior Disorder Guidelines *(Continued)*

D. Program Implementation

1. There is evidence of a clear focus on teaching alternative skills   1   2   3   4   5   N/A
    rather than simply focusing on decelerating disruptive or
    challenging behavior.

2. There is evidence of a consistent environment that includes a   1   2   3   4   5   N/A
    token economy (for example, scheduled routines, point-level
    system, procedures for feedback about behavior).

3. There is evidence of social skills training.   1   2   3   4   5   N/A

4. There is evidence of academic skills training (may be developmental   1   2   3   4   5   N/A
    academics or functional academics).

5. There is evidence of vocational preparation.   1   2   3   4   5   N/A

6. There is evidence of the involvement of parents or future   1   2   3   4   5   N/A
    caregivers in psychoeducational programming (parent training).

7. There is evidence of promoting involvement of individual with   1   2   3   4   5   N/A
    prosocial peers (for example, through community-based functions
    such as YMCA, Boy Scouts, church, sporting events, and so on).

CRITERIA: Treatment focuses on skill acquisition as well as deceleration of challenging behaviors.

* * * * *

E. Measurement and Outcomes

1. Progress monitoring data are collected, in a repeated fashion   1   2   3   4   5   N/A
    (for example, points, level status, rating scales), and there is evidence
    that this information is used to inform individual program plan
    development.

2. Consumer satisfaction measures are collected, in a repeated fashion,   1   2   3   4   5   N/A
    and there is evidence that this information is used to inform
    program implementation.

CRITERIA: Program planning and implementation are data-driven and based on consumer satisfaction.
The program emphasizes continuous quality improvement through ongoing data collection and analysis.

Chapter 6

The Professionalization of Direct Care Staff

Barry L. McCurdy, Catherine Ludwikowski, Mark Mannella

AMONG PROGRAM administrators, there's a common understanding that the ultimate worth of a treatment program is found in the expertise of the frontline staff. However, for many personnel directors, the experience of hiring talented direct care staff is analogous to taking target practice blindfolded. Point in the right direction and eventually, after enough attempts, you'll hit the target. But that doesn't mean you get a bull's-eye. In most cases, you settle for a warm body who's willing to stay awake from 11 P.M. to 7 A.M. and who, if asked nicely, might even agree to check on a client or two (as long as it doesn't interrupt the David Letterman show). From that point on, you find yourself repeatedly crossing your fingers and uttering novenas in hopes of avoiding a calamity brought on by the pairing of an inexperienced direct care staff with a client.

Organizations dedicated to the treatment of individuals with behavioral health care needs have become increasingly dependent on the role of the direct care provider (DCP) in the delivery of treatment services. Long considered the most integral link to the therapeutic process, DCPs assume responsibility for many components of treatment, often with little or no training. They perform a critical role in both community- and facility-based organizations (for example, in home-based services, treatment foster care, and residential treatment centers). DCPs operationalize treatment planning efforts. Whether conducting a problem-solving session with an adolescent who has a conduct disorder, implementing a discrete-trial routine with a child who has autism, or facilitating meal planning with an adult who has mental retardation, DCPs share in the important responsibility of translating the activities described in the treatment plan into a program of service delivery for clients. As part of the process, DCPs have additional responsibilities for data collection and summarization. These are demanding tasks for even the most experienced worker. Why then is there not a greater emphasis placed on professional development for DCPs? To answer this question, let us first examine the historic development of the DCP role.

The Direct Care Provider: Striving to Be Recognized

Historically, the role of the DCP has been linked to our institutional methods of care. For example, prior to the Civil War, institutions for children and adolescents with mental retardation emphasized teaching adaptive skills (Gardner & Chapman, 1993). By the turn of the century, however, a greater emphasis was placed on preparing residents for labor. Between the years of 1940 and 1967, when the number of individuals with mental retardation who were placed in institutional care nearly doubled, custodial care became routine. DCPs ministered primarily to the physical needs of the individual.

For children with more delinquent tendencies, the evolution of institutional care took a somewhat different path, allowing for greater DCP role definition. At about the middle of the nineteenth century, small cottage-type homes were favored as residential alternatives to the practice of placing children with farm families. Married couples, who served as foster parents to a group of children, staffed these homes. Although considered part of the treatment team, the DCPs (foster parents) still maintained a nonprofessional status. Much later, with the publication of the classic text, *The Other Twenty-three Hours* (Trieschman, Whittaker, & Brendtro, 1969), the concept of milieu therapy emerged, and the DCP role was elevated to treatment team partner.

Today, thirty years after the publication of the book that defined the role of the DCP, the struggle for recognition continues. Although there have been several attempts to professionalize the role, including unionization and the establishment of a new and autonomous profession (the child care worker), these attempts have been largely unsuccessful.

Empowering the Direct Care Provider

Despite awareness of the importance of the milieu or the environment in treating children with emotional disturbance, many residential programs that were founded in the early part of this century maintain a predominantly medical orientation toward treatment. Based on this view, emotional disturbance is considered to result from an underlying, intrapsychic conflict (Hobbs, 1982; Munger, 1997). Educational and recreational programming are considered "adjunctive" to the important work of treating the underlying cause of the problem which, of course, is the sole domain of treatment specialists: the psychiatrist, the psychologist, and the clinical social worker.

Today, older residential treatment facilities and child care institutions have had to grapple with the realities of providing service to a much more diverse and challenging client population and to do so within a shorter period of time. Many of the children and youth served in residential care have come from situations where parents or other caregivers have been ineffective in dealing with their behavior. Worse yet, they may come from situations where parenting has been seriously and negatively impaired by substance abuse or where parents are completely absent from the home due to abandonment, incarceration, or even death. These children have not had the benefit of training that is typically derived from an early, stable family life. Many are seriously deficient in both social and academic skills. Moreover, without significant and focused intervention during their stay in residential treatment and later, within their natural environment, they are unlikely to ever make a positive adjustment to community life. Accepting the need for change, providers began to look for other means of support in providing treatment.

Benefiting from Professionalization

One of the most obvious means of support in a large organization is the DCP. Direct care staff work closely with clients and their families. They are a ready source of information to the treatment team and, with training, can easily implement the specifics of a treatment plan. Also, by creating a more professional role for DCPs, there may be a positive impact on organizational commitment and turnover—two issues that are highly related to sustaining an effective treatment program.

It is our opinion that the professionalization of the DCP is an important consideration for treatment programs offering more intensive services. With the level of care needed to provide quality treatment, relying exclusively on the services of highly trained professionals such as psychologists and psychiatrists is inefficient and economically unfeasible. However, to move toward a model of service delivery that places greater recognition on the role of the DCP will require a substantial commitment to organizational change in two ways. First and foremost, there must be an organizational commitment to what was originally called milieu therapy and has now been expanded to include an ecological approach to treating the whole child (Hobbs, 1982; Munger, 1997). By understanding emotional disturbance as a consequence of environmental factors rather than as something within the person, the stage is set for others within the treatment facility such as the DCP to take a more prominent role in the process of treatment delivery.

Second and as previously discussed, there must be a commitment to professional development for individuals in the role. This involves clearly identifying the role responsibilities and specific tasks of the DCP (for example, implementing treatment plans, teaching skills) and selecting or developing materials for training. Following are several examples of competency- or skill-based training curricula that have been used to train frontline staff in the delivery of treatment services. In particular, the focus is on training people who have not had the benefit of more traditional and formalized clinical training.

Professionalizing Through Training

As is true with any field, professionalization is defined by the amount of specialized training an individual receives. The question is: How should an organization approach the training of DCPs? A variety of different approaches were reported in the survey. Surprisingly, the nature and amount of support did not seem to depend on the size of the organization. For instance, Cayuga Home for Children, a small organization (Ann Sheedy, personal communication, January 1999), the Baby Fold, a medium-size organization (Deborah Armstrong, personal communication, January 1999), and Villa Maria, a large organization (Jan Carson, personal communication, January 1999) all provide ongoing, inservice training, funds for conferences or training outside the organization, tuition reimbursement, and some type of merit raises for an advanced degree. One possible difference in relation to staff development and size of the organization was that larger organizations such as Villa Maria have a more formal structure (for example, an ongoing staff development and training committee) for identifying staff training needs.

Almost any administrator will tell you that training is costly and time consuming but desperately needed. Because of these realities and the overwhelming need for direct care professionals who can provide quality care, careful decisions about how to provide training are necessary.

Two approaches to staff training are (1) training in the natural environment and (2) general case training. Training in the natural environment involves using real-life situations for skill training and practice (Page, Iwata, & Reid, 1982). Alternately, general case training is conducted in simulated settings and refers to using multiple teaching examples that are carefully chosen to represent what the actual experience will be like. Ducharme and

Feldman's (1992) findings support the general case strategy as an effective approach to promoting skill generalization. They demonstrated that staff training that uses a simulation format (versus real client situations) can produce robust generalizations. These findings translate into an option of training skills to direct care staff via role-play scenarios and practice in order to generate positive training results. Advocates of general case training claim that it is not necessary to use actual clients or cases, which may be more inconvenient, time consuming, and costly. Therefore, when agencies design skill-based staff training programs, a general case approach may be an efficient and beneficial method.

Using Skill-Based Training

Training via the general case method requires a skill-based as opposed to knowledge- or content-based format. Program-specific skills must be identified and defined within the training curriculum. Training must include repeated opportunities for participants to practice skills in role-play situations and receive instructor feedback.

Numerous examples of skill-based training programs have been developed in recent years. One of the earliest and best known of the curricula was designed by researchers responsible for the development of the Teaching-Family Model at Achievement Place and captured in the *Teaching-Family Handbook* (Phillips, Phillips, Fixsen, & Wolf, 1971).

Components of the early teaching-family model training program included (1) an overview of the program, (2) information about motivation systems, including identification of the privileges to be earned, (3) ways to use the point system and deliver point consequences, (4) self-government systems, (5) responsibilities of a Teaching-Parent, (6) establishment of social behavior goals, (7) instruction in appropriate classroom behavior, and (8) instruction in self-care behaviors. The initial attempt to apply the curriculum to couples interested in replicating the Achievement Place program involved the use of classroom-based instruction, as well as an observation of the successful Achievement Place program in operation (Braukmann et al., 1975).

Unfortunately, after the initial training, potential Teaching-Parents were not successful in establishing replication sites, and researchers further identified the need to teach necessary and specific skills as a way to ensure future success. As a result, the training program began to place greater emphasis on training the practical skills involved in operating a Teaching-Family home. Skill demonstrations, practice, and feedback became an essential part of the initial fifty-hour workshop. This was followed by a three-month practicum and evaluation period in which trainers operated their own programs and were provided with guided supervision from experienced Teaching-Parents (consultants) through frequent phone contacts.

Today, various replications of the Teaching-Family model are employed in all certified Teaching-Family programs, including Father Flanagan's Boys' Home (Boys Town), the Center for Innovative Family Achievement, and the Devereux Teaching Family Program. Although training topics may differ somewhat, the commitment to skill demonstration, practice, and feedback remain constant. By providing trainees with a variety of opportunities to practice skills and receive feedback in the training environment (the general case strategy), there is a greater likelihood that skills will generalize across time, setting, and client programs (Ducharme & Feldman, 1992).

The Positive Education Program (PEP) in Cleveland, Ohio, offers another outstanding example of skill-based training (Osher & Hanley, 1996). PEP serves about fourteen hundred children and youth with emotional-behavioral disorders from thirty-one school districts within the metropolitan Cleveland area. Based on the core philosophical principles of Project Re-ED (for Reeducation) (Hobbs, 1982), PEP incorporates an ecological-behavioral treatment approach that works to help troubled children and their families capitalize on their strengths. At this treatment facility, PEP staff are committed to returning children to their local schools and helping older youth transition to work. Staff who deliver direct services include special educators, psychologists, social workers, parents, and paraprofessionals.

Similar to other skill-based training efforts, PEP incorporates a comprehensive curriculum consisting of eight essential skill areas: (1) an introduction to the Re-ED philosophy and the ecological model, (2) safety and crisis management, (3) knowledge and application of behavioral principles, (4) ecological interaction, (5) assessment and skill teaching, (6) teamwork and collaboration, (7) developing group process, and (8) ecological programming and planning for transitions (M. L. Cantrell, personal communication, March 2000). Like other skill-based training programs, PEP incorporates video, skill demonstrations, feedback, and active training techniques to enhance acquisition and promote skill generalization (Demchak, 1987; Ducharme & Feldman, 1992; Silberman, 1990).

One unique component of the PEP program is the Early Intervention Center (EIC) (Osher & Hanley, 1996). The EIC provides services to families with children from birth through six years of age. Children may be referred due to problems of an emotional-behavioral nature, developmental delay or disability, language delay, or simply parental concern. The EIC is modeled after the Regional Intervention Programs of Tennessee (Timm & Rule, 1981). The program emphasizes a parent-family training model in which the parents are trained to implement all intervention activities with the help of professional and parent-paraprofessional staff. The goal of the EIC is to provide children with the skills and behaviors necessary for integration into the educational setting. Once trained, parents may continue to develop their skills by teaching other, newly referred parents. This is part of the EIC's unique, voluntary payback procedure. Training components are embedded within a variety of experiences, including assisting in the child's classroom, parent-child play sessions, theory classes, and home programming. Specific skills may include using praise to encourage behavior, redirecting behavior, using time out, and using transactional intervention, which includes parental directiveness, interpreting the child's behavior developmentally, and balanced turn taking (Mahoney, 1988, 1996).

Measuring the Success of Training Programs

Successful training programs for direct care staff must meet four criteria (Reid & Parsons, 1994; Reid, Parsons, & Green, 1989). First, they must be performance-based. The training program must focus on how staff perform the skills required to do their job. Many training programs focus instead on providing information about doing the job but never teach the actual skill. The problem with this approach is that staff do not implement the expected competencies with consistency; as a result, clients do not benefit in the long run. A staff trainer should never be convinced that he has trained an individual staff member until that individual is observed successfully using the skill or competency with a client.

Second, the implementation of a staff-training curriculum alone is insufficient to change staff performance. It is highly recommended that a system of repeated and routine observations of staff be implemented as a way to ensure fidelity of treatment (Reid & Parsons, 1994). Unless staff are observed routinely and provided with frequent supervisory feedback, performance on the job is unlikely to improve despite the training received.

Additionally, training programs must be efficient in terms of time and money (Reid & Parsons, 1994). Training programs that require staff to be "off the floor" for extended periods of time are costly. Unless there is a substantial and immediate benefit in terms of organizational advantage, such programs are not likely to receive the full support of program administrators. Therefore, it is recommended that efficiency be a primary consideration in the development of any staff training program. Train only the "need-to-know" information and avoid the "nice-to-know" information.

And finally, a training program for direct care staff will only be successful if it possesses social validity—is considered acceptable by staff (Reid

& Parsons, 1994; Wolf, 1978). If staff dislike the training program or view it as a meaningless or unnecessary task, they will be unwilling participants. In turn, unacceptability will adversely affect the performance of the staff trainer. She will be less inclined to work hard at training all staff if the training program is negatively perceived.

A Model Training Program

Based on the four criteria just reviewed, Reid and Parsons (1994) developed a skill-based staff training program for direct care staff who work with individuals with moderate and severe disabilities. *The Teaching-Skills Training Program* (Reid & Parsons, 1994) is based on years of research on successful training programs. Piloted and studied extensively at the Western Carolina Center in North Carolina, *The Teaching-Skills Training Program* has been shown to be effective in improving the teaching performance of direct care staff and successfully done as one-day training; it is also acceptable to staff. The most important outcome is that, if implemented with integrity, *The Teaching-Skills Training Program* helps clients make significant gains in their adaptive skill development (Parsons, Reid, & Green, 1993).

The format of *The Teaching-Skills Training Program* consists of three phases: (1) classroom-based instruction, (2) "on-the-floor" monitoring and feedback, and (3) maintenance and generalization (Reid & Parsons, 1994). The classroom-based instruction component serves to familiarize staff trainees with basic behavioral terminology and to introduce the trainees to the performance skills, including (1) teaching from a task analysis, (2) using least-to-most assistive prompting, (3) using positive reinforcement, and (4) implementing error correction. To further assist trainees in learning the information, pretests and posttests are used to assess trainee progress. Performance modeling and practice, along with instructor feedback, are implemented during the classroom-based instruction session to help trainees acquire the skills.

In the second phase—on-the-job monitoring—staff who have been trained observe the trainees as they engage in a teaching episode with a client (Reid & Parsons, 1994). The trainers provide corrective and positive feedback in order to shape desired skill performance. Following the observation, the trainer evaluates the proficiency of the trainee's teaching skill and specifies any occurrences of incorrect implementation. Corrective feedback follows and defines how the trainee can rectify the performance. On-the-job monitoring continues until the trainee is observed conducting two client-teaching programs with 80 percent accuracy.

The final phase of *The Teaching-Skills Training Program* includes the maintenance and generalization component, which ensures that staff continue to use and to improve their teaching skills (Reid & Parsons, 1994). Essentially, a schedule of observation is developed so that supervisory personnel (or the staff trainers) are able to periodically observe the staff implementing the teaching skills. Trainees receive positive and corrective feedback. How often these observations occur depends on staff performance over time. As the trainee becomes more proficient at implementing the program, the observation can be curtailed.

Another Model: Devereux's Skill-Based Training Program

As a final example of a skill-based training program, let's look at a curriculum recently developed by Devereux's Institute of Clinical Training and Research titled *New Directions: Essential Skills for Direct Care Providers* (McCurdy et al., in press). The *New Directions* program is a skill-based staff development package intended for DCPs who work in residential treatment centers. It includes the Social Learning strand, for staff who work with children and adolescents with emotional-behavioral disorders and the Life Skills strand, for staff who work with children, adolescents, and adults with moderate to severe disabilities. Each strand is divided into ten to twelve training modules (see Figure 6.1). Although each presents different information, the two strands maintain a similar emphasis: building staff-client relationships and teaching adaptive, alternative skills (replacement behaviors) to clients. This is accomplished through a focus on training specific skills, including active listening, delivering praise, alternative skill teaching, encouraging communication, using the least-to-most-prompt hierarchy to teach adaptive skills, and incidental teaching.

Like the other programs mentioned, *New Directions* is a skill-based program that incorporates multiple opportunities for staff trainees to observe skill demonstrations, practice skills, and receive instructor feedback on skill performance. The program also incorporates content-based pre- and posttests, as well as performance-based observational posttests. As in *The Teaching-Skills Training Program,* staff are considered "trained" and then certified only when trainers observe them implementing competencies on the job. The program is unique because it is a first attempt to use a standardized training package across a multisite national agency such as Devereux. As such, it incorporates a well-developed train-the-trainers program. During a one-week course, trainers are trained in basic behavioral principles (which form the foundation for much of the curricular content), skill execution, trainee observation, and performance feedback. When they return to their programs, trainers maintain contact with curriculum developers by e-mail. The trainers are surveyed on a quarterly basis to assess the amount of training conducted at their program and to obtain feedback

---

FIGURE 6.1

New Directions Training Modules

Social Learning Curriculum	**Life Skills Curriculum**
• Introduction	• Introduction
• Building Relationships	• Encouraging Communication
• Listening to Understand	• Reinforcing Behavior
• Praising Effectively	• Teaching Life Skills: Using the Prompt Hierarchy
• Making Requests That Work	• Teaching Life Skills: Teaching from a Task Analysis
• Observing, Counting, and Recording Behavior	• Reinforcement and Error Correction
• Verbal Warnings	
• Using Time Out	• Collecting Performance Data
• Teaching to Promote Positive Behavior	• Incidental Teaching
• Problem Solving	• Redirecting Challenging Behaviors
• Routines and Transitions	
• Leading Activities	

Source: *McCurdy et al., in press. Used with permission.*

---

about effective or ineffective elements of the program. The curriculum is edited based on this feedback.

Recent evaluation of the effect of the *New Directions* curriculum on Devereux programs demonstrates that it is having a positive impact. Results of two initial investigations suggest that the curriculum (Social Learning strand) is an effective tool in teaching relevant verbal and performance skills to residential direct care staff (McCurdy, Ludwikowski, Serafin, & Maher, 1999). Moreover, once staff acquire these skills, they are able to maintain them over time (for up to ninety days after training). There is also initial evidence that trained staff may improve on a measure of job burnout. More specifically, they tend to feel less impersonal toward the recipients of their care (the residents). Finally, staff trainees report a high degree of acceptability for the training curriculum and specifically cite trainer instructions and feedback as the most helpful components in their own skill acquisition.

Implementing Training for Direct Care Providers

The idea of training staff often evokes an approach-avoidance conflict among managers and others at the top of the organization. On one hand, everyone knows that having experienced and well-trained staff is a necessary ingredient for running an effective treatment program. In fact, 100 percent of the organizations surveyed mandated some type of training for their direct care staff. On the other hand, the costs associated with training can be staggering and if not well planned from the start can result in minimal or no programmatic gains. This may explain the variability in the comprehensiveness of the training programs of the organizations surveyed. Survey findings revealed that organizations' training programs ranged from one to as many as sixteen mandated courses.

Given this risky state of affairs, what is the best advice for organizations with regard to staff training? Our experience suggests that staff training is important and should not be overlooked. But to get the best results, the training program must be implemented in such a way that it becomes an integral part of the organizational culture.

Establishing Training as an Organizational Priority

At Devereux, the first step in implementing the recently developed *New Directions* curriculum was to have senior management establish training as an organizational priority. Program administrators were given an option: train *New Directions* or substitute an existing training program currently used in your program (if it was on par with *New Directions*). Training center staff forwarded information about *New Directions* to each program site and requested managers to commit to a full or partial implementation of the *New Directions* curriculum (or another curriculum, if approved) during the next year. Figure 6.2 depicts a copy of a completed partial implementation plan, showing how one program site proposed to implement *New Directions* along with one module from a different curriculum.

Program administrators who were given the option of choosing a partial implementation plan were able to meet the training requirement without undue financial hardship. This is a point worth emphasizing when attempting to promote an organizational culture of training. By starting slowly, one avoids aspects of change that can overwhelm the organization. The advice is germane for small organizations in particular. Keep the commitment to training minimal at first and build gradually.

Selecting a Method of Implementation

The second step in promoting a program of training for DCPs is to decide on the method of implementation to be adopted. There are many options, including centralized training, a train-the-trainers model, or, for the truly techno-savvy organization, distance learning. The choice of implementation methods will vary depending on the size of the organization. For multisite

FIGURE 6.2

New Directions Partial Implementation Plan

Listed below are the "basic" modules to be trained at your Center to meet compliance with the *New Directions* partial implementation goal for the 1996–97 year. Please identify which modules are currently trained at your Center. If training in *New Directions* is not occurring, please identify the expected date when training can begin *or* identify an alternative module from your own training program that may serve as a suitable substitute for the modules listed (please see *New Directions* module descriptions attached).

Center: <u>Massachusetts</u>   Date: <u>10/24/96</u>

Name of Person Completing Form: <u>Charles Smith</u>

Social Learning Curriculum:

Module Title	Currently Trained? Yes/No	Target Date to Start Training	Title of Module to Substitute from Existing Training Program
Building Relationships		11/5/96	
Listening to Understand		12/17/96	
Praising Effectively		1/7/97	
Making Requests That Work		2/4/97	
Verbal Warning		3/4/97	

Life Skills Curriculum: N/A

Module Title	Currently Trained? Yes/No	Target Date to Start Training	Title of Module to Substitute from Existing Training Program
Encouraging Communication			
Reinforcing Behavior			
Informal Teaching			

organizations, it is probably better to consider a train-the-trainer or distance learning model. Single-site organizations are obviously better suited to a centralized model of training.

Centralized training involves appointing one or more individuals within the organization to a training position. This can be a full-time position or, through flexible scheduling, a part-time position for an experienced staff member interested in a developmental opportunity for career growth. There are clear advantages to adopting a centralized training program, including cost savings (no need to develop a program to train trainers), as well as convenience (all training is located in one area).

Multisite organizations usually cannot adopt a centralized training model without incurring significant costs for travel. Depending on the location of the other sites, this may be a prohibitive expenditure. In such cases, train-the-trainer and distance learning models are more efficient. By adopting a train-the-trainers model, the organization is committing to developing a cadre of trainers who will spend much of their time training others in the skills of the curriculum. One necessary component of a train-the-trainers model is a second curriculum to train trainers. It's important that trainer candidates be proficient in skill execution and that they understand and can use the principles of adult learning theory in the delivery of instruction. Also, consideration must be given to recertification or periodically checking the individual's skill performance to ensure that the program is being taught with integrity.

Distance learning—another option for large, geographically diverse organizations—includes a wide range of training modalities. In recent years, with advances in technology, the widespread use and availability of personal computers, and the ease of access to the Internet, distance learning has become an affordable and realistic option for organizational training. Computer-based training—one form of distance learning—includes the use of both CD-ROM and Web-based formats. Many training programs are currently available in an interactive CD-ROM program. These are a viable option when overtime and staff availability is an issue. Training programs are usually structured so that staff can work through one segment at a time while the program tracks their progress. Similar training programs are now widely available on the Internet. Usually, this involves a subscription fee to a training Web site. These sites have evolved quickly and employ a variety of sound bytes, video clips, and activities that make the whole experience an interactive one.

A second form of distance learning is videoconferencing, which is rapidly becoming a preferred communications tool for the fast-paced, corporate environment. It is useful for bringing one speaker or trainer to many locations simultaneously. It combines broadcast-quality video with high-speed digital telephone equipment for the sole purpose of achieving a face-to-face connection with individuals who may be thousands of miles away. The visual communication accessed through videoconferencing offers one additional advantage over computer-based training: participant skill performance can be observed and trainers can provide specific, corrective feedback as if on site. Although videoconferencing is designed to reduce costs associated with travel, the initial layout for equipment may limit the utility of this implementation model, especially for smaller organizations.

All of the distance learning techniques can be intertwined into existing training programs. Given the importance of skill-based training, distance learning models (with the exception of videoconferencing) are not necessarily recommended as the total training solution. They can, however, be a cost-effective adjunct for knowledge-based training, allowing the trainee the option of completing a training segment on his own time. Creative use of distance learning techniques may be worthy of further investigation for many organizations, large and small.

Evaluating and Maintaining the Training Program

The final two components of a program of training for DCPs involve evaluating outcomes and maintaining implementation integrity. Kirkpatrick (1996) identifies four levels of evaluation that should be employed in evaluating training programs. They include (1) satisfaction with training, (2) information acquired (learning), (3) participant behavior change, and (4) program outcome. The first two levels are easily accomplished as part of any training program. For example, in training the *New Directions* curriculum, trainers routinely ask DCPs to complete satisfaction surveys assessing their reaction to training. Additionally, the trainer can evaluate what the participants have learned by administering the pretest and posttest measures developed for each module.

Looking for positive changes in staff behavior, as well as improved overall program outcomes, are more sophisticated investigations and should not be undertaken without significant resources (funding, research personnel, and so on). Most respondents to our Organizational Survey reported the use of satisfaction measures (level one), as well as knowledge and skill assessments (level two). Unfortunately, a minority of the organizations reported the use of follow-up evaluations (level three).

The final step in promoting the training program as part of the organizational culture is to build it into the quality infrastructure. At Devereux, both the amount of and the procedures for training *New Directions* and *Crisis Prevention/Intervention,* two internally developed packages, are evaluated biannually through the site visit review process. Using a standard protocol (gap analysis; see Figure 6.3), information is obtained regarding the certification of trainers, the amount of training delivered to staff, and the site-specific process of staff certification. At one point during the review process, analogue assessments are conducted to evaluate DCPs' skill performance. Based on the outcome of the site review, recommendations are then made to administrative staff regarding the continued implementation of the program.

FIGURE 6.3

Quality Site Visit Review Checklist and Gap Analysis

Center

QUALITY SITE VISIT REVIEW CHECKLIST AND GAP ANALYSIS

Compliance with Devereux's established quality standards should be rated on the following scale:

Complete Compliance 1	Substantial Compliance 2	Partial Compliance 3	Marginal Compliance 4	Non-Compliance 5

Where a rating is not applicable, this should be indicated by recording N/A. **The threshold for immediate action planning is any score of 3, 4, or 5. Please describe and comment upon all minimum standards that are found to be below threshold.**

STANDARDS

III. DIRECT CARE STAFF TRAINING

A. *New Directions*

1. The program has at least one person certified as a *New Directions* instructor.　　1　2　3　4　5　N/A

2. The program maintains a copy of the certificate of all *New Directions* certified instructors.　　1　2　3　4　5　N/A

3. The program maintains a record of all direct care staff certified in *New Directions* modules.　　1　2　3　4　5　N/A

4. All *New Directions* modules are trained by certified instructors only, as evidenced by the instructor's signature on module certifications awarded to staff.　　1　2　3　4　5　N/A

5. Certification in a *New Directions* module is awarded to staff only when the knowledge posttest is passed at 80% accuracy and the performance posttest (skill) is passed at 100% accuracy.　　1　2　3　4　5　N/A

6. The program has a written implementation plan for training *New Directions*.　　1　2　3　4　5　N/A

7. There is evidence that all modules constituting the program's implementation plan are being trained.　　1　2　3　4　5　N/A

8. Any substitution of Life Skills basic modules (Encouraging Communication, Reinforcing Behavior, Informal Teaching) from the *New Directions* curriculum will have written approval from ICTR.　　1　2　3　4　5　N/A

9. Any substitution of Social Learning basic modules (Building Relationships, Listening to Understand, Praising Effectively, Making Requests that Work, Verbal Warnings) from the *New Directions* curriculum will have written approval from ICTR.　　1　2　3　4　5　N/A

(Continued)

FIGURE 6.3

Quality Site Visit Review Checklist and Gap Analysis *(Continued)*

10. Staff maintain competency in all *New Directions* skills in which they have attained certification, as evidenced by a behavioral role play test (rating criteria: **1 = 100% steps performed, 2 = 75% steps performed, 3 = 50% steps performed, 4 = 25% steps performed, 5 = 0 steps performed**).	1	2	3	4	5	N/A
11. There is evidence of supervisory monitoring and feedback to staff about the use of *New Directions* skills in the treatment environment (on the floor).	1	2	3	4	5	N/A

CRITERIA: The program will demonstrate appropriate utilization of the *New Directions* curriculum as the program of choice for direct care personnel.

* * * * *

B. *Crisis Prevention and Intervention*

1. The program has a designated curriculum for training in crisis prevention and intervention.	1	2	3	4	5	N/A
2. There is evidence that training in crisis prevention and intervention is conducted by certified/credentialed instructors of the designated curriculum.	1	2	3	4	5	N/A
3. The program maintains a record of all staff certified in crisis prevention and intervention.	1	2	3	4	5	N/A
4. There is evidence that all staff currently working with clients are trained in crisis prevention and intervention strategies.	1	2	3	4	5	N/A

CRITERIA: Devereux policy mandates that each Center's written plan for orientation and staff development includes procedures to ensure that all direct care staff receive appropriate crisis prevention/intervention training.

Committing to Positive Change

A commitment to the professionalization of DCPs is a commitment to organizational change. For organizations dedicated to treating children and adolescents, we believe that this commitment is paramount to providing quality care. At Devereux, a number of changes have cleared the way for this commitment to occur. They include the development of best practice guidelines that promote an ecological-behavioral view of treatment, the recognition of the DCP as an integral part of the treatment process, and the development of a quality infrastructure and the implementation of a process for quality oversight. It is our belief that, of all the changes that have occurred, role refinement and training for DCPs have been instrumental to Devereux's success in achieving better treatment outcomes in the current managed care environment.

## Chapter 7

Becoming a Data-Driven Organization

Linda A. Reddy, Paul A. LeBuffe

IN THIS ERA of accountability, one should consider what separates providers that thrive from those that fail. There is no doubt that objective outcome data help ensure organizational survival and offer an advantage over competitors who lack such information. The existence of objective data, like a pair of reading glasses tucked away in a pocket to be used as needed, enhances the provider's professional image and increases credibility with consumers, third-party payers, and the public alike.

As we have seen, the implications of managed health care practices are far-reaching in that now more than ever organizations must be demonstrably *data-driven*, producing quantifiable benefits to clients and their families. Beyond documenting the effectiveness of behavioral health services, outcome evaluation produces the necessary foundation for quality improvement (QI) initiatives such as the expansion or refinement of a service continuum, modification of existing programs, and development of innovative treatment approaches. Moreover, outcome evaluation also provides valuable information that can be used to develop treatment guidelines and establish standards of care.

In order to become a data-driven organization, a provider must undergo a metamorphosis, both philosophically and structurally. The transformation from caterpillar to butterfly is largely a function of the provider's attitude. For example, some providers may see the movement toward outcomes and accountability as an administrative nightmare—a helter-skelter effort that encroaches on precious fiscal and personnel resources and produces little, if any, clinically useful data about agency and client functioning. Others may view this movement as an opportunity for self-assessment, organizational growth and refinement, and goal attainment. No matter which perspective a provider adopts, the task of evolving into a data-driven organization is no small feat. This transformation can be particularly challenging, given the many fiscal, professional, regulatory, and administrative pressures in today's behavioral health care arena.

To become data-driven, providers must do some serious soul searching. To be maximally effective, outcome evaluation should reflect the core values, mission, and philosophy of the organization. Expending resources on measuring tangential, irrelevant, or inconsequential aspects of care is wasteful and will ultimately result in staff losing interest in the evaluation process. The self-evaluative process inherent in outcome evaluation helps refine an organization's mission and goals and looks objectively at what is actually provided to clients and what an agency would like to provide to clients in the future. This process is critical for planning and conducting successful first-generation outcome evaluation and QI projects.

This chapter answers two commonly asked questions: Why become data-driven? and What should be measured? In response, we offer pragmatic approaches and conceptual and methodological considerations for designing useful and rewarding outcome evaluation systems. In addition, a three-stage developmental model, outlined in this chapter and in Chapter Eight, is offered to help guide providers through the outcome measurement and QI process.

Why Become Data-Driven?

The expectation that providers objectively verify the effectiveness of clinical practices originated in a number of areas in the behavioral health care arena. These areas can be conceptualized as two categories: internal forces and external forces.

Internal Forces for Outcomes and Accountability

By far the most important reason to engage in outcome evaluation is to improve the quality and effectiveness of services provided to our clients. In this regard, outcome evaluation and QI share an important reciprocal relationship that promotes the survival and advancement of behavioral health care systems. In fact, QI is a critical internal factor for the long-term success of outcome evaluation efforts. Unless staff see outcome evaluation studies resulting in tangible improvements in client care or operations, they will lose interest in the endeavor and see it as meaningless busy work imposed on their already busy schedules. Outcome studies provide a tool for making informed, data-based decisions regarding the merits of different treatment interventions and services that are most effective with specific clinical populations and age groups.

Outcome evaluation also serves as a valuable source of information for QI projects. It affords a way to refine existing programs, as well as to create new, state-of-the-art programs such as early preventive services (for example, in-home parent training) and alternative community-based programs (for example, treatment foster care and family preservation models).

The benefits of outcome data extend far beyond programmatic issues. Outcome data offer behavioral health care entities a tool to examine operational and administrative efficiency. Outcome evaluation generates an objective baseline to track how an organization is operating and to determine what management changes are needed to enhance efficiency. Data on administrative procedures and management initiatives afford providers ways to make comparisons on their overall effectiveness and resourcefulness.

Advancements in computerized record systems make it much more feasible for providers to become data-driven. Computerized record systems provide administrators, clinicians, and staff improved efficiency in the collection, storage, retrieval, and use of clinical information. Many organizations routinely store substantial amounts of client information in computers. Existing databases offer rich sources for quickly accessing valuable information on clients and their families that can be easily used for outcome studies.

Computer technology also substantially reduces the time required for the completion of essential research endeavors such as literature searches of formal sources (books, specialized journals, *Psychological Abstracts,* and such services as Medline, ERIC, and Dialog). When evaluation planning is initiated, it is vital to survey the scientific literature and ascertain what has already been accomplished in the field of interest. This allows the provider to develop outcome evaluation plans on the basis of other outcome efforts and make informed decisions for program development based on best practices. Local universities and public and private libraries permit access to these services for nominal costs. For a straightforward review of methods and strategies of computerized reference access, see *Doing Psychology Experiments* (Martin, 1991).

The process of monitoring and documenting the effectiveness of therapeutic interventions and services fosters staff morale and team cohesion. Treatment outcome findings, regardless of their nature, should be shared with all levels of staff. Sharing positive findings will be rewarding and invigorating to staff. Disseminating negative findings internally is essential to program improvement efforts and may well validate the frustrations and negative expectancies that staff are experiencing anyway. Rather than suppressing negative findings, the open airing of such results can lead to very effective discussion regarding change. Outcome evaluation and quality improvement projects also can be used to evaluate staff goals, recognize efforts, and identify needs for staff development (see Chapter Six).

National advocacy organizations have spearheaded the demand for outcome evaluation research and education. The nation's largest mental health grassroots advocacy organization, The National Alliance for the Mentally Ill (NAMI), has forged several impressive campaigns for client rights, training, supports, and treatment services for those suffering from mental illness and their families. For example, NAMI established a policy in 1995 that encourages consumers and families to participate as active members of institutional review boards for facilities conducting treatment outcome research (National Alliance for the Mentally Ill, 1995). Providing treatment outcome data shows an organization's responsiveness to the legitimate demand of consumers for this kind of information.

External Forces for Outcomes and Accountability

The zeitgeist of managed care helps create the demand for outcome evaluation. Managed care in general calls for two objectives: the containment of costs and the maintenance of quality health care within a full continuum of services. Although these two objectives may seem simple, many providers must struggle mightily to achieve them. Managed care entities are commonly viewed as being preoccupied with cost containment. However, as most providers know, managed care entities are often concerned with quality in addition to cost. To maintain a preferred provider status, providers must be able to document outcomes. In addition, managed care entities require providers to be data-savvy during treatment as well. As one example, providers must now collect reliable data on client progress or lack thereof to substantiate requests for extended lengths of stay.

There is little doubt that some form of managed care is here to stay, at least for the near future. Whether a provider flourishes or perishes under the managed care system will depend, in large part, on the outcome results generated from program evaluation efforts.

The intense concern about behavioral health care services and program outcomes can also be seen in all funding sources, private and public, including grant-making foundations. Governmental agencies such as the National Institute of Mental Health (NIMH), Center for Mental Health Services (CMHS), Administration for Children, Youth, and Families (ACYF), and Child and Adolescent Service System Program (CASSP), as well as private foundations, now require outcome evaluation plans as an integral part of the grant application.

Despite increased funding for outcome research, few investigations pinpoint the key processes and treatment components that are most effective in serving various child populations (Kazdin, 1989; Reddy & Pfeiffer, 1997). Responding to the growing need to document outcomes of residential, group home, and therapeutic foster care, the Child Welfare League of America (with the cooperation and support of its member agencies) is conducting one of the largest national, multiple-site, prospective studies of child and youth outcomes in behavioral health care. To be completed by 2001, The Odyssey Project (Curtis & Brockman, 1999) is expected to provide valuable information on the type of services and the children who benefit most from out-of-home care.

Therefore, it is incumbent on providers to demonstrate convincingly that treatment decisions are data-based and result in short- and long-term client benefits. Future outcome studies are needed to demonstrate that clients with specific pathologies benefit from different types of interventions and treatment placements (for example, residential care, in-home interventions, and treatment based on family preservation models) (Goldman & Feldman, 1993; Lyman & Campbell, 1996).

Within the highly competitive health care arena, providers undertake treatment outcome evaluation to ensure market share. Funders are demanding that behavioral health care facilities demonstrate both treatment efficacy and cost-effectiveness for the clients whom they refer (Yates, 1996).

Many national accreditation and state regulatory agencies require behavioral health care entities to participate in prescribed outcome evaluation efforts. For instance, the Joint Commission on Accreditation of Healthcare Organizations (JCAHO), one of the largest accreditation bodies, requires providers to identify and integrate clinical care indicators into the outcome evaluation and performance improvement process through its ORYX initiative (Joint Commission on Accreditation of Health Care Organizations, 1997). In addition, behavioral health care providers are placed in a tailspin by many other national—for example, the Council on Accreditation (COA), the Health Care Financing Administration (HCFA)—and state-level initiatives.

These external and internal forces significantly affect the demand for outcome evaluation initiatives. Faced with the multiple demands just discussed, a provider may feel overwhelmed. The remainder of this chapter and Chapter Eight present a three-stage developmental model to assist providers in responding effectively to these demands.

Stage One: Preliminary Decisions

As we have said previously, embarking on outcome measurement requires the careful consideration of a number of important questions. We have outlined some of the critical decisions that are necessary for ensuring clinically useful outcome evaluation and QI initiatives.

What Should Be Measured?

Once the provider commits to becoming a data-driven organization, the decision about what to measure is critically important. All too often, this part of the evaluation process is given little attention and consideration, resulting in the identification of outcomes and indicators of care that are trivial, irrelevant, vague, impossible to measure, incompatible with the expectations of stakeholders, or inconsistent with the goals and mission of the program or agency. Think "haste makes waste." It is important to carefully consider your organization's mission and the goals and functions of each program and service. After all, this stage, in and of itself, can significantly affect the success or failure of an outcome evaluation and QI project.

Consider Your Audience

First and foremost, providers should carefully examine the expectations and perceptions of the constituents involved in the organization. Stakeholders may include clients, family members, frontline workers, managers and administrators, referring or transferring agencies, and funding sources. The expectations of *all* stakeholders must be carefully considered. Historically, program staff, in conjunction with third-party payers and regulators, have almost exclusively determined components of care, policies, and procedures without obtaining input from internal stakeholders such as clients and families. Eliciting feedback from key external and internal stakeholders can be one of the best investments an organization can make for future outcome projects. Here, give credence to the motto, "The customer is always right."

It is important to realize that stakeholders will have varying viewpoints on important issues. In a study conducted at Devereux and presented at the Institute of Behavioral Health Care's Children Services Outcome Management Conference (LeBuffe, Biggs, Hatch, Miller, & Roth, 1998), we investigated the different perspectives of clinicians, clients, parents, funders, and regulators regarding key outcome study parameters. One intriguing finding from this study was that stakeholders' perceptions of the goals of treatment often differed. For example, clinicians and parents tended to view the primary goal of treatment as being the reduction of psychiatric symptoms such as depression. In contrast, clients viewed the goal of treatment as helping them attain greater social competence or skills. Many funders saw the goal of treatment as being family reunification—a goal shared by the client but not necessarily by the family. The responses to this one question indicate that different stakeholders have different goals for treatment, and no single, narrow outcome indicator will address everyone's interests.

By asking constituents what the three most important things they hope to get out of a program are, evaluators can, in part, refine program goals and identify treatment elements that may accomplish these goals. Feedback from both external and internal constituents also offers comprehensive systemic and individual perspectives of the program and its functioning. For example, placement permanency (clients remain in the same placement) may serve as an expected or anticipated outcome for higher management and third-party payers, whereas the improvement of interpersonal and family relationships may be expectancies shared by family members or clients.

Behavioral health care entities like Devereux have begun to address this need by incorporating the perspective of various stakeholders into the outcome evaluation process. The process of "listening to the customers" can be accomplished through telephone interviews, surveys, client-based organizations, local advisory boards that include family members and community leaders, and focus groups.

Invite a Multidisciplinary Perspective

Adopting a multidisciplinary, multidepartmental team approach to outcome development is critical. Representation from *all* relevant areas of the organization should be included in the outcome development process. Insufficient involvement of any one constituency (for example, physicians or direct care staff) can seriously jeopardize the outcome evaluation project. For example, constituents who have not been invited to give their input may feel insulted, become resentful, and indirectly sabotage the outcome evaluation process. That is why providers should invite *all* constituents who may be potentially involved in the project. If this is not possible, an alternative is to establish teams that encompass a cross-section of key players nominated by their peers.

Keep in mind that a successful outcome evaluation project requires a collaborative team effort. Welcoming and eliciting staff and consumer input is one way to begin the buy-in process (see Chapter Eight). Although a multidisciplinary approach can be exhilarating, time consuming, and even threatening to some people involved, it is unquestionably an invaluable part of the outcome evaluation process that supports the best interest of the clients served.

Use an Outcome Framework

Given the complexity and the importance of creating an effective outcome measurement system, it is advantageous for providers to organize the possible array of outcomes into a framework that embodies the overall mission, goals, and culture of the organization. This task can be approached in a number of ways. Providers might visit and consult with other agencies that serve similar populations and offer comparable services. Additionally, providers may wish to examine well-established models or approaches. Also, providers may wish to out-source the outcome-defining and measurement process by obtaining support and guidance from consultants.

The Devereux Foundation has used all three approaches in defining and organizing its outcome evaluation program. In collaboration with the Corporation for Standards and Outcomes (CS&O), Devereux has launched a systemwide outcomes measurement initiative to assist Devereux centers with defining and evaluating outcomes for their specific treatment programs. CS&O's nationally recognized ten-step *Define It* process and outcomes-based management (OBM) model (Driggs, 1997) was used to guide Devereux's leadership committee in formulating and implementing this initiative. The OBM approach encompasses several guiding principles that direct all resources in an organization to the outcomes it must fulfill.

The leadership committee conducted a two-day retreat to define Devereux's outcome initiative mission and objectives and to critically examine those internal and external forces that might motivate or impede the initiative. The leadership committee solicited feedback from staff throughout the organization to assist in this process. Four primary client groups were targeted: (1) children under twenty-one years of age with emotional-behavioral disorders, (2) children under twenty-one who were dually diagnosed with emotional-behavioral disorders and mental retardation, (3) individuals with mental retardation, and (4) individuals with autism or pervasive developmental disorders. Based on these targeted groups, a Devereux-wide central database will be created to store, manage, and analyze core client and program characteristics, as well as outcomes. One advantage of using external consultants and services such as CS&O is that they provide an opportunity to benchmark or compare an agency's outcomes to the outcomes of similar agencies.

Using Models to Conceptualize Outcomes

In conceptualizing its outcome initiative and in selecting indicators, the Devereux steering committee also used models that have been described in the professional literature. In particular, the Logic Model (Hernandez, 2000) was used to confirm and support the *Define It* and OBM processes.

The Logic Model requires providers to critically examine whom they serve, what services and interventions they provide, and what outcomes these services are believed to promote. As stated by Hernandez (2000), "Logic modeling is a way to facilitate the dialogue between evaluators and program staff in articulating both a program's theory and the data elements that will be collected and analyzed. A logic model is a series of statements linking social and/or client conditions with the service strategies that will be used to address the conditions, and the anticipated outcomes." Figure 7.1 graphically depicts the Logic Model in its simplest form. The area on the left specifies the client and system conditions, that is, who is being served. The area in the middle describes the service strategies intended to address the concerns and needs of the client and system. Short- and long-term outcomes and associated indicators are specified on the far right. The key concept underlying the Logic Model is the specification of the interrelationships among these three areas. In other words, the model shows how the service strategies address the specific needs of the clients and lead directly to the expected outcomes. As Hernandez states, "Associating information from all three areas as an analysis strategy creates the potential for the effective utilization of outcomes by stakeholders interested in improving service delivery. Without such a tool, when only outcome information is collected, service system stakeholders loose the ability to begin to understand why results occurred."

An alternative model for conceptualizing outcomes has been developed by Rosenblatt and Attkisson (1993). Their model consists of four treatment outcome domains (what to measure), five respondent types (who provides the outcome information), and four social contexts of measurement (where to measure it). Four broad domains of treatment outcome are outlined: (1) clinical status, (2) functional status, (3) life satisfaction or fulfillment, and (4) welfare and safety. The clinical status domain encompasses impairment in both the psychological and physical health of clients, including the classification and severity of psychopathology and symptomatology. The second domain, functional status, refers to the client's ability to effectively fulfill social and role-related functions in a variety of social settings such as interpersonal and familial relationships, school or vocational training, and work. Life satisfaction and fulfillment, the third dimension, captures the client's personal fulfillment in life such as the promotion of well-being, quality of life, and happiness. Welfare and safety, the fourth outcome domain, consists of the overall welfare problems typically posed by serious mental illness to the individual, family, social network, and community. Examples may include lack of hygiene, infectious diseases, self-injurious behaviors, suicide, and the committing of illegal acts.

FIGURE 7.1

Logic Model/Analysis

Logic Model/Analysis

Service
Strategies

Client and
System
Conditions

Outcomes
and
Indicators

What are the interrelationships between the three areas? Analysis:

Source: *Hernandez, 2000.*

This model also emphasizes the importance of collecting outcome data from multiple respondents such as clients, family members, members of social networks, clinical staff, and researchers. In addition, the researchers advocate that information be collected across social contexts (individual or self, family, work or school, and the community).

Within this and other outcome frameworks, providers can begin to identify and define outcomes that are most salient to their organization's mission and goals. We offer six recommendations to begin the outcome development process:

1. Carefully evaluate stakeholders' expectations and needs.

2. Revisit the philosophy and mission of the organization.

3. Start small—identify no more than two programs to evaluate in the organization.

4. Keep it simple—choose only one or two measurable outcome goals for each program or treatment service.

5. Make goals relate directly to what the intervention is expected to change.

6. Determine what data are already being collected. If existing data assess the outcomes you have identified, use them as a foundation to start your first outcome evaluation project.

Select Clinical Indicators of Care

Another important step in the outcome evaluation process is to identify clinical indicators. A clinical indicator is a measurable variable in the process of treatment that assesses aspects of the quality of care in a program or organization (Bernstein & Hilborne, 1993). Clinical indicators are closely linked to outcomes, in that indicators define the parameters by which outcomes are measured. Clinical indicators are primarily designed to evaluate aspects of the quality of treatment services in a program.

In March 1999, the American College of Mental Health Administration (ACMHA) held the first summit on defining clinical indicators for the behavioral health care arena. ACMHA, in collaboration with five national accreditation organizations, developed a taxonomy that includes three types of indicators: access, process, and outcome. The top ten indicators were classified by type and are given in parentheses. They include the following ("ACMHA Summit," 1999, p. 10):

(1) The rate of persons served who are better, worse, or unchanged at the termination of treatment compared to the initiation of treatment (outcome), (2) the average number of days from a first appointment to a second appointment (access), (3) the rate of persons served who receive timely, face-to-face follow-up care after leaving a twenty-four-hour facility (process), (4) the rate of persons served who receive a timely course of treatment following diagnosis of a behavioral health disorder (process), (5) the rate of persons served who are better, worse, or unchanged at a standard interval following the termination of treatment (outcome), (6) the rate of participation in decisions regarding treatment by families of children and adolescents when indicated (process), (7) the rate of suicide, homicide, and unexpected deaths (process), (8) the rate of persons served who are diagnosed with co-occurring mental illness and substance abuse disorders (process), (9) the rate of persons served reporting that they receive services they need (access), (10) the rates of persons served compared to those eligible for services, analyzed by age, gender, ethnicity, location, and diagnostic group (access).

At Devereux, clinical indicators are measured and tracked via a Quality Indicator Report (see Figure 7.2 and Appendix T). A task force of eight members, representing facilities within the organization, developed this report. The task force identified fifteen core organizational indicators (for example, informed consent, staff turnover, sentinel events, client, and parent-agency-staff satisfaction), based on a comprehensive review of the professional literature and feedback from key stakeholders. A draft of the report was disseminated to all QI coordinators throughout Devereux for feedback and

FIGURE 7.2

Quality Indicator Report

Function: Care of the Individual/Treatment

Indicator #4: **Use of behavior management techniques or special treatment procedures.** *Special treatment procedures include seclusion, mechanical restraint, and personal hold (exclusion of escorts). Seclusion should be defined according to individual state requirements for monitoring: a locked room or any area from which there is no egress, etc. PRNs will be a separate calculated category that includes only medications administered for behavioral control. Quarterly figures should be discrete regarding the number of individuals receiving STPs. (Each individual should only be counted once even if they received personal holds in each month of the quarter.)*

*Injuries are defined as those **requiring external medical attention (clinic or hospital remedies)**.*

Calculation:

Data elements:

> \# of individuals receiving STPs
>
> \# seclusions per policy definition for the month or quarter
>
> \# mechanical restraints for the month or quarter
>
> \# personal holds (excluding escorts) for the month or quarter
>
> Average Daily Census for the month or quarter
>
> \# of client injuries secondary to STP for the month or quarter
>
> \# of staff injuries secondary to STP for the month or quarter

Formulas:

A. Ratio of STP occurrence:

> $\dfrac{\text{\# of seclusions + \# mechanical restraints + \# personal holds for the month or quarter.}}{\text{Average Daily Census for the month or quarter}}$

B. Average number of STPs per individual receiving STPs:

> $\dfrac{\text{\# of seclusions + \# mechanical restraints + \# personal holds for the month or quarter}}{\text{\# of individuals receiving STPs for the month or quarter}}$

C. % of individuals receiving STPs:

> $\dfrac{\text{\# of individuals receiving STPs for the month or quarter}}{\text{Average Daily Census for the month or quarter}} = \text{x } 100$

D. Rate of client injuries secondary to STP:

> $\dfrac{\text{\# of client injuries secondary to STP for the month or quarter}}{\text{Total number of STP occurrences for the month or quarter}}$

E. Rate of staff injuries secondary to STP:

> $\dfrac{\text{\# of staff injuries related to STP for the month or quarter}}{\text{Total number of STP occurrences for the month or quarter}}$

> Average Daily Census:
>
> $\dfrac{\text{(Sum of the \# of residential clients listed per day of the month or quarter)} + \text{(Sum of the \# of day + partial clients listed per day of the month or quarter/3)}}{\text{Total \# of days in the month or quarter}}$

Sample size:	All occurrences
Population:	All programs

FIGURE 7.3

Outcome and Clinical Indicator Worksheet

Mission of the Organization:

_____

_____

_____

Program Name: _____

    Outcome goal (1): _____

        Clinical indicators: _____

            _____

            _____

    Outcome goal (2): _____

        Clinical indicators: _____

            _____

            _____

            _____

---

recommendations and was revised based on their input. In the spirit of QI, the report is reviewed routinely for usefulness and modified accordingly. It has since been streamlined to seven indicators and serves as Devereux's core clinical quality measurement system. This system generates data that guide decision making and track the success of performance improvement initiatives.

In selecting indicators, use the following criteria: (1) Is the indicator a reliable measure of quality over time? (2) Does the indicator possess sensitivity to change? (3) To what degree does the indicator measure what it is supposed to measure (specified outcome)? (4) Will data that measure the indicator be accessible and easy to collect? (5) To what extent is the indicator meaningful and easily comprehensible to all professionals or lay audiences? Figure 7.3 presents an outcome and clinical indicator process worksheet to assist providers.

Defining Outcome Success

As mentioned, the outcomes and indicators that are selected are critically important in designing successful evaluation projects. It is equally important to define the criteria for determining effectiveness or success for a particular program or service. To date, consensus on what defines outcome success is lacking. Some have gone so far as to say that there are as many outcomes as there are definitions of success. How do providers determine when interventions and services are "truly" successful for the clients they serve?

A number of methods can be used to conceptualize and operationalize outcome success. We have found three strategies to be particularly useful:

1. *Operationalize program goals into quantifiable units.* Assessment instruments or procedures can be particularly useful in helping providers quantify program goals. For example, the goal of "improved adaptive functioning" can be defined as "at discharge, clients will score ten points higher on a standardized test for adaptive functioning than at admission."

2. *Set thresholds for favorable, equivocal, and unfavorable outcomes.* A threshold is a predetermined cut-off point that indicates whether or not a program goal was achieved. For example, the goal of "reduced alcohol consumption" can be defined as the extent to which clients refrain from consuming alcohol at least six out of seven days per week. The goal of "increased school attendance" can be defined as clients attending class 80 percent of the time during the semester. In these two examples, both goals would be defined as favorable outcomes. Conversely, attendance at school less than 30 percent of the time would be conceptualized as a negative outcome, and alcohol consumption that reflects no discernable change between two points in time would be classified as equivocal.

3. *Use the dual criterion of statistically reliable and clinical meaningful change, when possible.* A particularly useful and rigorous approach to examining outcomes is to use dual criteria, specifying that changes in functioning or symptomatology must be both statistically reliable and clinically meaningful. The first criterion, statistically reliable change, asks how large the change in scores must be to conclude that the clinical change reflects more than chance variance. In other words, does the difference in scores obtained at admission and at some other point during the course of treatment reflect "real differences, as opposed to ones that are questionable or unreliable" (Jacobsen & Truax, 1991, p. 12)? By considering the criterion of statistical significance first, providers avoid interpreting changes as significant when they may be nothing more than measurement error or regression effects (Atkinson, 1991; Lord & Novick, 1968).

The second criterion, a clinically meaningful change, asks whether the change in outcome represented by the change in scores reflects a real difference in the lives of the clients. Clinical meaningfulness may be conceptualized as clients entering a program as part of a dysfunctional population (for example, at high risk for suicide) and departing from a program no longer belonging to that population (Jacobson & Truax, 1991). However, in many cases, a client's progress in treatment does not reflect a dichotomous—positive or negative—change; rather, progress is placed on a continuum of therapeutic change over time. For example, an adolescent placed in a treatment foster care home might obtain a scale score of 85 on a depression inventory at admission and a scale score of 70 on discharge from the program (the inventory has a mean score of 50 and standard deviation of 10). At first glance, it appears that this youth's depression has abated considerably, reflecting a 1.5 standard deviation difference between scale scores from the time the adolescent entered and left the program. However, although the 15-point change may be statistically significant, the reduction in the adolescent's depression may not be clinically meaningful, in that a score of 70 may still reflect considerable remaining dysphoria and clinical impairment.

One assessment instrument that offers an explicit methodology to examine the statistical significance and clinical meaningfulness of outcome change is the Devereux Scales of Mental Disorders (Naglieri, LeBuffe, & Pfeiffer, 1994). To determine whether outcome change is statistically reliable, the Devereux Scales include tables (see pages 210–225 in the technical manual) that specify a range of posttest scores clients must exceed in order for the change from pretest to be deemed statistically significant. If the change is statistically reliable, the clinical meaning of the change is determined by comparing the client's score at discharge to a normal standardization sample. Scores at discharge that reflect reliable change and are within one standard deviation of the mean are considered to indicate an "optimal outcome." A computerized scoring program that automatically makes these determinations is available (LeBuffe, Naglieri, & Pfeiffer, 1996). For a detailed description of the methodology developed for the Devereux Scales of Mental Disorders, see LeBuffe and Pfeiffer (1996).

Having completed the preliminary steps of surveying stakeholders and determining what should be measured and how, providers are prepared to approach outcome measurement in a systematic and meaningful fashion. The stage has been set for the second stage in our development progression—using existing data.

Stage Two: Using Existing Data

Look at the data sources you already have. Do they measure the outcomes that you are assessing? Most providers collect a wealth of information that reflects the progress the client is making toward outcome goals. For example, current psychological and psychiatric evaluations, school achievement records, family visit reports (for residential programs), sentinel event reports, medical records, and so on can all be used as indicators of clinical progress.

There are distinct advantages to using existing data. To begin, it does not create additional expense for the agency or burden for the staff. It provides an opportunity for staff to engage in the analysis and interpretation of data and the use of results in QI efforts without changing their current workflow or responsibilities. And the use of existing data can be an important opportunity to teach staff the importance of having reliable, accurate data sets. Finally, by being involved in the use of existing data to examine and improve outcomes, staff will be more receptive to the eventual requests or demands to collect additional data such as postdischarge surveys. In fact, a skillful outcomes manager can lead a staff to request the additional information.

When examining existing data sets for information useful to outcome evaluation, providers should not limit their scope to client-related information. Data about staff (turnover, training, morale, worker's compensation claims, grievances), consumers (satisfaction surveys, complaints, commendations), and program operations can be very useful for maximizing positive outcomes. At Devereux, an example of existing program data that are intricately linked to client outcomes is Devereux's gap analysis reports.

The gap analysis has been developed by the coauthors of this volume as an innovative approach to analyzing the quality and efficiency of mental health services at the organizational and program level. The analysis was developed to systematically evaluate whether Devereux programs and centers successfully implemented performance standards (compliance with licensure, governance and management, human resources, program planning, and implementation). The gap analysis guides programs in assessing *where they are* and *where they need to be* (that is, accomplishing benchmarks). The gap analysis is a two-stage evaluation process that includes the completion of self-assessment surveys on performance standards followed by a site visit by an independent team of evaluators. Results of the independent evaluation are then shared with the agency to clarify perspectives, identify resources, and create opportunities for developing consultative relationships in the organization. If gaps exist, corrective plans are designed and implemented. An example is presented in Chapter Five (see Figure 5.4).

In general, the use of existing data sources is often best suited to evaluating processes. Process evaluation can be used to analyze indicators of care at the individual program or organization level. The method of process evaluation, which will be discussed in more detail with respect to program analysis, is an empirical approach for assessing the extent and nature of service delivery across a mental health service system. Process evaluation is used to determine whether programs are delivered consistently and as intended. For example, an agency may wish to evaluate the efficacy of a training program for parents of children with disruptive behavior disorders. Information on how the parents were trained, the number of training sessions that parents attended, completion of homework, and the implementation of behavioral techniques in the home may be collected and analyzed.

Other variables and processes that are commonly used in process evaluation include (1) the decision-making processes (centralized, participatory) used in an organization, (2) the overall culture and commitment to program refinement and innovation, (3) allocation of resources (physical space, staff, equipment), and (4) the type and extent of internal and external demands placed on the organization's functioning.

A good example of the clinical utility of process evaluation is illustrated in a study conducted by the Devereux Florida Treatment Network (Joint Commission on Accreditation of Healthcare Organizations, 1999). The multidisciplinary staff was concerned that the historical use of behavioral PRNs (prescribed medications used as needed to control behavior) and mechanical restraints with acutely assaultive clients was inconsistent with the program's goal of long-term behavioral change that maximizes the potential of each client and increases independence. They also felt that these two procedures were at variance with the unit's values that interventions should be normalized, functional, and capable of generalization to the community. They examined existing records and determined that they were averaging twenty-seven PRNs per month. Following QI procedures, they instituted a change in procedures that required a behavioral analyst to intervene for fifteen minutes using replacement techniques such as progressive relaxation or planned ignoring before a behavioral PRN could be administered. In the ten-month period following this change in procedure, the total number of PRNs was reduced to four. This near-zero level has been maintained for a number of years. In addition, clients were now spending more time in program. The replacement skills that were taught were more normative and more likely to generalize to a nontreatment setting. In addition, parent and funder satisfaction increased. This study illustrates the value of being data-driven and the advantages to be gained by using existing data within a multidisciplinary, goal-oriented, QI system.

Use of Process Evaluation

Process evaluation, which can often be accomplished using existing data, generates detailed information on the quality of ongoing service delivery, on who receives services and to what extent, what program components contribute to the attainment of goals, and how program services can be successfully implemented. In contrast to impact evaluation, which focuses on inferring what outcomes (intended or unintended) result from a given program, process evaluation clarifies what a program consists of and whether it is being delivered (in terms of duration, dosage, and so on) as intended to targeted audiences.

Process evaluation serves as a valuable tool for program development. As a first step, all program components need to be outlined. In collaboration with stakeholders, evaluators should delineate the strategies, behaviors, activities, products and supplies, and technology required to deliver a program. Program components may include whom the program will serve (for example, consumers' age, income level, health status), where the program will be implemented (for example, in a clinic, home, school, community agency), and how the program will be delivered. Although specifying program elements can be labor intensive, it is an important process for defining programs and evaluating program services.

As providers begin the program specification process, it is helpful to apply a set of criteria for specifying and measuring program components. Yeaton (1985) and others (see Sechrest, 1979) advocate that evaluators (1) define program activities as observable behaviors rather than as goals, (2) clearly differentiate each program element from each other and measure each, (3) link each aspect of the treatment program to theory, and (4) identify aspects of the program that are intended to be delivered and those that are to be adapted for a specific setting.

Three methods are particularly useful in the specification of programs. These include (1) formative evaluation, (2) evaluability assessment, and (3) the identification of program theory (Wholey, 1987).

Formative evaluation is a valuable technique for obtaining preliminary data from stakeholders about the feasibility of treatment activities and their fit with the targeted consumers and setting. Through systematic and frequent data collection, providers can document and track the key processes involved in implementing, modifying, and designing program services over time.

A second useful technique for program specification is evaluability assessment. This is a systematic approach to specifying the intended use of program data and clarifying the underlying theory of programs before launching a full-scale evaluation. Making site visits, accessing feedback from stakeholders, and examining organizational flow charts and records all aid in initiating this process. For a more detailed discussion of this approach, see Wholey (1987). Formative evaluation and evaluability assessment are particularly helpful for evaluators who are either less seasoned or are conducting first-generation outcome evaluations.

Another method for program specification is the examination of program theory. Understanding the theory that underlies a treatment program helps clarify the assumptions and values that run the program. This method encourages providers to examine the current literature and to critically appraise alternative theories that relate to clinical change. Furthermore, the delineation of program theory also explains which processes lead to service delivery and clinical change and what measures are needed to assess these processes.

Process evaluation can also aid in the measurement of program implementation. Data on the extent and nature of program implementation is essential for outcome evaluation. Implementation data provide information on the type, strength ("dosage"), and quality of program components that were delivered and the scope of treatment provided (number of consumers served and their characteristics). Implementation data also offer providers a tool to monitor interventions in order to identify and resolve problems as they occur during the course of treatment. Data on the variability of program implementation also can be used to generate hypotheses as to why service delivery is and is not carried out as intended. In addition, data can offer valuable insight on how interventions affect outcomes at the program and individual client level. Most important, because client outcomes are the result of processes, it is only through understanding and altering processes that we can improve client outcomes. As providers, we cannot directly change client outcomes. We can only change what we do and how we do it and hope that if we have specified our theory of change (for example, using the Logic Model) well enough that these changes in process will directly influence client outcomes.

Ultimately, client outcomes are the most important. It is the documentation of lasting and tangible effects on the client such as reduced symptoms or increased skills that lie at the heart of accountable systems of care. Having explored the use of existing data to study processes, we turn to the third and culminating phase of being a data-driven provider: the examination of client outcomes.

Chapter 8

Designing and Conducting Outcome Evaluations

Linda A. Reddy, Howard A. Savin

THERE'S NO DOUBT that the accountability and outcomes movement has served as a wake-up call for many behavioral health care providers. Outcome evaluation is no longer an event that must be completed each year but rather a journey that organizations must engage in during the entire course of service delivery. For some, outcome evaluation is a means to an end—an annual event requiring organizations to produce data that reflect "real" value for the clients and families served. Those who view outcome evaluation QI as simply another task to complete may limit their ability to reach their full potential and growth. The routine and periodic examination of outcome data helps organizations make informed decisions about interventions and services, as well as establish treatment guidelines and standards of care. The process of outcome evaluation and QI also instills pride, ownership, and cooperation among key stakeholders.

The outcome evaluation and QI journey is a consciousness-raising experience. Outcome data help providers look critically at their strengths and weaknesses and generate plans for improvement. To successfully engage in this process, however, organizations must be willing to self-evaluate, take chances, and experience some uncertainty. Once an organization has crossed this bridge, it can begin the third and final developmental stage of outcome evaluation—designing and critically examining the outcomes and processes in their programs. As outlined in Chapter Seven, the first two stages—making preliminary decisions and accessing and using existing data—create the momentum for conducting successful and rewarding outcome evaluation and QI projects.

As an organization begins the third stage, it needs to address a number of practical and conceptual issues. This chapter offers a simple, step-by-step approach for designing and conducting outcome evaluation and QI initiatives. It is written for providers who are relatively inexperienced and possibly uncomfortable with the evaluation and QI process.

Facilitating Organizational Buy-In

We mentioned this previously but it is worthy of reiteration that launching a successful outcome evaluation and QI process is contingent on organizational buy-in. A successful outcome assessment requires commitment and support at all levels: the agency, staff, and client and family levels.

Agency Buy-In

A treatment outcome system requires the support and commitment of the highest levels of the organization. Administrative leadership must convey a clear and strong endorsement of the outcome evaluation and QI system. The practical and relevant day-to-day clinical benefits generated from this process must be communicated to all staff. For example, administrators may point out to clinicians that outcome measures can be used to assist in diagnostic decision making, evaluating a client's progress over time, and determining the overall effectiveness of programs and services. An evaluation system that includes outcomes that are observable and functional to the daily lives of clients (for example, school attendance, job skills, or reduced alcohol consumption) can also help clinicians see how their efforts facilitate clients' change (Bengen-Seltzer, 1999).

It is important to note that rhetoric alone is not enough to successfully promote organizational buy-in. Administrative leadership must demonstrate, in addition to financial support, a hands-on commitment to the process such as attending meetings and participating in decision making. Organization leaders need to be ready to roll up their sleeves and work hand-in-hand with staff on developing the initial outcome evaluation system. Staff may become resistant to the evaluation process if administrators are perceived as lacking interest or are absent.

Administrative leaders should introduce the outcome evaluation system as a tool to foster organizational growth and stability rather than as a means to identify staff or operational failure. It is essential that leaders create a nonthreatening learning environment—one that encourages staff to question why certain interventions are not working, what could be done differently in the future, and what has been learned from past experience. By focusing on trends and the relative effectiveness of various interventions rather than the performance of individuals or groups of clinical staff, administrators create an open and collaborative atmosphere for developing practice guidelines. If staff do not trust the merits or intentions of the system, they are likely to focus on how they are viewed by others rather than how service delivery could be improved.

It is important to set expectations at the outset that the outcome evaluation and QI system will be an ongoing process, not a single event. First-generation projects will likely be imperfect and may not yield clinically robust findings. Outcome evaluation projects typically go through a series of developmental stages of increasing complexity and sophistication. With time, the system will become easier to implement and more refined, and will produce more clinically useful information.

Staff Buy-In

The leader of the system must set realistic goals with the team—goals that can be achieved. It is equally important that the treatment outcome team demonstrate to the organization the value of the outcome evaluation process. The champion serves a critical function in promoting staff enthusiasm and knowledge of the project, as well as sharing ownership of many components of the project (for example, selecting instruments, collecting data, and explaining the purpose of the study to clients and families). As the process becomes fairly routine, it takes less effort for the team to promote the value added to the organization.

It is critical that the team conveys to staff and administrators the "real" time and resources (personnel, finances, equipment) needed to run the outcome system. Realistically outlining the key parameters needed to successfully implement the system will help secure future collaborative and trusting relationships with all involved.

Another way to foster staff buy-in is to elicit feedback about the outcome evaluation process. Periodic meetings, formal surveys, and e-mail are three ways to obtain feedback and promote staff buy-in. An anonymous suggestion-grievance box may be particularly helpful for staff who may wish to provide confidential feedback to the outcome team.

A mentoring program for clinicians is another effective way to foster buy-in at the agency and staff level (Bengen-Seltzer, 1999). This approach is based on the premise that clinicians who are trained by other clinicians would be more likely to use an outcome-based system than those trained by administrators. As one example, the Los Angeles County Department of Mental Health implemented a mentor program to improve clinicians' proficiency in using an outcome system. The program resulted in a double buy-in; mentors became increasingly more invested in the system as they trained others, and clinicians who were trained used and trusted the system more (Bengen-Seltzer, 1999).

Client and Family Buy-In

It is essential to enlist the interest and commitment of the clients and families to secure the success of an outcome evaluation and QI system. Client and family involvement is best secured at the time of admission. During the admission process, the treatment philosophy of the facility, including aspects of supervision and the quality of client care, should be clearly explained to clients and their families.

It is also important (Reddy & Pfeiffer, 1996) to do all of the following:

- Explain the purpose of the outcome evaluation system and provide an example of a recently completed study and its ties to changes in client treatment and the delivery of services.

- Offer strict assurances of confidentiality.

- State ways that information will be collected and provide an example of a standardized measure, as well as an explanation of the derived data and its uses to the parents.

- Establish a schedule with respect to the data or information that will be collected.

- Illustrate ways that the system will improve program effectiveness.

- Present specific projects that were helpful in the past to clients and their families. The extent to which clients and families understand and relate to the benefits produced by the outcome evaluation system will influence their participation in the process.

It is vital to maintain the interest and commitment of clients and families in the evaluation system during the course of and after termination of treatment. Strategies that help secure client and family participation and commitment to outcome projects include (Reddy & Pfeiffer, 1996):

- Distribute informational newsletters.

- Present the purpose and findings of recently completed outcome projects during agency or community meetings or Family Day visits.

- Offer compensation in the form of nominal stipends ($5 or $10) to clients or families for participating in projects.

- Send holiday and birthday cards to former clients in order to routinely collect follow-up data and keep a record of correct names, addresses, telephone numbers, or e-mail addresses.

Assembling a Treatment Outcome Team

A key component to initiating a successful outcome assessment and QI system is to identify knowledgeable and enthusiastic staff to participate on a treatment outcome team. Initially, this may appear to be a simple task, but in reality it's important to give careful consideration when selecting staff for this endeavor. For example, a team member must effectively communicate, collaborate, and manage tasks with other team members in order to successfully design and implement an outcome assessment project.

A treatment outcome team typically includes personnel at four levels: (1) project coordinator, (2) data manager, (3) data collector, and (4) informants. A team of four usually works well. Having too many people on the team can make it difficult to establish meeting times that accommodate everyone's schedule. Decision making can also slow to a crawl because too many viewpoints and expectations must be considered. Conversely, too few team members can limit exposure to different perspectives and result in a paucity of legitimate ideas. There are a number of ways to gather ideas from staff members without increasing the team size, such as soliciting suggestions through memos, e-mail, and occasional large-group meetings to share progress and gain ideas.

Defining Roles and Responsibilities

Once staff members are invited to participate in the treatment outcome project, it is critical that *roles* and *responsibilities* be defined for each team member.

The project coordinator typically is a clinical director or administrative director of a treatment facility or program. This person generally possesses the skills of a "change agent" in communicating, problem solving, and championing the overall project. In particular, the project coordinator must have leadership qualities and strong communication and interpersonal skills. The project coordinator serves as both task manager and liaison between clinicians, staff, and the outcome team technical or support staff (Davies et al., 1994).

The data manager is a staff member who is knowledgeable about QI principles, computers, and database management. This person usually is responsible for designing questionnaires (for example, parent, client, and agency satisfaction surveys), managing large data sets, and analyzing results. The data manager also supervises data collection, manages data storage, conducts quality control procedures, and presents outcome findings in a clear and concise manner. Behavioral health care providers like

Devereux often support clinical operations with statistical and data management consultation.

The data collector is typically an administrative assistant who is centrally located at the treatment facility and accessible to the data manager and informants on the outcome team. The data collector is responsible for collecting data from informants and organizing and storing data. This person is also responsible for identifying missing data.

Informants are not formal members of a treatment outcome team. Informants provide data that are essential for the quantification of treatment interventions and outcomes. They may include teachers, direct care staff, parents or guardians, clients, clinical staff, support staff, employers, or outside agencies. Informants must be trained in completing standardized instruments such as behavior rating scales, clinical checklists, surveys, and other measures. In addition, informants must be sufficiently familiar with aspects of the source (for example, client and clinical procedure) to be measured.

The type of informants who assist the team depends on the program's objectives and clinical indicators of care. For example, teachers may serve as informants for assessing the academic skills and emotional and behavioral problems of clients during school. Direct care staff, however, may serve as informants for evaluating clients' independent living skills, pathological behaviors, and hygiene.

The worksheet provided in Figure 8.1 assists in identifying team members and conceptualizing the roles and responsibilities of a treatment outcome team. If an organization has limited resources or is unfamiliar with the outcome evaluation and measurement process, it may wish to outsource the evaluation process.

Determining the Scope

Determining the scope of an evaluation is an essential step in designing a successful treatment outcome and QI system (Reddy & Pfeiffer, 1996). The scope of an outcome project is influenced by the overall mission of the organization and its treatment programs. The scope defines the criteria for including clients and variables in the data collection effort. An outcome team should address two broad questions: (1) What kinds of clients will be included in the system, and (2) How many clients will be included in the system? With regard to the first question, many studies focus on specific clinical groups or interventions. For example, a study may include only clients with diagnoses of conduct disorder and attention deficit hyperactivity disorder (ADHD). Studies may include clients who are self-referred,

FIGURE 8.1

Assembling a Treatment Outcome Team

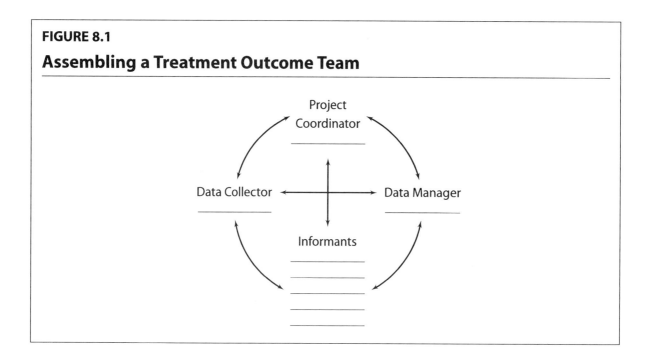

who have dropped out of treatment, or who have participated in both individual and family therapy.

In a similar fashion, outcome projects may be designed to include clients of specific age groups or special characteristics. For example, projects may study children between the ages of five and twelve years, adolescents with substance abuse dependency, or adults between the ages of twenty-five and forty years with mental retardation. It is certainly possible, however, to design a project to include a cross-section of clinical populations, age groups, and methodological procedures. Such cross-sectional groups can be designated as *experimental* groups. The experimental group is compared to the control group and is the one for which there is an expectation of change, depending on the type, intensity, and duration of the intervention. For example, conduct-disordered adolescents usually respond to groups whose primary intervention is teaching more mature levels of interpersonal problem solving. With increased interpersonal problem solving, there is often an associated reduction in the client's levels of aggression, hostile attributions, and cognitive distortions involving others.

Let's turn to the other question in determining the scope of the evaluation: How many clients will be included in the system? A team may chose to include all or just some of the clients in a program or agency. Less experienced treatment outcome teams typically include a large number of clients from a program and subsequently collect inordinate amounts of data on many variables. All too often this results in a study that is overwhelming and unmanageable. It is recommended that first-time outcome teams include a modest number of clients and a few variables in their outcome evaluation and QI efforts.

A team may use a selection procedure to identify a sample of clients in a program. For example, outcome data may be collected on every other or every third client admitted for services. Also, a team may wish to randomly select clients in a program or agency. For example, a team may randomly select 20 percent of the clients in a vocational training program for adjudicated youth and 30 percent of the clients served in a substance abuse dependency program. Selection procedures are designed to reduce the probability of selecting groups that are biased on a characteristic or variable that is related to the benefits of the actual intervention. It is particularly helpful to use either selection procedure for programs (for example, outpatient clinics or inpatient hospitals) that offer short-term treatment services to a large volume of clients.

When designing outcome studies, it's a given that treatment outcome teams will want to insert additional variables of clinical interest into the research design. The insertion of additional variables such as gender, age, and number of risk factors at admission, however, results in an enormous data pool. The addition of more variables greatly increases the amount of effort required to collect data and decreases the likelihood of having complete data sets on each individual involved in the study. Beware—the addition of just a few more variables may render an outcome study so cumbersome that it cannot be completed.

Identifying and Enhancing Resources in the Agency

An important task for the outcome team is to determine what, if any, additional resources are needed to successfully execute the system. Most treatment programs have a rich supply of resources readily available at the facility. It is the outcome team's responsibility to identify, access, and enhance resources in the treatment environment. Resources typically found in most facilities include database or spreadsheet software, copying machines, knowledgeable and skilled staff in the procedures of outcome evaluation and QI at the facility, assessment instruments (for example, personality inventory, adaptive behavior scales, behavior rating scales, and questionnaires (client, employer, and parent satisfaction surveys), and staff with strong leadership and communication skills who can effectively train or mentor staff (Reddy, 1995).

Strategies that can be used to enhance resources include the following (Reddy, 1995):

- Use existing data or data that will be routinely collected as an integral part of the treatment process when possible. In many instances, information found on intake forms, psychosocial histories, treatment progress notes, psychological assessments, and psychiatric evaluations offer a wealth of information that can be used in treatment outcome projects.

- Seek out skilled and knowledgeable staff at the facility.

- Conduct in-service training for staff on the principles and methods of outcome evaluation and CQI. Staff respond best when examples of past studies are used, particularly when the studies were conducted at their facility.

- Obtain additional resources such as outside consultants, supplemental training, and access to library materials.

- Collaborate and share knowledge with other provider entities.

Avoiding Pitfalls in Outcome Evaluation

Staff personnel typically encounter a range of difficulties when conducting treatment outcome evaluation and QI. Two important functions of the treatment outcome team are to anticipate potential problems and to use effective strategies to overcome these difficulties (Joint Commission on Accreditation of Healthcare Organizations, 1993; Reddy, 1995). Five common constraints and strategies to overcome these problems include the following:

Staff Resistance

You may recall that in Chapter One the authors discussed the common pitfall of staff resistance during the evaluation process. Staff resistance may be manifested in a number of ways, including anxiety about indirect or direct self-evaluation, ambivalence about carrying out the study (extra work), or opposition to the implementation of the system itself. The team must carefully assess the staff's concerns and motives regarding the system before attempting to intervene. For example, ambivalence may be attributed to staff not fully understanding the purpose and implications of the project. Or resistance may be related to staff misunderstanding the intent of the project and viewing it as a means to review personnel or account for expenditures. Only through understanding the nature of staff resistance is it possible to intervene constructively and address the underlying issues of the resistance. It is possible to circumvent staff resistance constructively by presenting a few past outcome studies. As an integral part of these presentations, it is necessary to link the results of the outcome project to QI and programmatic changes. In this way, staff view the direct linkages between outcome evaluation and QI. Here are some strategies to overcome staff resistance (Joint Commission on Accreditation of Healthcare Organizations, 1993):

- Enthusiastically "market" the project and clearly describe staff's roles and contributions to the overall success of the project.

- Offer training on treatment outcome evaluation.

- Set expectations about the project early with newly employed staff.

- Disseminate outcome results and consequent programmatic changes that were effected in CQI on a routine basis and formally commend staff for their efforts and participation.

- Elicit staff feedback periodically.

Limited Time and Resources

Limited time and resources are commonly encountered when clinical or administrative activities are added or improved. Resources may include staff, skilled personnel, data, equipment, assessment instruments, and space. Ways to overcome limited time and resources may include:

- Begin with a small pilot project and then build the complexity of the outcome project with success.

- Set strict time limits on meetings. Write and distribute minutes of meetings. Use memos and e-mail whenever possible.

- Maintain a high degree of group focus and organization. Such goals will maximize the use of available space, resources, and time.

- Seek out available internal resources such as assessment instruments, preexisting data, and skilled and knowledgeable persons.

Collecting Too Much Data

A common difficulty in an outcome system is collecting a lot of data that provide little information on the issues being studied (Joint Commission on Accreditation of Healthcare Organizations, 1993; Reddy, 1995). Few situations are more discouraging to program staff who have invested their time and energy into logging client activities, surveying, and collecting data on clients than to learn that the data were never used or did not answer basic questions of the study. All too often, less experienced outcome staff "want to do it all," expanding their outcome projects before adequately testing their effectiveness. Here's how to avoid collecting too much data (Joint Commission on Accreditation of Healthcare Organizations, 1993; Reddy, 1995):

- Don't jump into a project; keep it simple and carefully consider the program goals and clinical indicators.

- Review findings regularly to see whether data elements should be added or dropped. It is equally essential that the data be obtained from measures that have the requisite psychometric properties of reliability, validity, and sensitivity to change over time.

- Elicit input from staff who are actually collecting and coding the data. Ask staff what is working in the process and what problems they have encountered. Ask for suggestions for improving the process.

Collecting Too Much Detail

Another potential pitfall inherent in outcome evaluation systems is asking for a level of detail that is too time consuming, invalid, or inappropriate (Joint Commission on Accreditation of Healthcare Organizations, 1993; Reddy, 1995). Even the most conscientious staff member at times neglects to complete all requested information. The result is a project that is difficult to manage and analyze; if it is methodologically unsound, the missing elements or data may be irretrievably lost. Such a study is ultimately an expensive waste of time and resources. Ways to avoid requesting too much detail include (Joint Commission on Accreditation of Healthcare Organizations, 1993):

- Keep the level of detail in check by starting with clear program goals and a few specific clinical indicators.

- Revisit the level of detail in the data set whenever a new data element is proposed. This enables the data manager to ensure that the data sets have integrity and are compatible with data to be used for future projects.

- Balance the level of effort required for data collection and the usefulness of the data in improving the quality of the program.

Limited Financial Resources

Implementing an outcome system requires fiscal support. The hiring of new staff, contracting with consultants, and purchasing of measures, equipment, and materials can drain most providers' budgets. As pressures mount to curtail costs, providers may find it increasingly difficult to support even the smallest outcome projects. These strategies are helpful in overcoming financial difficulties:

- Include only the core outcomes needed to evaluate the program. Streamline what is to be measured, and keep the detail of the data in check.

- Use existing data whenever possible. This will help contain the costs of purchasing measures and data entry.

- Develop a training partnership with local colleges and universities. Create an externship placement for undergraduate and graduate students. An outcome evaluation system offers excellent training opportunities for undergraduate and graduate students interested in the field of psychology. Creatively including students in the implementation of the outcome system will be rewarding for the students and the agency.

- Access support and consultation services from national organizations. For example, the Child Welfare League of America (CWLA) and the National Association of Psychiatric Treatment Centers for Children (NAPTCC) offer professional training workshops, electronic bulletin boards, and consultative services to their members.

- Consider fee-based outsourcing assistance from recognized consultants or research groups.

Selecting Appropriate Measures

A critical step in designing an outcome measure is the selection of appropriate measures. A number of sources are available that review outcome assessment instruments for children, adolescents, and adults. The Devereux's Institute of Clinical Training and Research developed a *Consumer's Guide to Mental Health Treatment Outcome Measures* (Pfeiffer, Soldivera, & Norton, 1992) that critiques over twenty-five different rating scales, structured interviews, and specialized assessment measures. Green and Newman (1996) offer an extensive overview of references for locating outcome assessment instruments. *Assessing Outcome in Clinical Practice* (Ogles, Lambert, & Masters, 1996) is a text that identifies assessment instruments that have been used extensively in outcome research and reflect adequate psychometric properties.

As providers begin to select outcome assessment instruments, it is important to consider how well these measures assess the outcomes being studied. It can be helpful to apply a set of outcome assessment criteria to select among assessment instruments (Reddy & Pfeiffer, 1996). Figure 8.2 outlines criteria for selecting outcome assessment instruments.

FIGURE 8.2

Criteria for Selecting Outcome Assessment Measures

- Practicality (including credentials or training required, administration time, and scoring).

- Relevance to the target group (scales that have been tested on persons similar to the population being evaluated with high rates of reliability and validity).

- Objective referents (items specified in behavioral terms).

- Opportunity for multiple respondents (scales are available for which the same or a related version may be used by different types of respondents such as employers, significant others, teachers, and parents).

- Psychometric strengths (includes indices on reliability, validity, classification accuracy, and sensitivity to change).

- Costs (purchasing costs, administration, scoring, and use of results).

- Offensive language (for example, sexism or racism).

- Ease of understanding by nonprofessional audiences (requires basic reading skills, clear instructions, results and scores are understandable to various audiences).

- Compatibility with clinical theories and best practices guidelines (extent to which the measure reflects a strong theoretical base and a high standard of treatment practices).

- Usefulness in clinical practice (scales that are clinically relevant to organizational and staff concerns).

- Availability of valid norms (scales include norms for a range of age groups, races, gender, races, and comparable clinical populations).

Methods for Data Collection and Management

After selecting the measures but prior to initiating an outcome assessment project, it is important for the team to identify procedures for collecting and managing data. A number of methods can be incorporated into an outcome evaluation system; three that are particularly helpful include using a data collection schedule, a data collection checklist, and an informant feedback form.

After defining outcome success and adopting an outcome assessment approach (see Chapter Seven for details), the team is now ready to create a timeline or schedule that outlines what data will be collected and coded. A data collection schedule can be helpful in prioritizing tasks and using staff time efficiently (see Figure 8.3). A data collection schedule typically does the following:

- Lists the measures to be used and domains to be assessed.

- Specifies when the measures will be administered.

- Indicates how often the data will be collected.

- Identifies who will collect the data.

FIGURE 8.3

Data Collection Schedule

Instruments/Measures	Domain	Data Collection Schedule		
		Admission	Discharge	Follow-Up
Youth Self-Report (YSR)	Level of behavioral problems	Parent/guardian; client	Parent/guardian; client	
Program-specific assessment instrument	Perception of problem areas	Parent/guardian; client	Parent/guardian; client	
Number of discipline referrals	—	Home school staff		Home school staff
Number of referrals to juvenile justice agencies	—	Home school staff		Home school staff
Number of policy contacts	—	Home school staff		Home school staff

A second method that is useful for outcome evaluation is a data collection checklist (see Figure 8.4). A data collection checklist is an important tool for organizing, tabulating, and managing incoming data. The checklist offers the team a method to determine (1) when data are to be collected, (2) when data were collected, and (3) what data were collected from which clients.

A third method that has been proven valuable in conducting outcome research is an informant feedback form (see Figure 8.5)—a formal way to elicit informants' feedback and suggestions during the evaluation process. This provides the team with important insight about (1) what is working during the data collection process, (2) what problems have been encountered, and (3) what might be done to improve the process. This form also asks informants about whether they received training on completing the instruments used to collect the data and if they feel the training on instrument administration was adequate. In addition, this tool offers a way to acknowledge the important contribution informants make to the overall success of the outcome project.

Database management is the process of obtaining complete and accurate data in an efficient time frame. This task presents arduous difficulties for many behavioral health care providers. Data management usually involves two important tasks: (1) data entry and (2) data quality control.

FIGURE 8.4

Data Collection Checklist

Instrument/Procedure Used:

Client Name	Admission	Discharge	Follow-Up
1			
2			
3			
4			
5			
6			
7			
8			
9			
10			

FIGURE 8.5

Informant Feedback Form

Thank you for doing your part as a member of our treatment outcome project. Please take a couple of minutes to give us your thoughts about the outcome evaluation process.

DID YOU . . .	YES	NO
Receive training on completing the instruments?		
Feel that the training was adequate?		

1. What is working in the outcome evaluation process?

   _____

   _____

2. What problems have you encountered during the outcome evaluation process?

   _____

   _____

3. Please offer suggestions for improving the outcome evaluation process:

   _____

   _____

Once data are collected, providers must then code and enter the information into a structured framework (a database).

Prior to coding and entering outcome data, however, the team should address three questions, as follows:

1. *Is it important that data be entered in "real time," or can data entry be delayed?* It has been our experience that it is easier to delay data entry until several completed forms can be entered at the same time. This is called batch data entry and is conducted most efficiently in a centralized area of the center (Davies et al., 1994). However, for many reasons data should be entered immediately after the assessment form is completed. This is real-time entry. For example, a clinician may want to compare a client's level of depression with last month's depression score or with that of other clients in the program. If real-time entry is required, data entry will need to be conducted in the treatment program.

2. *Will data entry be manual or automated?* A team can choose to enter data manually or through automated systems. Manual data entry is a clerical function that can be time consuming but performed successfully with minimal training. Automated data entry methods such as scanners, touch

screen technology, or computer assisted telephone interviewing systems are time efficient but are more expensive to build and install than manual methods. Automated data entry is the recommended data entry method if a team anticipates processing a large volume of data or prefers to have real-time data feedback (Davies et al., 1994).

3. *Who should be responsible for performing the data entry function?* Determining who will be responsible for entering and managing the database depends on which data entry method is used (Davies et al., 1994). For example, if delayed data entry is acceptable, it is probably easier for the data manager to handle these tasks. However, if the clinical staff require real-time data feedback, more than likely the clinical staff will need to assume part or all of the responsibility for data entry.

Outcome data must be carefully checked for completeness and accuracy throughout the project. Here are some methods that are helpful in assisting provider networks with managing data and enhancing the quality of data (Davies et al., 1994; Reddy, 1995):

- During data collection, identify missing or incomplete data so informants can immediately correct the problem.

- Before data entry, identify faulty data forms.

- Establish set times for data to be checked for completeness and accuracy.

- Use two persons to independently enter the same data: "double entry."

- Database software can be used to check for values that are out of range, illogical, or missing. Hand-scored data can be checked with software scoring programs.

- Provide quality control summary reports to the project coordinator at set time intervals.

Methods for Data Analysis

Once outcome data have been entered and checked for quality, providers can begin the analyze and reanalyze phase. A number of approaches can be used to evaluate the operational efficiency of an organization, effectiveness of treatment programs, and the relative impact of services on clients' lives (also see Chapter Seven). The analyze and reanalyze stage offers providers an empirical baseline for formulating improvement plans.

One useful technique for evaluating the performance of an organization or program is outcome monitoring, which requires the periodic measuring and reporting of system or program results. In contrast to process evaluation, outcome monitoring focuses on measuring the impact of an organization or intervention on the functioning (for example, reduction in anxiety, improved skills) of clients and staff. For example, a provider may evaluate the effectiveness of a parent-training program by assessing parent stress levels and the frequency of behavioral incidents at home prior to the start of the program, during the course of training, and after the program has been completed. Data could be analyzed by comparing changes in parental stress and the frequency of behavioral incidents between different points in time.

Outcome monitoring requires the routine and frequent monitoring of system or program indicators. This approach helps providers identify system constraints and enhance resources for promoting organizational performance. A report card (summary) generated at all levels of an organization serves as a comparative analysis of the effectiveness of different programs and services. In addition, performance summaries can foster a healthy sense of competition among key stakeholders and promote creativity and innovation in system improvement.

A second approach to analyzing outcome data examines change at the individual client level to assess the quality and efficacy of interventions. Process evaluation and impact assessment techniques can be used separately or in combination to evaluate client change. A variety of outcomes and clinical indicators can be examined at the consumer level. For example, the reduction or improvement of client symptomatology, skills, well-being, quality of relationships, or adaptive functioning during treatment (formative evaluation) or after treatment has ended (summative evaluation) are outcomes that can be included in a client evaluation.

A number of methods can be used to evaluate individual client change. We have found two methods helpful for measuring improvement in client functioning: (1) the goal attainment scale (GAS; Kiresuk, 1973) and (2) the computation of effect size. Since the 1970s, GAS has been used as a technique to assess changes observed in client behavior. The GAS offers a simple approach for evaluating treatment goals that are unique for individual clients. Goals are established at the beginning of treatment, often in collaboration with clients. Each goal is defined in specific behavioral terms (80 percent of the time, the client will work on the task: completes morning personal hygiene five out of seven days). Client progress toward goals is periodically evaluated (hourly, daily, weekly, every three months, and so on), ideally by someone other than the clinician treating the client. If the client remains in treatment or his needs change, this process is repeated. The GAS method offers providers a flexible and efficient way to manage, track, and evaluate treatment process for individual clients.

The computation of effect size is another useful way to assess the impact of an intervention on an individual's functioning. Busk and Serlin's (1992) single-subject design effect size (ES) can be used to assess the magnitude of clinical improvement observed in a client during the course of treatment. Data collected prior to the start of treatment are compared to data obtained at a specific point in the treatment process, taking into account the variability of client performance during treatment. Busk and Serlin's (1992) ES equation produces an ES value that can be easily interpreted. ES values of .20, .50, and .80 signify small, medium, and large changes observed on an outcome variable (Cohen, 1988). ESs can have negative or positive values. For example, a large negative ES value of -.85 indicates that an outcome (for example, number of referrals, attendance) significantly deteriorated during treatment; a large positive ES value of .85 indicates that an outcome (for example, positive peer interactions, learning of math skills) substantially improved during treatment.

Deciding to Use Statistical Analytic Methods

A number of conceptual and methodological factors need to be considered when deciding whether or not to use data analysis tests for outcome evaluation. A modified version of Newcomer's (1994) criteria for choosing appropriate data analysis methods is presented in Figure 8.6.

The decision as to whether or not to use statistical tests partly depends on the number of consumers included in the evaluation study. A project with an adequate (large enough) sample size provides more statistical power or sensitivity to detect whether reliable differences exist between groups (for example, individual versus group treatment or satisfaction ratings of male and female clients). A common problem in most initial outcome evaluation projects is that samples tend to be small, often yielding statistical test values that reflect no significant differences, usually due to a lack of power. Thus the provider has a less than satisfactory result, which can be disappointing and lacks clinical usefulness.

Where does this leave the behavioral health care provider who offers treatment services to a small number of clients over an extended period of time and wants to evaluate outcomes? It is important to remember that inferential statistics are tools to help providers make judgments and draw conclusions. As previously mentioned, in some situations, adopting only statistically reliable criteria for determining outcome success may be inappropriate.

FIGURE 8.6

Considerations for Using Data Analysis Methods

1. Question-related considerations

   • Is replication of the outcome evaluation results desired?

   • Is the impact of the program the focus?

   • Are the evaluation question(s) relevant to regulatory and accreditation requirements?

   • Is the quality and consistency of service delivery the focus?

2. Methodological-related considerations

   • Are multiple clinical indicators used to evaluate outcomes?

   • How many participants will be included in the project?

   • Will more than one group or intervention be compared?

   • How many times will participants be observed (for example, 1, 2, or 3 times)?

   • How reliable and valid are the measures used?

   • Are there participants that scored extremely low or high (outliers) in the sample?

   • Are multiple informants being used to define and evaluate outcome success?

3. Stakeholder-related considerations

   • Will outcome findings be useful for policy, program, and fiscal decision making?

   • Are sophisticated statistics (for example, MANOVA repeated measures) comprehensible?

   • Do descriptive statistics (for example, means, percentages) and graphic presentations (for example, pie charts, bar graphs) enhance stakeholders' understanding and use of outcome findings?

   • Do stakeholders understand the difference between statistical and clinical significance?

Methods of Summarizing Outcome Data

We have found it helpful to summarize outcome data so that we can make inferences about how well clients are profiting from programs and services. One method is to compute and report percentages of clients in various outcome categories. For example, an outpatient clinic may not statistically test its data but instead compute the percentages of each group who remained in treatment and dropped out of treatment, and those who dropped out and eventually returned for services. Similarly, a provider of residential care may wish to examine the number (percentage) of families who participate in team meetings, attend campus functions, and participate in family outreach services (for example, parent training, respite, and support groups).

Another method is to graphically represent clients' average scores over time; this provides an appealing venue to show the effectiveness and quality of programs and services. This method can also dramatically highlight findings and accelerate an understanding of the purpose and usefulness of the evaluation process. For example, an evaluator may share with program staff a descriptive summary of the characteristics and background information on the clients served in a program and graphically illustrate (for example, bar graph) the percentage of clients discharged to home, group home, and residential care. It is important to carefully select graphics (pie charts, bar graphs) that are familiar and easily understood by the target audience. A number of sophisticated and user-friendly graphic programs are available, such as Lotus Freelance Graphics and Microsoft PowerPoint.

Another approach is to establish justifiable criteria among stakeholders for improvement or clinical change. Once criteria are agreed upon, data can be reported in terms of the percentage of clients who improved and clients who did not.

Weighing Advantages and Disadvantages

The decision about whether or not to use statistical analysis isn't simple. Such analysis offers benefits as well as challenges. A benefit of *not* using statistical analysis is that providers have to develop reporting methods and formats that are more comprehensible and useful for stakeholders who need to make informed decisions. Providers who don't use statistical tests, however, have a greater professional responsibility to interpret the data they do have and draw appropriate conclusions.

We advocate that providers use a conservative approach to outcome analysis, keeping consumers in mind, using statistical technology when appropriate, and seeking consultation when needed. For those who wish to statistically analyze their own data, there are a number of sophisticated and user-friendly statistical software programs that include data spreadsheet and data scanning capabilities. For example, SPSS for Windows and MINITAB are two of many statistical software programs that can be used to enter, store, and analyze outcome data. These programs offer providers the capability to compute descriptive statistics (percentages, means, standard deviations, correlations), basic inferential tests (*t*-tests, chi-square tests, analysis of variance), as well as more advanced analytic techniques (multivariate tests, trend analysis). In addition, easy-to-read guides that bridge the conceptual and mathematical application of analytic techniques are also available for each of these programs (see Norusis, 1988; Wilkinson, Blank, & Gruber, 1996).

Integrating Outcome Evaluation and CQI: Illustrative Examples

It is important that results from outcome evaluations yield useful and practical information for improving the effectiveness of service delivery. The ability for an outcome evaluation system to meet this objective relies largely with the program's team and clinicians. Linking outcome information to clinical practice is more easily accomplished if program goals, outcome measures, and analyses are designed with this purpose in mind.

We present here three illustrative examples of outcome evaluation and QI projects. All three cases demonstrate how outcome evaluation can be used to generate plans for QI. The first case presents an outcome study conducted at Cleo Wallace Centers—a continuum of programs for children and adolescents with emotional and behavioral disorders disorders (Mike Montgomery, personal communication, July 1999). The second case depicts an outcome study conducted in the Devereux Texas Treatment Network's Alternative Education Program for students who are emotionally or behaviorally disturbed (Betters, Shea-Clauson, Daniel, & Varisco, 1998). The third case presents an outcome study that assesses the effectiveness of a teen pregnancy prevention program at Devereux's Florida Treatment Network residential treatment facility for youth with emotional and behavioral problems (Patty Hurst, personal communication, July 1999).

Case 1: Parent Satisfaction at Cleo Wallace Center's Programs for Children and Adolescents

The facility set out to conduct a parent satisfaction survey to determine parents' perception of the treatment programs and develop plans for QI (Mike Montgomery, personal communication, July 1999). Staff decided to include all parents, guardians, and caseworkers of current clients in their continuum of care. Programs included residential treatment, inpatient hospitalization, and day treatment. The goals were (1) to increase parent involvement in program development through survey methods, (2) to increase parent satisfaction, and (3) to improve the program.

Cleo Wallace developed an internal survey that assesses parents' satisfaction on several dimensions: quality of treatment, experience with family therapy, education and support received around medication administration, staff competence, level of involvement, admission process, and discharge and aftercare experience (Mike Montgomery, personal communication, July 1999). The entire population of parents is surveyed annually by mail, and a random sample is interviewed by telephone.

After collecting the outcome data, staff began to analyze and generate hypotheses regarding the results of the survey process (Mike Montgomery, personal communication, July 1999). The results from the satisfaction survey revealed general satisfaction with the program overall. Specific dissatisfaction centered on staff's inability to make parents feel welcome on the units when they visit. Subsequently, the facility trained staff on specific techniques to improve parents' level of comfort during visitation.

Staff began to question the reliability and validity of the survey findings after obtaining similar results over a number of years. Their primary concern was the potential bias built into the findings due to the self-selective nature of a mail-in survey approach. Return rates were relatively low—below 40 percent. Usually only those that are extremely satisfied or extremely dissatisfied with services are motivated to complete and return a survey. Therefore, the survey process fails to capture the perceptions of those who fall in the middle; this leads to biased data. Cleo Wallace addressed this concern by contracting with Gallup, an independent company, to conduct a satisfaction survey. Gallup designed a new survey in collaboration with Cleo Wallace staff. They then surveyed the parents. The response rate increased considerably. Over 540 cases were randomly collected, providing statistically valid results. The findings provided a more critical assessment of Cleo Wallace's programs, confirming staff's initial concerns about bias in the original findings from their internal process. Gallup was also able to rank order the factors with the greatest impact on parent satisfaction. Most significant from the Gallup survey data was the high correlation between the clinical case manager and parent satisfaction, which had tremendous implications for the training and recruitment of clinical staff.

The outcome results offered Cleo Wallace a baseline to improve the process of clinical services in the program (Mike Montgomery, personal communication, July 1999). After sharing the results of the project with staff, the program created plans for improving the overall quality of the treatment services. As discussed in Chapter Five, the programs adopted a solutions-oriented approach to treatment as part of a larger biopsychosocial model, developed a manual, and trained all clinical staff on its implementation. The approach emphasizes respect of patients' and families' inherent strengths and the enhancement of adaptive functioning over pathology. The organization has taken steps in the right direction, which with follow-through will result in a positive outcome.

Given the staff's confidence in the findings from the Gallup survey and the usefulness of the information obtained for their programs, Cleo Wallace has permanently switched to outsourcing, that is, using an independent local survey group to conduct future surveys on a routine bases via telephone interviews (Mike Montgomery, personal communication, July 1999). Data will be collected to assess the effectiveness of programmatic changes to improve parent satisfaction.

Case 2: Alternative Education Program for Children and Adolescents with Emotional-Behavioral Problems

An outcome evaluation system was developed at the Devereux Texas Treatment Network to assess the effectiveness of their Alternative Education Program for students who are emotionally or behaviorally disturbed (Betters et al., 1998). The program consisted of education class for four subjects (math, science, English, and social studies), group counseling, and physical education, with heavy emphasis on behavior modification throughout. The program also provided individual and family counseling. Placement varied from six to twelve weeks.

The outcome study included seventy intermediate and high school students from a large school district in Southeastern Texas (Betters et al., 1998). The main goal of the program is to enable students to be successful in school as well as in society. The program offers a placement alternative to those students who otherwise would be without placement services and as result would be at higher risk for future delinquent behavior. Individual program goals include (1) reduce the number of students' discipline referrals by 80 percent upon returning to their home school, (2) decrease students' referrals to juvenile justice agencies by 70 percent upon returning to their home campus, (3) decrease students' number of police contacts by 70 percent, and (4) reduce the number of behavior problems.

The outcome assessment plan incorporated two assessment instruments: the Youth Self-Report (Achenbach, 1991) and a program-specific pretest designed to measure parent and student perceptions of problems (Betters et al., 1998). After program completion, follow-up on student progress at home and school was completion at two- and six-week intervals for one year. Figure 8.3 outlines the assessment plan used in this study.

The YSR was used to assess the level of behavioral problems of the students in the school (Betters et al. , 1998). The instrument comprises a Competence Scale and a Problem Scale. The Competence Scale provides a total Competence Score and three additional subscale scores: an Activities Scale, a Social Scale, and a Mean School Performance Scale. The Problem Scale offers Externalizing and Internalizing scores and subscores for eight syndrome scales (Withdrawn, Somatic Complaints, Anxious/Depressed, Social Problems, Thought Problems, Attention Problems, Delinquent Behavior, and Aggressive Behavior).

This study produced primarily positive results (Betters et al., 1998). Program staff found a 97.1 percent reduction in student discipline referrals upon completion of the Alternative Educational Program, a 95.3 percent decrease in referrals to juvenile justice, and an 82.4 percent decrease in police contacts. Assessment of YSR results indicated significant improvements in Attention Problems, Aggressive Behavior and Total Problem Score. Decreases in the areas of Somatic Complaints, Anxious/Depressed, Social Problems, and Thought Problems approached statistical significance. Students demonstrated improvement in the Competence Scale scores as expected; however, it was not statistically significant. The only surprising outcome was a slight increase in the scores on the Withdrawn Scale.

The outcome results from this study offer school psychologists, special educators, and administrators valuable information on the quality and effectiveness of the Alternative Education Program (Pam Helm, personal communication, July 1999). After analyzing the outcome data, program staff developed a plan for future assessment and program improvement. The staff realized that the existing evaluation method failed to account for differences in length of stay. Therefore, staff concluded that it was necessary to conduct additional assessment to control for such differences and to reconfirm initial findings. Staff decided to complete additional follow-up of program graduates to assess the program's impact on long-term gains in behavior change as additional validation of the program's effectiveness.

Case 3: Pregnancy Prevention Program for Young Teens

Given the sexual history and incidence of teenage pregnancy of the clients served in the residential treatment setting of Devereux 's Florida Treatment Network, the facility implemented a nationally recognized program called Baby Think It Over (Jurmain & Jurmain, 1999), designed to help teens postpone pregnancy. The program was designed to teach teenagers the responsibilities and realities of becoming a parent, with the intended effect of demystifying the romanticism of having a child. The program uses realistic, life-sized, and multicultural mechanical dolls that simulate the need for attention and care of a real baby.

Baby Think It Over is one element of a nine-week course that includes an educational component on postponing sexual involvement, a safe sitter program (participants receive certification in baby sitting), training in infant medical issues (sudden infant death syndrome, head injury, narcotic-addicted infants, cardiopulmonary resuscitation), and two weeks of actual parenting (Patty Hurst, personal communication, July 1999). Participants must manage all aspects of infant care, including arranging day care while in school (hence the safe sitter program), budgeting for supplies, purchasing supplies, attending well-baby check-ups, and car safety. Those who complete the program can obtain school credit.

The program development team developed an outcome evaluation system to assess its impact on participants' attitudes and behaviors regarding sex and pregnancy (Patty Hurst, personal communication, July 1999). The specific goals of the program are (1) to teach teens the skills to resist pressures to become sexually involved, (2) to teach the consequences of early pregnancy, (3) to teach teens how to take care of young children in a babysitting situation, (4) to teach the responsibilities of becoming a parent, and (5) to teach teens to avoid pregnancy by postponing childbearing until adulthood.

The outcome assessment plan included a pre- and posttest of participants' attitudes toward sexual activity and childbearing, the percentage of participants who successfully complete the Safe Sitter Program, and a follow-up question on pregnancy after discharge (Patty Hurst, personal communication, July 1999). The pre- and posttest assessment plan evaluates attitudes related to participants' desire to have a child, time frame within which they want to have a child, impact of a child on a couple's relationship, and the difficulty of being a single parent.

Preliminary results indicate positive improvements on participant attitudes (Patty Hurst, personal communication, July 1999). Specifically, 100 percent of the participants reported they would have a child in less than ten years at pretest and in more than ten years at posttest. Seventy-five percent of participants reported that it is more difficult to have a child in a single-family home at posttest compared to 50 percent at pretest. Fifty percent of those surveyed changed their mind completely about wanting a child, reporting at posttest that they did not want a child, whereas during pretest they did. The most telling information regarding effectiveness of the program were the participants' comments. These included, "I used to want a baby; now I know I'd be miserable" and "I just want you to know I am a born-again virgin!"

Given the impact of the program, as suggested by the initial findings, the team decided to continue implementing the program to clients identified as appropriate by the treatment team (Patty Hurst, personal communication, July 1999). The real test will be in the program's ability to postpone pregnancies in teens after their discharge from the program. Therefore, the team plans to incorporate follow-up assessment of incidence of pregnancy during aftercare and to compare the rates of participants to nonparticipants and the general population.

Designing and conducting outcome evaluations requires a multidimensional effort. When outcome evaluation information and QI efforts are integrated, administrators, policymakers, clinicians, and clients have significantly more information about the processes and outcomes of care. The complementary relationship between outcome evaluation and QI offers practical and rich information that can be used to inform decision making, improve service delivery, and establish best practices.

Chapter 9

Finishing Touches

AS WE REVIEW what we have learned in the process of writing this book, it is readily apparent—perhaps to no one's surprise—that behavioral health care providers striving to put their houses in order have been faced with major challenges. The threats and pressures of managed care and the increased requirements of the major regulatory bodies such as JCAHO, COA, and NCQA, have been with us for some time, stimulating the movement toward quality and accountability. With the proverbial gun to their heads, provider organizations, large and small, have struggled to sustain operations with static or declining revenue per unit of service. At the same time, these providers have been taking steps to illustrate the effectiveness of their services and to demonstrate broad stakeholder participation in their systems of care.

Survey results from the book's diverse sample of behavioral health care providers, interviews with a number of organizational leaders, and the authors' experiences at Devereux suggest that during the past decade our industry has more or less survived rather than thrived. Although we have regained our collective equilibrium from the incursion of managed care and various regulatory bodies into our organizational lives, the challenges of blended funding initiatives, movement toward privatization, and the possible effects of computer snafus lie ahead. Is there no rest for the weary?

As they forge ahead, behavioral health care provider organizations can expect to find themselves financially at risk yet fully accountable for the quality and specific outcomes of their services. Sorry, there is no going back to the days of unmanaged care. All care is now more or less managed. Employers and government agencies have increasingly opted out of the fee-for-service health care and human services business. In addition to established commercial and public sector managed care paradigms, new worries have emerged with regard to funding.

Historically, only mental health and substance abuse services were funded by managed insurance programs, but more recent behavioral health care initiatives have been broadened to include developmental disabilities, child welfare, and juvenile justice services, along with the related needs and interests of the broad base of stakeholders. Writing on this theme in *Open Minds*, a popular behavioral health care industry newsletter, McManus (1999) states that accountability in the form of performance benchmarks "is a requisite part of any system reform. It is therefore essential that providers and consumers insist on this level of accountability that is responsible to multiple stakeholder groups" (p. 4).

Furthermore, payers are beginning to look beyond traditional managed care models to fund the delivery of care. Privatization and the related use of sophisticated provider groups (sometimes referred to as professional service organizations) is a case in point. When government entities elect to privatize various programs and services, they look to a large, sophisticated provider organization—with or without the involvement of an existing managed care organization (MCO)—to provide administrative, direct care, or care management services.

Thus as we start the new century, providers must be prepared to embrace "sophistication." To be sophisticated is to be operationally autonomous, data-driven, and quality managed. Provider networks will be transparently linked via information technology to offer rapid access to a full continuum of care. Either an administrative entity will be created to provide network management or a large provider organization with requisite capabilities will be chosen to serve as a lead agency. Having gathered input from various stakeholders, payers will move toward purchasing outcomes versus services from provider organizations. For instance, the issuance and renewal of contracts can be expected to orbit about consumer satisfaction with various processes of care in addition to objective measurements of consumers' quality of life in such areas as sustainable schooling, work, and community living.

To survive and thrive in the era of accountability, it is helpful to begin with a review of where our organizations are today in relation to where we need to be tomorrow. Behavioral health care organizations have begun to comply with mandates for accountability. Primarily with paper-based methods, we have begun gathering data and using it to make "snapshots" of consumer satisfaction and other outcomes of care. And most provider organizations have installed some type of QI team. In aggregate, however, we remain fairly reactive to operating challenges and cannot yet rightly consider ourselves to be quality managed and data-driven.

In this concluding chapter, we reexamine the major themes that run throughout this book and look at what we've learned and how the behavioral health care provider of the future will operate. Let's review the collective provider organization "punch list" and subsequent suggestions for putting the finishing touches on our homes.

Key Themes

From our survey, the most universal finding is that nearly all behavioral health care organizations have been making good faith efforts to document programmatic outcomes and improve quality. Regardless of size, most organizations have been earnestly engaged in some form of outcome measurement for at least a few years. Typically, the path has been difficult, with many false starts, setbacks, and a steep learning curve. Yet providers have persevered. It is, in part, to help other providers avoid these pitfalls that we have written this book.

Often a provider's first attempt at establishing accountability of its services has been driven by external demands for outcome data versus an intrinsic desire to be outcomes managed. As we noted previously, payers, regulators, and consumers have demanded data to demonstrate the value of services. It seems that this demand for outcome data has helped spawn an enabling climate for quality management initiatives. Accordingly, most providers have seemingly "backed into" QI as an approach to improving the data that are reported to outside constituencies.

Fortunately, in the routine collection of outcome-related data, many providers and their staffs take an essential first step in the quality quest. The next move in this evolution is to begin to use outcome data as part of a fully integrated QI system. This progression is of vital importance. Indeed, it seems logical that in the near future our field will migrate from the current focus on outcome measurement to a more sophisticated and dynamic mode of operation that is *based on* outcome management. Increasingly, we will see the use of real-time programmatic data to manage client care and improve outcomes. In other words, the emphasis will shift from reporting data to using data to continuously improve systems of care.

The embryonic nature of quality management systems within our field has emerged as a closely related theme. Although most surveyed providers have been able to develop systems of accountability for addressing basic standards of care, they are generally provider-specific and low-tech. An illustration of this is found in client record systems. Each provider entity tends to have its own unique client record with provider-defined fields and operational definitions. In many cases these records are built on word processing programs rather than relational databases. This significantly limits the utility of client records for data analysis and outcome management within a given provider organization. Additionally, the idiosyncratic nature of these records makes it difficult to compile reliable client information across providers and systems of care and to track trends and support research and advocacy efforts.

It will be necessary to adopt sophisticated, generic, and nimble technological systems in order to maximize the communication of relevant "apples to apples" client information within and across broad health care networks. (More than likely, many of these new systems will be Web-based.) Such systems will enable consistency of reporting and permit comprehensive data analyses. For example, movement toward the standardization of client records will facilitate admission and discharge planning processes. This, in turn, can result in better access to care and more timely care as well.

Encouragingly, the credentialing of professional staff stands out as one area where standardization and the use of technology has already resulted in improved efficiency. Behavioral health care provider organizations can now use a number of Web sites on the Internet to obtain primary source verification of much of the needed information. Alternatively, provider groups are increasingly outsourcing this function to a few nationally established credentialing firms. Outsourcing can result in better accountability and improved cost-effectiveness. The result is a win-win for consumer and provider.

Another trend to emerge from our survey is the movement to standardize behavioral health care interventions through the use of clinical practice guidelines (CPGs). This is also an encouraging development and appears more widespread than we initially anticipated. The move to employ CPGs suggests that undesirable variability in clinical care is being reduced. Thus it is now less likely that clinicians will rely solely on personal treatment biases or the school of thought that dominated their graduate training program in delivering care to their clients.

Nearly all providers in our survey have adopted or are developing evidence-based practice guidelines. In most cases, including that of Devereux, these guidelines have been developed by the provider organizations' professional staff in response to organizational specifics and operational realities; they are not being adopted wholesale from more generic, published guidelines. Given that such provider-specific guidelines are empirically based and theoretically sound, we view this as a positive finding. It is also a decided plus that a representative, multidisciplinary group of clinicians were involved in the CPG development process. This not only serves to ensure that the standards reflect local concerns and conditions but it facilitates buy-in from the treatment providers who will be expected to implement the guidelines.

Prior to a discussion of where our industry appears to be, where it needs to go, and how it will get there, it is useful to briefly review salient findings that typify surveyed providers.

The Modal Provider

The array of services offered by the typical provider in our sample is bimodal. That is to say, the delivery of comprehensive mental health (33 percent) and child welfare (34 percent) services were of equal prevalence, with provision of juvenile delinquency and mental retardation and developmental disability services making up the balance. Given that the organizations in our survey primarily serve children, adolescents, and families, our modal behavioral health care entity strives to meet the needs of America's youth.

With regard to the adoption of QI methodology and infrastructure, it was most common to find that behavioral health care provider groups complied as an organizational duty (business as usual); they were neither "noncompliant" nor "fully internalized and acted upon as a corporate value." Although our surveyed providers typically have standing QI leadership committees that meet monthly, most do not include clients, parents, or guardians as members. However, there is mandated QI staff training in most instances. On the other hand, the role of QI coordinator is usually layered on top of existing primary work responsibilities and is not a full-time job. Finally, although it is common for today's behavioral health care provider to use computerized financial systems, clinical records and other care management functions are still handled manually.

With basic standards of clinical care, we see high levels of accountability in the areas of credentialing and supervision. Although our typical provider group makes use of a uniform client record, there is still suboptimal use of client strengths and functional assessments. Further, many of the surveyed provider groups do not routinely include discharge criteria or permanency goals in their clients' records. Additionally, the continuing education and training of a facility's professional staff is encouraged, but it is typically an area that is neither formally pursued nor monitored by the provider organization.

From the vantage point of client rights, ethics, and advocacy, our typical provider organization is attuned to such issues but does not have a bona fide client rights or ethics committee. Instead, there are varied means of access for clients, family members, and staff wishing to present their issues for review. Although most surveyed providers do have specific policy and procedure in this area, the means for review range from using an outside agency, to any staff person, to a designated staff person, or to a review committee.

It also appears that psychiatrists have not been taken into the bosom of most of our surveyed provider groups, with the exception of acute care hospital settings. Licensing and accreditation regulations notwithstanding, physicians can seldom be found actively participating on QM or senior management teams. Although it is common to find a part- or full-time psychiatrist functioning as medical director, there are few instances of empowered medical advisory committees with input into program design and clinical best practices. Typically, we find psychiatric consultants whose primary role is to assess and medicate.

As we have already suggested, the use of practice guidelines is a positive and evolving area for our modal provider. Although there is significant variability as to what any given provider may reference as practice guidelines, both child welfare and mental health care organizations are actively seeking to improve and standardize their clinical workflows. It is common for organizations to adapt evidence-based or actuarially derived guidelines to their own client populations and settings of care. Although conceptual and methodological issues are being tended to first, targeted and focused interventions are being sought to address the specific behavioral health care needs of clients.

What a positive discovery it was to learn that every provider organization we surveyed mandated some type of training for frontline staff. We found substantial variability in the comprehensiveness of training, needs assessment, and evaluation. Our typical provider requires staff to participate in several training programs. Most providers, however, do not have formal mechanisms for identifying staff training needs or validating the use of targeted training skills in subsequent client interactions. Instead, training often consists of courses that are either mandated by a payer or regulator, or deemed theoretically relevant by senior management. Effectiveness of training is then usually gauged by trainee satisfaction surveys and use of immediate posttests to measure knowledge and skills. Unfortunately, acquired knowledge and skills are not commonly sampled "on the floor" or at specified intervals after the training.

Finally, we learned that surveyed providers did not typically belong to multiprovider computer networks that permit within- and across-organization benchmarking. In fact, our modal provider claimed to use a clinically oriented computerized system for outcome management only. Although it was reported that QI staff commonly use computerized systems to carry out their duties, this was not the case for clinical staff. The good news is that data are being collected and outcome reports are being generated. However, clinical operating data are not yet the common driver of managerial decisions. Similarly, outcome findings are not always broadly shared with key stakeholders or developed into multiyear studies that fuel the QI cycle.

So in retrospect, when we think about where the profession has been and where we are now, we've come a long way. Behavioral health care, as both a profession and an industry, has been around for approximately one hundred years. For most of that time, treatment approaches have been extremely varied and desirable results have been hard to objectify. During the past decade, we began to adopt QI methodology into our organizations, comprehensively define standards of care, quantify processes and outcomes of care, and involve a full gamut of stakeholders in evaluating and enhancing our systems of care. We have a blueprint for organizational development and a set of powerful tools. We have, in fact, built solid foundations for our future.

Getting from Here to There

The sophisticated behavioral health care provider of tomorrow—the one that remains viable in this increasingly competitive, ever-changing environment—will be able to apply the lessons in this book and erect a sturdy house from a solid foundation. This will require the provider to have building blocks in place in order to construct effective systems of accountability (see Figure 9.1). These blocks should include

- A solid QI infrastructure—through leadership commitment—to drive the systems

- Standards of care

- Safeguards to help ensure the provision of ethical care

- Psychiatric involvement in treatment planning and services

- Practice guidelines

- A commitment to the professionalization of frontline staff

- An outcome-based management approach to making operational and clinical decisions

Taken individually, implementation of any one of these elements seems straightforward and manageable. The provider that will flourish, however,

Figure 9.1

Building Blocks for Systems of Accountability

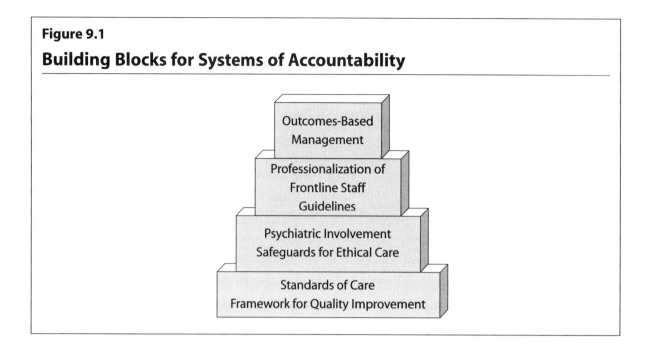

is the one that is able to integrate these elements into a seamless system of accountability. This may seem like an insurmountable task, but it isn't.

We have looked at the modal or typical provider's profile in the implementation of systems of accountability that defines where we are today. As we peer into the future, we expect that major progress in developing accountable systems of care will result from two major trends. The first, already described, is the shift from data collection to data utilization. After gaining experience with outcome reporting, providers are now beginning to use those data in true QI initiatives. Although still comparatively rare in our field, using data in the QI process (to assess, analyze, hypothesize, implement process changes, reassess) will become more commonplace. It is in the implementation of true data-based QI efforts that the promise of improved outcomes will be realized.

The second major trend will be the horizontal and vertical integration of the various quality management areas and functions around the theme of improved client care. Practice guidelines will be integrated with staff training, client outcomes, and consumer satisfaction. This trend is under way at Devereux. In the past, our internal quality site visits have operated in a traditional mode. Different staff members were assigned to review various programmatic areas such as credentialing, record keeping, and staff training. These reviews would occur concurrently and in isolation from each other.

We are currently moving to a different, more integrative model in which a multidisciplinary team will randomly select clients for review and all aspects of those clients' care, as well as their integration, will be reviewed in depth. In this emerging model we will be interested, for instance, in the inter-relationships of client assessment, treatment planning, implementation of practice guidelines, and clinical outcome management and outcomes. We would also review the training, credentialing, supervising, and continuing education of all staff working with these few selected clients. Such a system, with a more holistic systems approach, will present a clearer view of the actual processes of care and their influence on outcomes.

These shifts in emphasis from data collection to data-process integration and utilization will require a corresponding shift in staff attitudes. We must move from the current view of quality management as an organizational duty (as noted in our survey) to fully embracing QI as part and parcel of the provider's corporate culture.

Only when QI becomes the mission of all staff and not just of those few professionals who have labored to erect the quality management infrastructure, will we truly know that we have placed our house in order. Let's look at the strategies that the sophisticated provider of tomorrow would use to "get from here to there."

Committing from the Top Down

We've said it before and here we must say it again, achieving accountable systems of care begins with commitment from the top. This point cannot be overemphasized. The model provider seeks and supports leaders who embrace the tenets of QI as the operating drivers of change. QI, as a management philosophy, is internalized by staff at all levels as the one and only way to operate. As such, QI is not another process that one begrudgingly implements but rather is transparently woven through the entire fabric of the organization's operation. It becomes second nature to staff's way of doing things. Only when this value is embraced can a provider truly begin to address other elements of the system.

Staff at a provider agency may have good intentions and the motivation to implement continuous quality improvement. However, without the support and commitment from senior management to "walk the talk," the process will not take root. Beginning at the top will ensure that the cultural change is taken seriously, resources are allotted, decisions made are consistent with implementing QI, and others throughout the organization accept the change. It goes without saying that leaders must practice what they preach. It takes unswerving support and nurturing from the bottom up to foster conviction in this new way of doing things. So how does a provider organization engender leadership support?

One of the best ways to convince top management of the value of something is to speak their language: the language of "bottom line." Demonstrate the cost of *not* implementing QI and you're sure to grab their attention. For instance, the value of QI will certainly be appreciated when presented in the context of the avoided cost of referrals withheld, accreditation lost, and litigation encountered when the organization proactively addresses restraint-related injury through QI.

It is essential for senior management to obtain training in QI so that they can model the behavior they expect of others. Once they have bought into the process, the leaders provide direction to others by setting the organization's global mission, vision, and objectives.

Sharing the Vision

With the big picture established, the model provider goes on to foster a corporate culture that supports QI implementation. This may involve modifying reward systems, financial and information systems, and training systems to be consistent with the organizational change (Packard, 1995). Staff are trained in principles and tools of QI so they can use them in all aspects of performance.

Internalization of QI does not come easily. The process is slow; inevitably, there will be setbacks. This is one of those cases in which patience is definitely a virtue. Senior management's training in QI will come in handy to give them the tools they need to maintain staff motivation and faith in the process during the early stages when resistance and obstacles may seem formidable (Packard, 1995). It's up to leadership to do what it takes to see that staff can get the job done. As staff embrace the principles of QI, they can begin to participate in the organization's metamorphosis. The structure of QI provides the parameters and rules of engagement to which staff adhere in their interaction with one another. That is, all staff at all levels participate in organizational improvement, leaving their egos at the door.

Building the Dream Through Data

It is staff's role to translate leadership's mission and vision into reality. To do so, the model provider seeks their agreement on the specific goals, planned methods, and desired outcomes of the agency with all stakeholder involvement (for example, clients, families, staff, management, funders, agencies, and other major constituents) (Hernandez & Hodges, 1996).

We have seen how consensus increases both the likelihood of buy-in and commitment to the goals and objectives at all levels. This requires understanding stakeholders' assumptions about service provision. Who do stakeholders believe the agency is intended to serve, what services do they believe fulfill their mission, and what outcomes do they believe the agency is intended to meet?

The next step involves determining the factors that may be contributing to the outcome, such as characteristics of the population served, the processes or services engaged in, and so on (Hernandez & Hodges, 1996). This is achieved by collecting and assessing information about the agency's population, the services provided, and the outcomes obtained. Accurate measurement of both outcomes and key processes is essential to identify the potential factors contributing to or affecting the outcome. The gaps between the assumptions and reality will define the bases for all other elements of the accountability system and help staff focus resources.

Implementing the Remaining Elements

The model provider uses the findings from data analysis to build and shape its programs. When staff are aware of the gaps between goals and reality, they can apply the standards of care relevant to their target population that will guide the processes believed to affect desired outcomes. Let's look at an example. Staff at Provider A determined that the target population is children between the ages of five to twelve with attention deficit disorder, and the desired outcome is integration back into regular education. If this provider were a model provider, it would establish the standards of care that reflect the processes relevant to those parameters.

In this provider's case, credentialing standards would be developed that specify the need for the agency to verify its staff's age-specific competence relative to the diagnosis. Clinical records standards would provide guidelines for incorporating and emphasizing educational goals and progress in the treatment plan. Supervision would be hinged on the appropriateness of clinical decisions and staff development needs relative to serving the target population. Training and education of professional staff would be related to the competence with the target population and the achievement of educational goals. Finally, QI initiatives would assess the extent to which the processes the agency staff engaged in achieved the identified program objectives (integrating clients back into regular education). This would be accomplished by selecting relevant process and outcome indicators (number of group problem-solving training sessions, number of days in school, and so on) for which data would be routinely collected, analyzed, and used in program improvement.

Standards that are universal will apply to any population, regardless of the desired outcome. One can readily appreciate how the standards will ultimately affect the outcome. The required elements stressed in the credentialing standards will determine the quality and competence of the staff hired. The quality of a treatment plan will affect the services provided, the comprehensiveness of care given, the selection and focus of the interventions used, and so forth. How the goals are written will limit the options of intervention and the focus of services provided. If a treatment plan is not designed to elicit and use client strengths in treatment, then goals will likely emphasize decreasing challenging behaviors rather than increasing skill acquisition. Ultimately, this affects the agency's level of success in achieving the desired outcomes.

Conducting an Ethical Practice

Policies and provision of ethical conduct are applicable regardless of the population served. However, the model provider goes one step further and uses the process of defining its population to identify unique considerations that may need to be incorporated into safeguards for quality care. For instance, if children are your primary population, then the method of communicating and enforcing their rights will be different than if your population is adolescents. You will need to be sure that the children can comprehend your client handbook. Satisfaction surveys will need to be designed for administration with children. And the children should be able to effectively use the client advocacy structure.

As we learned earlier, adolescents provide an entirely different set of considerations. In particular, emancipation introduces unique concerns related to establishing and obtaining informed consent (Kaplan, 1988). How much does the adolescent truly understand? How capable is the adolescent in making competent, informed decisions? What factors may influence the adolescent's competency—cognitive development, life stressors, complexity of the decision? All of these individual client factors need to be considered when developing a system to ensure ethical care.

Involving Psychiatrists

In the spirit of QI, it's important to welcome and embrace all staff of all disciplines as valuable contributors to service provision. The model provider recognizes, in particular, the essential role psychiatric staff play in the treatment process.

Aside from fulfilling a philosophical principle, psychiatric involvement meets a basic standard of care for ensuring the provision of competent services that are appropriate, comprehensive, and effective. Limiting psychiatrists' practice in an agency's program to the ancillary functions of prescribing and monitoring medications is short-sighted. The unique expertise and keenly developed skills of psychiatrists can add insight into the total care of the client.

Although it's true that financial constraints may be responsible for the failure to integrate psychiatrists into the total system of care, securing psychiatric commitment to certain responsibilities through minor modifications to the contract can make their involvement feasible without breaking the bank. This will enable programs to maximize the wealth of skills, knowledge, and talent within their reach and move ahead of the curve in state-of-the-art care.

Customizing Treatment Guidelines

Once again, the model provider uses the process of defining its population and identifying goals to guide staff in determining the guidelines that need to be developed in order to close the gaps between reality and goals. Knowing whom you serve is essential to this process. The data collected through the program's day-to-day operations of admission, treatment, and discharge will help to define the characteristics of the served populations. This information is critical to indicating the type of guidelines that need to be developed and implemented. For instance, one agency may discover via data analysis that the clients actually served are in fact much younger than originally intended, with a mean age of eight. Given the treatment requirements the population presents, staff will need to search for or develop guidelines that address their exact needs and that take into consideration the provider's service setting. Only by being data-driven can a provider remain aware of how its population changes month to month, year to year. This is what enables a provider to be responsive to the changing needs of its clients.

Guidelines will help ensure that the services provided are the most effective and efficient means of meeting the population's needs and ultimately achieving the expected outcomes. They will define the resources that are needed, the staff competencies that are required, the additional training that must be provided, and the services that are to be used. They will ultimately reflect the agency's theory of change—given client X, if we provide service Y, we will achieve outcome Z.

Training for Frontline Staff

Clearly, an agency's theory of change and established guidelines will affect the training requirements for frontline staff. The model provider adheres to these principles of treatment to determine the elements of its training program. The skills frontline staff will need to carry out the same objectives may vary from agency to agency, depending on the desired outcomes and the interventions that the agency espouses will lead to their achievement. You may recall that in Chapter Six we discussed how critical frontline staff are to the effectiveness of services. They are the ones who actually deliver the majority of the plan for services that is believed to achieve the desired outcome. That is why, before defining a staff member's development plan, it is essential for an agency to have asked the pertinent questions about whom the agency serves and what it does. This is how the agency determines the theory of change and the training needed to support it.

Managing for Outcomes

What exactly drives the outcomes framework? For the model provider, the theory of change or its beliefs about how outcomes are obtained lie behind the framework, including the process and the outcome indicators measured. By collecting data related to this theory of change, the agency can evaluate the effects of its services on the population served (Hernandez & Hodges, 1996). Specifically, staff can isolate the individual factors that most greatly contribute to the desired outcome (that is, which processes in combination with which client characteristics lead to which outcomes). The data collected are then used to make decisions regarding modifications to existing services, access of services to reach the intended population, and program development.

Let's say, for example, that the desired outcome for a defined population of adolescents with disruptive behavior disorders is the successful transition back to the home and reduced need for mental health services. An agency may attempt to achieve the desired outcomes by providing an after-school program that focuses on developing adolescents' social skills and a parent training program that emphasizes discipline techniques. Some indicators that the program may measure the number of parents involved in training, the number of training sessions provided, the acuteness and complexity of the needs of clients involved in the programming, demographics on the clients, the number of days in school, the amount of involvement with the police, and so on.

Providing a structure for how to operate (QI) and asking a few key questions (managing by outcomes) will enlighten staff and focus resources to the common goals of providing safe, high-quality, and effective care to individuals served. Laying the bricks and mortar and investing the resources up-front will pay off in clearly defined objectives, priorities, and expectations that everyone can understand and work to achieve. Once you have established the structure, the elements of implementing standards of care, incorporating relevant guidelines into processes, developing a mechanism to ensure ethical care and to integrate psychiatric staff, training front-line staff, and conceptualizing a framework for outcome evaluation will all be clearly attained.

With a solid foundation in place, you can begin to install the frame, walls, and roof that will support a complete system of accountability. It's a time-consuming, high-maintenance, labor-intensive task but one that is well worth the effort. After all, there is nothing quite so satisfying as to look around and see that finally, your house is in order.

Appendixes

Appendix A

Organizational Survey

Name of organization: _____

Headquarters location (city & state):

_____

Survey completed by:

Name: _____

Title: _____

Phone number: _____

1. Your organization's:

   Average daily census: _____

   Number of sites and programs: _____

   FTEs: _____

2. Is your organization accredited by any of the following? Please check all that apply.

   _____ JCAHO

   _____ NCQA

   _____ CARF

   _____ COA

   _____ Other (specify)

3. Type(s) of client(s) served. Please check all that apply.

   Age:

   _____ Preschoolers

   _____ Children

   _____ Adolescents

   _____ Adults

   _____ Geriatric

(Continued)

Organizational Survey *(Continued)*

Major Presenting Problems:

_____ Juvenile delinquency

_____ Abuse or neglect

_____ Mental health

_____ Mental retardation or developmental disabilities

_____ Substance abuse

_____ Dual Diagnoses (please specify)

Quality Improvement (QI) History

4. Please describe previous QA/QI/QM initiatives and their outcomes. Please describe how many previous initiatives your organization has undertaken, how long each lasted, and what was the impact.

_____

_____

_____

_____

_____

_____

_____

_____

Current QI Initiatives

5. Please describe current QI initiative(s). How long has the current initiative(s) been in existence?

_____

_____

_____

_____

_____

_____

6. Please rate 1–5 the degree of QI adoption by your organization, as evidenced by staff compliance with QI-related requests.

1 = noncompliance

2 = grudging compliance

3 = compliance as an organizational duty (business as usual)

4 = willing compliance

5 = fully internalized and acted upon as a corporate value

QI Staffing

7. What is the title of the individual who directs your organization's QI program?

   _____

8. What is his or her discipline or academic background?

   _____

9. How much of his or her time (expressed as an FTE) is devoted to QI management?

   _____

10. How many professional FTEs are devoted to QI as their primary job responsibility? _____

11. How many support staff (secretaries, data entry clerks, records management technicians) are devoted to QI as their primary job responsibility? _____

12. Is there a separate department or committee for QI? Y _____   N _____

    If yes:

       What is its annual budget? _____

       For comparison, what is your organization's total budget? _____

13. Is training in QI mandated? Y _____   N _____

    If yes:

       For what levels of staff? _____

       _____

       What does the mandated QI training consist of? _____

       _____

       How many hours/days is the mandated training? _____

       _____

QI Committee Structure

14. Is there a standing QI leadership committee? Y _____   N _____

    If yes:

       Who sits on this committee? _____

       How often do they meet? _____

       Is there a committee mission statement? Y _____   N _____ (If yes, please attach)

       Is there a standing agenda? Y _____   N _____ (If yes, please include a copy)

       How are issues from program staff brought to the committee?

       Do clients participate in the QI committee meetings? Y _____   N _____

          If yes, how? _____

          _____

       Do parents and guardians participate in the QI committee meetings? Y _____   N _____

          If yes, how? _____

          _____

(Continued)

Organizational Survey *(Continued)*

Do payers or regulators participate in the QI committee meetings? Y _____ N _____

If yes, how? _____

_____

_____

What other methods, if any, are used to involve clients, parents or guardians, payers or regulators, in the QI process?

If no:

How are quality issues handled at your program?

_____

_____

_____

Standards for Clinical Practice

15. Does your organization use practice guidelines or manualized treatment approaches? Y _____ N _____

If yes:

_____ Did you develop your own guidelines? or

_____ Adopt published documents? Please specify. _____

How do you implement and monitor compliance?   How do you handle exceptions?

_____

_____

If no:

What approach does your organization use to promote consistency of care? _____

_____

16. Does your organization use a uniform or standardized client record? Y _____ N _____

If yes:

_____ Did you develop your own record? Or

_____ Adopt a commercial product? Please specify. _____

Please indicate which areas are included in your record: (check all that apply)

_____ functional assessment

_____ client strengths

_____ discharge criteria

_____ permanency goals

How do you train staff in the use of the record? _____

_____

Is your clinical record computerized? Y _____ N _____

Information Resources

17. For which of the following functions do you use a computerized system? Please check all that apply.

_____ Financial functions (billing, A/R, A/P)

_____ Clinical record management

_____ Clinical case management

_____ Outcomes management

18. Please Indicate the degree to which the following categories of staff use computerized systems to carry out their duties:

1 = Never   Clinical: _____

2 = Rarely   Administrative: _____

3 = Occasionally   Direct Care: _____

4 = Frequently   QI: _____

5 = Continuously

19. Does your organization belong to any multiprovider computer networks that allow for within and across organizational benchmarking? Y _____   N _____

If yes:

Please specify _____

_____

_____

Ethics and Clients' Rights

20. Does your organization have a clients' rights or ethics committee? Y _____   N _____

If yes:

Who are the members of this committee? _____

_____

If available, please attach a mission statement for this committee. _____

_____

How do clients, clients' family members, and staff access this committee? _____

_____

How does this committee interface with the treatment team? _____

_____

If no:

What process does your organization use to address clients' rights issues? _____

_____

21. How does your organization provide for client advocacy services? _____

_____

(Continued)

Organizational Survey *(Continued)*

Culturally Competent Practice

22. Does your organization have *mandated* training to teach your staff how to be culturally competent?

    Y _____   N _____

    If yes:

    For whom is the training required? _____

    What does it consist of? _____

    _____

    How many hours or days is the training? _____

    Have you developed your own training program? Y _____   N _____

       If yes:
       Please describe your training program. _____

       _____

       If no:
       Did you adopt a published curriculum? Y _____   N _____

       If yes: Please identify. _____

       _____

    If no:
       Do you provide optional training on cultural competence? Y _____   N _____

       Please describe. _____

       _____

23. If you do not provide any training, how do you ensure that your staff demonstrate cultural competencies? _____

    _____

Medical-Psychiatric Leadership

24. Does your organization have a medical director? Y _____   N _____

25. Does your organization have a medical-psychiatric leadership committee (for example, National Medical Advisory Committee)? Y _____   N _____

    If yes:
       Who are the members of this committee? _____

       _____

       If available, please attach a mission statement for this committee.

       How do clients, clients' families, and staff access this committee? _____

       _____

       How does this committee interface with the treatment team? _____

       _____

If no:

How does your organization provide for medical-psychiatric leadership? _____

_____

26. How does your organization provide for peer-review (for example, internal review with staff or outside consultants)? _____

_____

27. How are medical-psychiatric findings integrated into programming? _____ _____

_____

Professionalization of Direct Care Staff

28. Does your organization have mandated training for direct care staff? Y _____ N _____

If yes:

What does it consist of? _____

_____

How many hours or days is the training? _____

Have you developed your own training program? Y _____ N _____

If yes:

Please describe. _____

_____

How do you assess the effectiveness of training? _____

_____

29. How do you support the ongoing professional development of direct care staff? _____

_____

Measurement and Performance Improvement

30. What indicators of clinical quality does your organization routinely measure? _____

_____

31. What kinds of reports are created based on these indicators? _____

_____

32. How are these reports disseminated and used? _____

_____

33. What are your major treatment outcome indicators? _____

_____

34. How does your organization compile treatment outcome data? _____

_____

35. Are summary reports written? _____

36. How are these reports disseminated and used? _____

_____

37. Does your organization use any outside service (for example, SumOne for Kids) to collect or manage treatment outcome data? Y _____ N _____

(Continued)

Organizational Survey *(Continued)*

38. Does your organization benchmark its performance against external criteria? Y _____   N _____

    How? _____

    _____

39. Does your organization participate in any treatment outcome consortia (for example, Odyssey Project)? Y _____   N _____

    If yes:
    Please list. _____

    _____

Other Information

40. Are there any organizational success or horror stories related to the previous questions that you would like to share with the readership of this book? Remember, success stories and innovations will be cited by organizational name; horror stories will not. Please describe: _____

    _____

    _____

    _____

41. Would you be willing to participate in a telephone interview to elicit more information on these topics? Y _____   N _____ (If yes, please make sure that you have provided your phone number at the beginning of this survey.)

Appendix B

Quality Management Committee Meeting Minutes

Date:

Attending: Recommended staff members, including (list names, degrees, titles):

            Quality manager/chair   Clinical director

            Executive director   Director of administrative services

            Marketing director   Physician

            Director of residential services (unit coordinator and/or program director)

            Principal/senior educator and/or vocational services

            Admissions director

            Client organization representative (rotating)

            Referral agency representative (rotating)

            Clients and family members (rotating)

Absent:

Excused:

Guests:

I. Proactive Concurrent Case Reviews

Case Study #: Use a code to protect the client's identity.

Date of Review: Only include if case review completed by outside team.

Reviewer Names: Review team should be interdisciplinary. Only include if case review completed by outside team.

Case Summary: If case review is attached, indicate here "See attached report" and omit following case review information from body of minutes. If incorporating report into the body of the minutes, proceed with the following headings and narrative as specified in the case study review form.

Program: _____ DOB: _____

Age: _____ Gender: _____ Admission Date: _____

Referral Agency: _____

(Continued)

Quality Management Committee Meeting Minutes *(Continued)*

Diagnosis:

Axis I

Axis II

Axis III

Axis IV

Axis V

Current Medications:

Intellectual Functioning: FSIQ: VIQ: PIQ:

Academic/Adaptive Behavior Functioning:

Last Psychiatric Review:

Special Diet/Allergies:

Recent hospitalizations/tests:

Last Physical: Physician:

Therapist: Psychiatrist:

1. Need Areas: Briefly summarize; not all areas will necessarily apply to your population.

   Areas of Focus: Comments:

   _____ Academic/Vocational (MR)

   _____ ADL—Activities of Daily Living (MR)

   _____ Socialization/Community (MR)

   _____ Medical

   _____ Residential

   _____ Family

   _____ Clinical

2. Strengths:

3. Current Treatment Plan Goals: Interventions: Current Progress:

   A.

   B.

   C.

   D.

   E.:

4. Target Behaviors (if behavior plan developed):   Restrictive Procedure: Y _____   N _____

5. Therapy Received: Response to Therapy
                                                        (Current Progress):

_____ Psychological:

    _____ Individual:

    _____ Group:

    _____ Family:

_____ Occupational:

_____ Physical:

_____ Speech:

_____ Other:

6. *Findings:* Summarize above information in terms of overarching concerns or issues needing to be addressed (if you conclude there are no concerns, provide clarification for your reasoning).

7. *Recommendations:* Describe globally, recommended modifications or suggestions to address concerns or issues identified in the findings.

8. *Planned Course of Action:* Outline specific steps that will be taken to effect desired outcome; provide rationale for taking the specified steps (for example, how you expect the specified steps to resolve the issue). Identify who will complete the steps and select a date for update on progress and deadline for completion.

		Completion Date &
Action Step:	Responsible Party:	Follow-Up:
1.		
2.		
3.		

9. Discharge/Aftercare Planning: (Review existing plans.)

Conclusions: Only include if case review completed by outside team. Record QM team's additional recommendations if any and approval of or suggested changes to review team's submitted recommendations.

Repeat above outline for second case.

Follow-Up: Report outcome of actions taken for cases discussed in previous meetings.

II. Credentialing & Recredentialing

Current Status: Record issues that need to be addressed. If all files are complete and up-to-date, then state so accordingly.

(Continued)

Quality Management Committee Meeting Minutes *(Continued)*

Planned Course of Action: Report what steps will be taken to address issues. If all files are current, then record n/a.

1.

2.

3.

Follow-Up: Report outcome of actions taken for issues discussed in previous meetings (whether actions taken were successful; if not successful, what is recommendation).

III. Outcome Studies

Study Being Completed: Briefly describe study of discussion so that reader knows which study current status is referring to in the case where more than one study is being conducted by the center.

Current Status: What steps are currently occurring towards completion of the outcome study (for example, twenty-five satisfaction surveys were received and are currently being analyzed; DSMDs were completed for eighty clients).

Next Steps: Report future steps that need to be completed, who will complete them and desired date of completion.

Step:	Assigned to:	Complete by:
1.		
2.		
3.		

Results: If study is complete, present the results and report how information will be used toward continuous quality improvement. A one-page addendum providing this information can be attached to the minutes (see sample).

IV. Grievances and Complaints

Topic of Grievance or Complaint: Briefly describe the grievance or complaint (do not use names).

Recommendations: Describe desired outcome and overarching recommendation to address issue.

Planned Course of Action: Record in detail the individual steps to be taken to resolve grievance or complaint and achieve desired outcome, who will complete tasks and when they will be completed.

Completion Date & Action Steps:	Responsible Party:	Follow-Up:
1.		
2.		
3.		

Follow-Up: Report outcome of steps taken to address grievances or complaints raised in previous meetings.

V. Sentinel Events

Problem Identified: Describe details of individual sentinel events related to categories on the National Policy Sentinel Event description list. Try to identify factors contributing to frequency of occurrence.

Recommendations: Describe overarching program, policy, or procedure changes and or additions that need to be made to effectively intervene in individual case and prevent future occurrence of similar event types.

Planned Course of Action: Outline specific steps that will be taken to reduce the occurrence of the events, who will complete the steps and select a date for update on progress and deadline for completion.

Action Steps:	Responsible Party:	Completion Date & Follow-Up:
1.		
2.		
3.		

Follow-Up: Report outcome of actions taken to address sentinel events raised in previous meetings.

VI. Action Items

Summarize in table form all steps to be taken for each agenda item. Include dates for follow-up.

Agenda Item	Action Item #	Action Item	Active Step	Person Responsible	Completion Date	Date Completed
Proactive Concurrent Case Review	1.	Provide social oppor-tunities	Investigate community programs	JR	1/1/96	
	2.					
	3.					
Credentialing	1.					
	2.					
Outcome Studies	1.					
	2.					
Grievances & Complaints	1.					
Sentinel Events	1.					
	2.					

VII. Other Administrative

_____   _____

Name and Title of Recorder   Date

Distribution:

Appendix C

Quality Council Meeting

Home of the Innocents, Inc.
Quality Council Meeting

11/10/98   2:00 PM to 2:55 PM   Board Room

Meeting called by: Type of meeting: Regular monthly

Attendees: Administrative Team
Please read: Previous meeting minutes
Please bring: Previous meeting minutes

Agenda		
1. Approve Minutes	MP	2:00–2:05 PM
2. Update on Current Performance Improvement Teams	AV (Extreme Team)	2:05–2:25 PM
	JB (SPM Team)	
	EF (Motley Crew)	
	EF (Recruitment-Retention Team)	
3. Approval Requests for New Teams		2:25 PM
4. Update on Outcome Measures		2:25–2:35 PM
5. Report on IOP Forms		2:35–2:45 PM
6. Changes to PI Procedures		2:45–2:50 PM
7. New Processes, Functions, Services		2:50–2:55 PM

Additional Information

Observers:

Special Notes:

Note: Reprinted by permission of Home of the Innocents, Inc. (1998).

Appendix D

Credentialing-Recredentialing Disclosure Form

NAME _____

Please respond to the following questions. If you answer yes to any of the questions, please provide an in-depth explanation for your response.

1. Has your license to practice been revoked, suspended, or denied?   Yes   No
   If yes, please explain. _____
   _____

2. Have your privileges at any facility been revoked, suspended, denied, or restricted?   Yes   No
   If yes, please explain. _____
   _____

3. Has your DEA certificate been revoked, suspended, or denied?   Yes   No   N/A
   If yes, please explain. _____
   _____

4. Since the last renewal, have you been convicted of a felony?   Yes   No
   If yes, please explain. _____
   _____

5. Are you unable to perform the duties of your position, with or without   Yes   No
   accommodations, as outlined in your job description or as defined in your
   independent contract?
   If yes, please explain. _____
   _____

6. In the past year, have you been the subject of a malpractice suit?   Yes   No
   If yes, please explain the circumstances.
   _____
   _____

7. In the past year, have you been subject to any disciplinary hearings or proceedings?   Yes   No
   If yes, please explain. _____
   _____

I attest that the information above is complete and correct to the best of my knowledge.

_____   _____
Sign   Date

Appendix E

Part A

B. ASSESSMENT RESULTS

Section B of the *Comprehensive Treatment Plan of Care* is an assimilation and integrative analysis of all historical information, assessment data, and clinical observations collected on the client. The purpose of the assessment summary is to synthesize and quantify all assessment data commensurate with the end of the admission assessment period in order to generate a comprehensive treatment plan. *Section B* is to be repeated a minimum of annually. Continuing assessment provides a more objective means to measure and monitor client progress/regress and to update and revise the comprehensive treatment plan dependent upon current outcome data.

1. Process Steps:

a. The assessment phase begins at intake and includes both required standardized instruments and other predetermined standardized instruments as listed on the *Assessment Matrix*. The clinician will select client-appropriate standardized instruments or will utilize standardized assessments as predetermined by the Center. Assessment also includes the core record intake and various additional (nonstandardized) assessment tools. If the need for more in-depth or specialized assessment arises, the clinician can select an appropriate assessment from the *Supplemental Assessment Matrix*.

b. All selected assessments are performed and are then reviewed by a licensed clinician at the end of the designated assessment period (established by the individual Center).

c. The licensed clinician is then responsible for completing *Section B*, based on the analysis of the assessment data. See Form Completion Guide below for instructions.

d. The licensed clinician will then use the resulting data to develop a comprehensive treatment plan (*Section C*).

e. Ongoing assessment and evaluation of the client continues throughout treatment (*Section D*). The licensed clinician shall reevaluate the client's status and complete a new *Section B* of the *Comprehensive Treatment Plan of Care* a minimum of annually.

f. The licensed clinician will then review and revise the comprehensive treatment plan based on the resulting outcome data.

(Continued)

Mental Health Core Record Instructions, Part A *(Continued)*

2. Form Completion Guide:

Section B is composed of seven primary dimensions: lethality, functional, challenging behaviors, support systems, mental status, health issues, and chemical dependency. Each primary dimension is divided into designated subdimensions that are considered to be critical elements in the determination of the level of overall performance within a dimension. Evaluation of performance within each subdimension is determined by administration of the selected standardized global assessment, biopsychosocial assessment, psychiatric evaluation, QPRT-P/QPRT, SASSI, and additional standardized assessments as needed.

a. Once the clinician has administered the assessments, he or she records the standard or T score for each subdimension in the appropriate column.

b. A determination is made as to whether the score indicates a "strength" or a "need" based on the following guidelines:

   1) a score that is one standard deviation above the norm is considered a strength;

   2) a score that is one standard deviation below the norm is considered a need; and

   3) a norm score may represent a strength or a need, based on assessment data and clinical judgment.

c. Findings from other assessments and observations are to be recorded in the column for other findings.

d. Based on the assessment outcomes as recorded, the treatment team must then make a decision as to whether the dimension or subdimension is to be a focus of treatment or deferred at this time.

   1) If the dimension-subdimension is to be a focus of treatment, then the respective box is checked in the goal column and an objective is to be recorded under the corresponding dimension on *Section C* of the *Comprehensive Treatment Plan of Care*. It is not necessary to record the goal or objective on *Section B*. Any dimension-subdimension that is identified as a "need" should be addressed in the treatment plan by an objective unless there is a clinical rationale to defer.

   2) If the treatment team makes a clinical decision to defer focusing treatment on an identified need at the time, the clinician is to check the appropriate box and record the clinical rationale in the goal column for *Section B*.

C. GOALS AND OBJECTIVES

1. Goal

Develop and document individual dimension goals that are determined as the focus of treatment, by the Assessment Outcome in section B of the Comprehensive Treatment Plan of Care. A goal written for the specific dimension should be written on its own page. More than one goal may be written per dimension.

2. Strengths Utilized

Indicate the client's strength that will be utilized to meet the above goal. This strength should be derived from the assessment results.

3. Date Initiated

Enter the date that the measurable objective was initiated. New dates will be entered as objectives are met/revised/discontinued and new objectives are generated.

4. Measurable Objectives

Enter narrative information regarding objectives, in measurable terms, that the client must achieve in order to meet his treatment goals.

5. Target Date

Enter the date the client is expected to achieve this objective.

6. Date Achieved or Status Change

Enter the date the client actually achieves the stated measurable objective or the date the objective's status was changed (revised or discontinued). When all objectives for a goal have been met or discontinued, the goal is inactive and does not need to be addressed.

7. Status

If there is a status change, indicate the nature of the change by checking the appropriate option (objective met/revised/discontinued).

8. Interventions, Strategies, Modalities

List the treatment interventions, strategies, and modalities that will be utilized by the client-staff to aid the client in meeting objectives.

9. Staff Responsible

List the names of the staff responsible for implementing the treatment interventions.

10. Repeat 1 through 9 for each goal identified in the assessment section.

11. Signatures

The signature and title of each member of the treatment team are required for completion of this document

D. TREATMENT PLAN OF CARE REVIEW

The Treatment Plan of Care Review form will be completed on a regular basis as indicated in center-specific policies and procedures.

1. Review Date

Enter the date that the Treatment Plan of Care is being reviewed by the treatment team.

2. Review Period

Please specify the time frame between the last plan of care review and the present review (30 days, 90 days, and so on).

3. Diagnosis

   a. If the diagnosis has remained the same from the last plan of care review, place an X in the box next to *Diagnosis Remains Unchanged.* Indicate the date of the last change to the diagnosis in the *Date of Last Change* field.

   b. If the diagnosis has changed since the last plan of care review, place an X in the box next to *The Diagnosis Has Been Changed as Indicated Below:* Then fill in all diagnoses, Axis I through V.

   c. If the diagnosis has changed, document the reason for the change in the *Rationale for Diagnosis Change Section.* Any time there is a change in diagnosis, rationale should always be listed here.

(Continued)

Mental Health Core Record Instructions, Part A *(Continued)*

4. Current Medications

List the names of the client's current medications.

5. Justification for Continued Treatment

Enter narrative information indicating whether the client still requires treatment at this level of care and why.

6. Brief Summary of Progress According to Dimensions of Care (Note if Goals and Objectives have also been changed)

Enter a narrative summary of the client's progress since the last plan of care review for each dimension that pertains to the client. The reports should summarize activity related to the particular dimension, covering the time frame from the date of the last treatment team meeting to the present. Be sure to include rationale for any status changes to objectives (met/revised/discontinued).

7. Discharge/Continuing Care Plan

Enter any changes to the discharge or continuing care plan.

8. Ecological Support Needs

a. Enter the date of the last Treatment Plan Review in which Ecological Support Needs were changed in the *Date of Last Change* section.

b. Enter any changes to ecological support needs noted since the last Treatment Plan Review on the corresponding line. Changes could include additional assignments or updates to status (change in target date, change in staff responsible, and so on). If there is a change to any item in this section, please insert needs information for all items. This will mean not only writing the change, but also copying forward-unchanged information from the last Review in which changes were made to this section. If there have been no Reviews, copy the information from the Master.

9. Treatment Team Certification-Recertification

This section is optional. Each center will enter information as required by their state regulatory agencies, or as policy and procedures dictate.

10. Recommendations

Enter any additional Treatment and Goal recommendations the team may have.

11. Parent-Guardian Impressions of Treatment and Goal Recommendations

Enter any comments that the parent or guardian may have regarding treatment and goals.

12. Signatures

Obtain signatures including their discipline or title and the date of the signature. Signatures should include the Therapist, Nurse, Psychiatrist, Client and Parent or Guardian if applicable.

E. MASTER PLAN SIGNATURES

Obtain signatures including discipline or title and date of signature. Signatures should include the Therapist, Nurse, Psychiatrist, Client and if applicable, the Parent or Guardian.

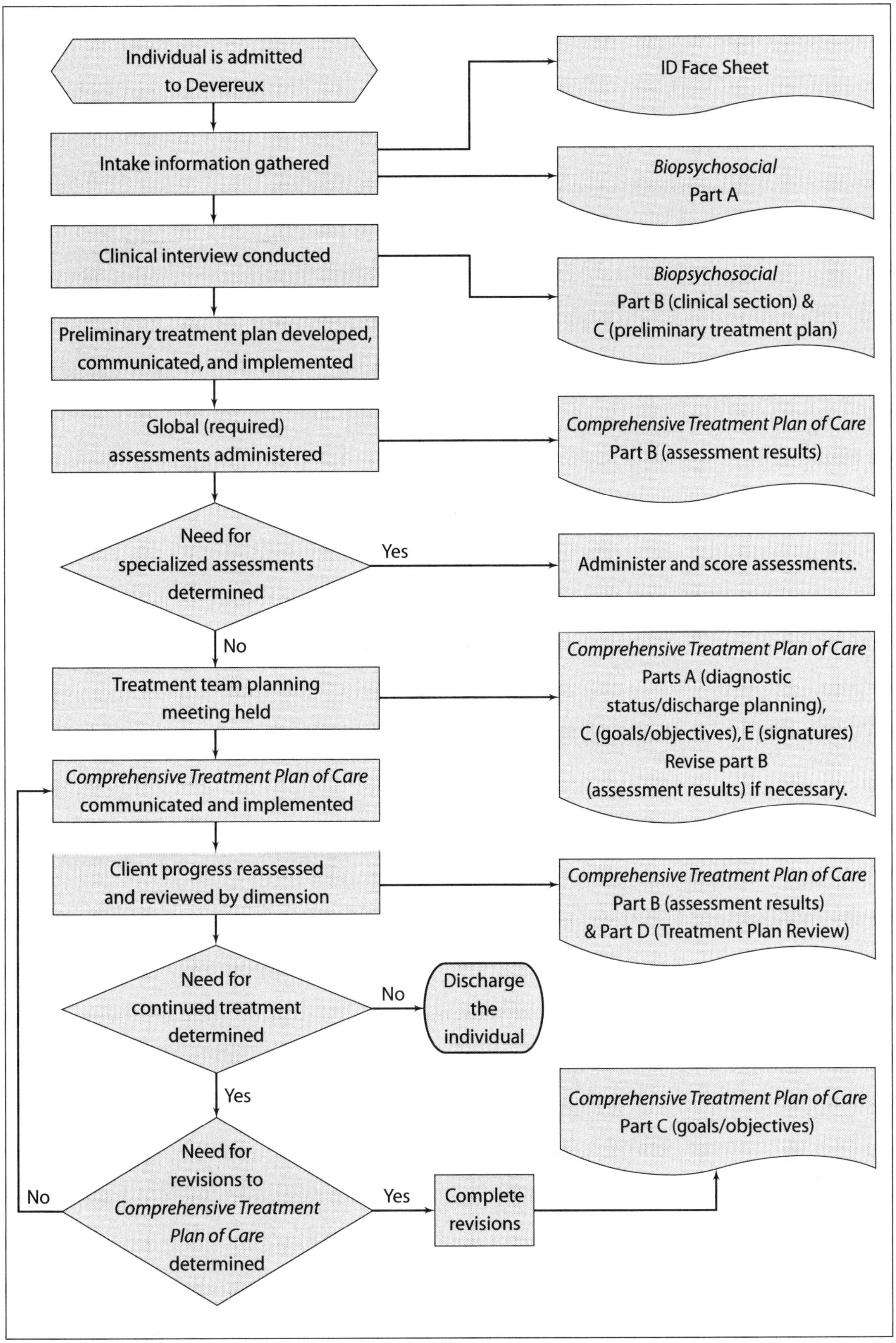
Individual is admitted to Devereux
Intake information gathered
Clinical interview conducted
Preliminary treatment plan developed, communicated, and implemented
Global (required) assessments administered
Need for specialized assessments determined
Yes
Administer and score assessments.
No
Treatment team planning meeting held
Comprehensive Treatment Plan of Care communicated and implemented
Client progress reassessed and reviewed by dimension
Need for continued treatment determined
No
Discharge the individual
Yes
Need for revisions to Comprehensive Treatment Plan of Care determined
No
Yes
Complete revisions
ID Face Sheet
Biopsychosocial Part A
Biopsychosocial Part B (clinical section) & C (preliminary treatment plan)
Comprehensive Treatment Plan of Care Part B (assessment results)
Comprehensive Treatment Plan of Care Parts A (diagnostic status/discharge planning), C (goals/objectives), E (signatures) Revise part B (assessment results) if necessary.
Comprehensive Treatment Plan of Care Part B (assessment results) & Part D (Treatment Plan Review)
Comprehensive Treatment Plan of Care Part C (goals/objectives)

Appendix E

Part B

Mental Health Core Record, Part B

❏ Master

❏ Master Update (completed no less frequently than annually)

Date: _____ Birth Date: _____ Admission Date: _____ Therapist: _____

Unit: _____ State: _____ Diet: _____

Axis	Code	Diagnosis
I		
II		
III		
IV		
V	**Current GAF:**	**Past Year GAF:**

List Current Medication(s):

Justification for Treatment:

Discharge Criteria:

(Continued)

Mental Health Core Record, Part B *(Continued)*

DISCHARGE/CONTINUING CARE PLAN   Anticipated Discharge Date: _____

Ecological Needs:	Not Applicable	Target Date	Staff Responsible
Level of Care			
Psychiatric or Psychologist Referral			
School / Educational / Vocational			
Interpersonal / Social			
Caregiver Needs			
Community Support Services			
Financial Needs			
Nutritional Care Needs			
Recreation-Related Needs			
Medical or Medication-Related Needs			
Other			

Dimension	Assessment Used & Subdimension (when applicable)	Assessment Outcome				Goal Planning Recommendation
		Standard Score	T Score	Strength(S) Need (N)	Other findings or additional assessment results	
Lethality	*Homicide* **Assessment:** ❑ Psych. Eval. ❑ Biopsychosocial ❑ Other:					❑ Focus of Tx; See Goal Sheet ❑ Defer; Provide Rationale:
	Suicide **Assessment:** ❑ Psych. Eval. ❑ QPRT-P/QPRT ❑ Biopsychosocial ❑ Other:					❑ Focus of Tx; See Goal Sheet ❑ Defer; Provide Rationale:

Dimension	Assessment Used & Subdimension (when applicable)	Assessment Outcome				Goal Planning Recommendation
		Standard Score	T Score	Strength(S) Need (N)	Other findings or additional assessment results	
Functional	**Assessment:** ❑ SSRS ❑ BERS ❑ SIB-R ❑ ABI ❑ ACLSA ❑ Other:					❑ Focus of Tx; See Goal Sheet ❑ Defer; Provide Rationale:
	Communication **Assessment:** ❑ SIB-R ❑ ABI ❑ ACLSA ❑ Other:					❑ Focus of Tx; See Goal Sheet ❑ Defer; Provide Rationale:
	Daily Living Skills **Assessment:** ❑ SIB-R ❑ ABI ❑ ACLSA ❑ Other:					❑ Focus of Tx; See Goal Sheet ❑ Defer; Provide Rationale:
	School Performance **Assessment:** ❑ SSRS ❑ BERS ❑ SIB-R ❑ ABI ❑ ACLSA ❑ Other:					❑ Focus of Tx; See Goal Sheet ❑ Defer; Provide Rationale:
	Vocational/ Prevocational **Assessment:** ❑ SIB-R ❑ ABI ❑ ACLSA ❑ Other:					❑ Focus of Tx; See Goal Sheet ❑ Defer; Provide Rationale:
	Leisure/ Recreational **Assessment:** ❑ SF-36 ❑ ACLSA ❑ Rec/Leisure ❑ Inventory ❑ Other:					❑ Focus of Tx; See Goal Sheet ❑ Defer; Provide Rationale: *(Continued)*

Mental Health Core Record, Part B *(Continued)*

Dimension	Assessment Used & Subdimension (when applicable)	Assessment Outcome				Goal Planning Recommendation
		Standard Score	T Score	Strength(S) Need (N)	Other findings or additional assessment results	
Functional (continued)	*Social Skills* **Assessment:** ❏ SSRS ❏ BERS ❏ SIB-R ❏ ABI ❏ ACLSA ❏ Other:					❏ Focus of Tx; See Goal Sheet ❏ Defer; Provide Rationale:
Challenging Behaviors	**Assessment:** ❏ DSMD (under age 18). ❏ SSRS ❏ BERS ❏ SIB-R ❏ Other:					❏ Focus of Tx; See Goal Sheet ❏ Defer; Provide Rationale:
Support Systems	**Assessment:** ❏ Biopsychosocial ❏ BERS ❏ Other:					❏ Focus of Tx; See Goal Sheet ❏ Defer; Provide Rationale:
Mental Status	*Thought Perception* **Assessment:** ❏ Psych. Eval. (no score) ❏ BSI (over age 18) ❏ Other:					❏ Focus of Tx; See Goal Sheet ❏ Defer; Provide Rationale:
	Mood/Affect **Assessment:** ❏ Psych. Eval. (no score) ❏ DSMD (under age 18) ❏ BSI (over age 18 only) ❏ Other:					❏ Focus of Tx; See Goal Sheet ❏ Defer; Provide Rationale:

Dimension	Assessment Used & Subdimension (when applicable)	Assessment Outcome				Goal Planning Recommendation
		Standard Score	T Score	Strength(S) Need (N)	Other findings or additional assessment results	
Mental Status (continued)	*Judgment* **Assessment:** ❑ Psych. Eval. (no score) ❑ Other:					❑ Focus of Tx; See Goal Sheet ❑ Defer; Provide Rationale:
	Attention/ Concentration: **Assessment:** ❑ Psych. Eval. (no score) ❑ DSMD (Under age 18). ❑ Other:					❑ Focus of Tx; See Goal Sheet ❑ Defer; Provide Rationale:
Health Issues	*Medical Illness:* **Assessment:** ❑ SF 36 ❑ Medical History ❑ Other:					❑ Focus of Tx; See Goal Sheet ❑ Defer; Provide Rationale:
	Wellness Practices: **Assessment:** ❑ ACLSA ❑ Medical History ❑ Other:					❑ Focus of Tx; See Goal Sheet ❑ Defer; Provide Rationale:
Chemical Dependency ❑ Adult ❑ Adolescent	**Assessment:** ❑ SASSI ❑ Other: ❑ Biopsychosocial questions that have a * beside them ❑ Chemical Dependency Section					❑ Focus of Tx; See Goal Sheet ❑ Defer; Provide Rationale: *(Continued)*

Mental Health Core Record, Part B *(Continued)*

Goal: _____

Strengths Utilized: _____

Date Initiated	Measurable Objectives	Target Date	Date Achieved OR Status Change	Status	Interventions, Strategies, Modalities	Staff Responsible
				❑ Obj. met ❑ Revised ❑ Discontinued		
				❑ Obj. met ❑ Revised ❑ Discontinued		
				❑ Obj. met ❑ Revised ❑ Discontinued		
				❑ Obj. met ❑ Revised ❑ Discontinued		
				❑ Obj. met ❑ Revised ❑ Discontinued		
				❑ Obj. met ❑ Revised ❑ Discontinued		
				❑ Obj. met ❑ Revised ❑ Discontinued		
				❑ Obj. met ❑ Revised ❑ Discontinued		
				❑ Obj. met ❑ Revised ❑ Discontinued		
				❑ Obj. met ❑ Revised ❑ Discontinued		

ADDITIONAL ROWS ADDED AS NECESSARY

Signatures/Disciplines and/or Title/Dates:	
Therapist	Date:
Registered Nurse	Date:
Psychiatrist	Date:
Client	Date:
Parent/Guardian (if applicable)	Date:
	Date:
	Date:

Review Date: _____ Review Period: (specify) _____

Diagnosis (select one of the following two rows):

❑ Diagnosis remains unchanged; date of last diagnosis ___/ ___/___

❑ The diagnosis has been changed as indicated below:

Axis	**Code**	**Diagnosis**
I		
II		
III		
IV		
V	Current GAF:	Past Year GAF:

Rationale for diagnosis change:

Current Medication(s):		

Justification for Continued Treatment:

Brief Summary of Progress According to Dimensions of Care (note if Goals/Objectives have also been changed):

Lethality

Functional

Challenging Behaviors

Support Systems

Mental Status

Health Issues

Chemical Dependency

(Continued)

Mental Health Core Record Instructions, Part B *(Continued)*

Discharge/ Continuing Care Plan   Anticipated Discharge Date: _____

Ecological Needs (select one of the following two rows):

❑ Ecological Needs remain unchanged; date of last update ___/ ___/ ___

❑ The Ecological Needs have been modified as indicated below:

	Not Applicable	Target Date	Staff Responsible
Level of Care			
Psychiatric/Psychologist Referral			
School/Educational/Vocational			
Interpersonal/Social			
Caregiver Needs			
Community Support Services			
Financial Needs			
Nutritional Care Needs			
Recreation-Related Needs			
Medical- or Medication-Related Needs			
Other			

Treatment Team Certification / Recertification (optional based on licensing or payer requirements):

Recommendations:

Parent/Guardian Impressions of Treatment and Goal Recommendations:

Signatures/Disciplines and/or Title/Dates:

Therapist	Date:
Registered Nurse	Date:
Psychiatrist	Date:
Client	Date:
Parent/Guardian (if applicable)	Date:
	Date:
	Date:

Participation in Treatment Plan of Care:		Mode of Participation		
Person/Place	Relationship to Client / Title	Telephone	Written	Attended Meeting

Signatures/Disciplines and/or Title/Dates:

Therapist		Date:
Registered Nurse		Date:
Psychiatrist		Date:
		Date:
		Date:
Client Signature		Date:
Parent/Guardian Signature (If applicable)		Date:

Appendix F

Quality Site Visit Review Checklist and Gap Analysis

Center _____

Compliance with Devereux's established quality standards should be rated on the following scale:

Complete Compliance 1	Substantial Compliance 2	Partial Compliance 3	Marginal Compliance 4	Non-Compliance 5

Where a rating is not applicable, this should be indicated by recording N/A. **The threshold for immediate action planning is any score of 3, 4, or 5. Please describe and comment upon all minimum standards that are found to be below threshold.**

STANDARDS

I. CLINICAL SERVICE DELIVERY

A. Credentialing and Recredentialing of Clinical Staff

1. A procedure is in place for temporarily credentialing each provider covered under this requirement. 1 2 3 4 5 N/A

2. The procedure includes the requirement that prior to the first day of employment a copy of a valid license or certificate must be on file. 1 2 3 4 5 N/A

3. For physicians who are being credentialed temporarily, there is a copy of a valid DEA Registration form. 1 2 3 4 5 N/A

4. There is evidence of malpractice coverage for each professional prior to granting temporary privileges. 1 2 3 4 5 N/A

(Continued)

Quality Site Visit Review Checklist and Gap Analysis *(Continued)*

5. Temporary Credentialing Form has been forwarded to the Vice President of Clinical Affairs for each staff member covered by this procedure.   1 2 3 4 5 N/A

6. The permanent credentialing process for those who are temporarily credentialed occurs within 90 days.   1 2 3 4 5 N/A

7. The permanent credentialing forms are sent to the Regional Vice President upon receipt.   1 2 3 4 5 N/A

8. There is primary source verification of the professional license or certificate of each candidate.   1 2 3 4 5 N/A

9. If no certificate is available, then documentation from the appropriate national organization has been obtained.   1 2 3 4 5 N/A

10. A report from the National Practitioners Data Bank is on file for all professionals covered by this requirement (physicians, dentists, etc.) at the time of employment and every two years hence.   1 2 3 4 5 N/A

11. There is primary source verification of specialty board certification for physicians.   1 2 3 4 5 N/A

12. There are three letters of recommendation in the professional's file attesting to his or her clinical competency and that professional practices (from previous facilities) are in good standing.   1 2 3 4 5 N/A

13. There is primary source verification for each physician of: 1 2 3 4 5 N/A
    - graduation from medical school
    - completion of internship
    - completion of residency training

14. A copy of each Health Care Professional's CV is maintained in his or her file and updated every 2 years.   1 2 3 4 5 N/A

15. There is primary source verification for other Health Care Professionals of their education and training, e.g., dieticians, pharmacists, behavior analysts, paraprofessionals.   1 2 3 4 5 N/A

16. The center follows state requirements for the utilization of unlicensed clinicians.   1 2 3 4 5 N/A

17. There is record of work history for each Health Care Professional.   1 2 3 4 5 N/A

18. There is a procedure in place to renew credentials annually that includes primary source verification of the clinician's license, malpractice coverage, and for physicians, their DEA certificate.   1 2 3 4 5 N/A

19. At the time of annual review, professionals complete a form indicating that they have not been subject to punitive actions by any state, local, national organizations or have any condition that would interfere with their clinical activities.   1 2 3 4 5 N/A

CRITERIA: All contracted Health Care Professionals at every Devereux center must meet the minimum standard of expertise by being properly credentialed.

* * * * *

B. Clinical Records/Chart Documentation

Total Number of Clients Served:

1. Complete Documentation of Client Charts
   Manual or on-line documentation to be included in all charts:

■ Medical History	1	2	3	4	5	N/A
■ Biopsychosocial Assessment	1	2	3	4	5	N/A
■ Strengths-Based Assessment	1	2	3	4	5	N/A
■ Treatment Plan	1	2	3	4	5	N/A
■ Medication Log	1	2	3	4	5	N/A
■ Specialist Contacts	1	2	3	4	5	N/A
■ Collateral Contacts	1	2	3	4	5	N/A
■ Progress Notes	1	2	3	4	5	N/A
■ Discharge Plan	1	2	3	4	5	N/A
■ Treatment Summaries	1	2	3	4	5	N/A
■ Informed Consents	1	2	3	4	5	N/A

CRITERIA: Treatment plans and progress notes, across disciplines, will reflect measurable objectives and be linked to specific remedial interventions. The treatment plan and progress notes must include:

- A thorough assessment of the presenting problem from biological, psychological and sociological perspectives.
- DSM-IV (Axis I-V) or appropriate functional diagnosis.
- Clear conception of the functional diagnosis with targeted behavioral objectives.
- Appropriate consultations with psychiatric or medical staff.
- Goals and treatment interventions based on the assessment of the client.
- All clinical records, documents, progress notes, etc. will bear the clinicians full signature and degree.

* * * * *

2. Legibility of Clinical Records   1   2   3   4   5   N/A

CRITERIA: All clinical records must be completed in typed form or handwritten in a manner that is readable by any and all reviewers.

* * * * *

C. Supervision of Clinical Services

1. A center's supervisory log notes the date, time, type (individual   1   2   3   4   5   N/A
   vs. group) and supervisee of each supervisory event.

2. Client "Progress Notes" indicate, via supervisor's signature, that   1   2   3   4   5   N/A
   supervisory review occurred and recommendations or treatment
   modifications were noted.

3. Nonphysician clinicians participate in weekly group supervision   1   2   3   4   5   N/A
   of at least one-hour duration.

(Continued)

Quality Site Visit Review Checklist and Gap Analysis *(Continued)*

4. Nonlicensed clinicians receive individual supervision from a licensed Devereux staff clinician that equals or exceeds state requirements.

  1 2 3 4 5 N/A

5. Psychiatric staff participate in monthly individual supervision with the senior or lead psychiatrist at each Devereux center.

  1 2 3 4 5 N/A

6. Supervising psychiatrists maintain a log of peer review activities and appropriate amount of weekly/monthly direct supervision.

  1 2 3 4 5 N/A

7. Clinical Directors and Senior Psychiatrists meet with the Senior Vice President of Clinical Affairs, or Senior Medical Director, at least semi-annually, for one hour of supervision.

  1 2 3 4 5 N/A

CRITERIA: All mental health clinicians providing direct care and related consultative services will participate in routine, scheduled supervision.

* * * * *

D. Training and Education of Credentialed Professional Staff

1. Each center maintains a list of professional staff that fall into this category.

  1 2 3 4 5 N/A

2. A validated log of CEUs indicates that each licensed mental health clinician has obtained CEUs that equal or exceed the state's licensing requirements.

  1 2 3 4 5 N/A

3. A validated log of CEUs indicates that each unlicensed mental health clinician has obtained CEUs that equal the state requirements for licensed providers in that discipline.

  1 2 3 4 5 N/A

4. The Training and Education Log is up to date.

  1 2 3 4 5 N/A

5. A CQI study of the effectiveness of training is conducted as part of center's Quality Management Plan.

  1 2 3 4 5 N/A

CRITERIA: All clinical and paraprofessional mental health staff will have demonstrated that they meet the CEU Guidelines from the State and Regulatory agencies.

* * * * *

E. Quality Management

1. Center has developed and implemented an annual QM plan approved by the Senior Vice President of Clinical Affairs and President's Council.

  1 2 3 4 5 N/A

2. Center's QM plan includes at least two CQI outcome studies, one of which is center-specific and one which is a regional study.

  1 2 3 4 5 N/A

3. QM committees meet at least one time per month and a minimum of 10 times a year. Membership on the committee and the reporting agenda conform with established standards.

  1 2 3 4 5 N/A

CRITERIA: A Quality Management (QM) Committee structure will operate at each Devereux center and at the Regional level. QM committees will proactively drive a continuing quality improvement (CQI) process.

Appendix G

**Devereux Florida Treatment Network
Campus Programs
Viera, Florida**

1. Peer Review: Quarterly—(Peer Reviews are done monthly; Committee meets quarterly)
   a. Conduct medication monitors
   b. Conduct psychiatric assessments

2. Safety Committee: Monthly

3. Milieu Committee: Twice weekly
   Monthly
   a. Review referrals
   b. Address appropriateness
   c. Identify risk issues
   d. Identify acuity issues
   e. Review sentinel events
   f. Identify and plan for special needs of prospective referrals
   g. Identify client (or family or other) complaints

4. Clinical Supervision
   a. Psychiatrists—Monthly
   b. Pediatrician—Monthly
   c. Case Managers or Therapists—Weekly
   d. Consulting Psychologist or Psychometrician—Monthly
   e. Consulting Sexual Disorders Specialist—Monthly

5. Treatment Team Meetings—2 to 4 times weekly

6. Quality Management Committee—Monthly

(Continued)

Psychiatric-Medical Quality Management and Risk Management Activities

7. Risk Management Committee—Monthly

8. Pharmacy & Therapeutics Committee—Quarterly
   a. Conduct drug utilization studies
   b. Review medication errors
   c. Monitor discharge medication safety issues
   d. Monitor medication room safety

9. Utilization Review Committee—Monthly

10. Clinical Case In-Depth Reviews—Minimum 24 per year

11. Unit Rounds—Five days per week

12. Credentialing-Privileging-Reprivileging Reviews

13. Inservices and CEU Presentations—As needed
    a. CEU seminars
    b. Nursing meetings
    c. Announcements updating recent findings re psychotropic and other medications

14. Identify At-Risk Client Populations—As needed
    a. Conduct Cylert study (for example, liver functions)
    b. Conduct Adderall study (for example, weight loss)

15. Special Projects—As needed
    a. Monitor and reduce behavioral PRN use, for example
    b. Reduce special treatment procedure use, for example

16. Monitoring Restraint/Seclusion Use—Daily

17. Internal Campus Investigations—As needed
    a. Participate in investigating significant events on campus that may represent adverse or at-risk situations

18. Devereux Florida Management Council—Quarterly

19. Southern/Eastern Regional Quality Management Committee—Biannually

20. National Suicide Prevention Task Force—Bimonthly
    a. Create training curricula to be used nationally for suicide prevention, intervention, and postvention

21. National Medical Advisory Committee—Monthly
    a. Review sentinel events nationally
    b. Review risk issues nationally
    c. Participate in investigations at national level of situations of high risk

22. National Quality Management Committee—Annually

Appendix H

Physician Peer Review Meeting Minutes

AGENCY X
March 18, 1999

Present: *Absent:*

Tom Thumb, R.N., Acting Director of Nursing

John Doe, Director, Medical Records

Jane Doe, M.D., Psychiatrist, Adolescent Services

John Q. Public, M.D., Psychiatrist, Children's Services

                                                             Guest:

I. CALL TO ORDER

The meeting was called to order at 1:05 p.m.

KEY ITEMS/ CONCERNS IDENTIFIED	DISCUSSION/ RECOMMENDATIONS: (WHO, HOW, & WHEN)	ACTIONS TAKEN OR TO BE TAKEN BY COMMITTEE	O/C/I*
1. Psychiatric Evaluation Peer Review	**The Committee reviewed the analysis of finding to show 100% compliance in all areas except:** Interests, skills and talents addressed; Criteria for this level of care addressed;	Tom Thumb to edit report to include in the Comments section that 6 reports were reviewed. Tom also to edit Psychiatric Evaluation worksheet as requested.	I
			(Continued)

217

Physician Peer Review Meeting Minutes *(Continued)*			
KEY ITEMS/ CONCERNS IDENTIFIED	**DISCUSSION/ RECOMMENDATIONS: (WHO, HOW, & WHEN)**	**ACTIONS TAKEN OR TO BE TAKEN BY COMMITTEE**	**O/C/I***
1. Psychiatric Evaluation Peer Review *(Continued)*	Estimated length of stay; Prognosis included. It was noted that 6 psychiatric evaluations were reviewed. To increase compliance in the above noted areas, the Physicians requested that the Psychiatric Evaluation worksheet (the form used to compile information to dictate from) be edited to include additional headers to cue dictators to include information and to add additional line for writing space.		
2. Psychotropic Medication Peer Review	The group noted 100% compliance in most areas.		I
a. Antipsychotics	Regarding the indicator titled Liver Profile At Admission And Every 6 Months, the Committee was asked to consider removing the words "every 6 months" as the same indicator is repeated under Laboratory. ("Liver profile within one month.") Also the frequency of CBC labs were questioned.	Dr. Doe to research the appropriate frequency of monitoring for these items and report back to the Committee. Dr. Doe will also create a Protocol for Antipsychotics.	O
b. Antidepressants	The Liver Profile indicator was reviewed for appropriateness.	Dr. Public to research appropriate frequency of monitoring and report back to Committee. Dr. Public will also create a Protocol.	

KEY ITEMS/ CONCERNS IDENTIFIED	DISCUSSION/ RECOMMENDATIONS: (WHO, HOW & WHEN)	ACTIONS TAKEN OR TO BE TAKEN BY COMMITTEE	O/C/I*
3. Diabetes Protocol and Peer Review Form	Dr. Doe gave recommendations for both these items. The Committee reviewed.	Dr. Public to take recommendation and draft Protocol and Peer Review Sheet.	O
4. Next Meeting	The next meeting was set for June 17, 1999.		I
Meeting adjourned 2:00 P.M.			
Dr. Public, Chairman, Peer Review Committee			

Appendix I

Pediatric Medicine Peer Review—Diabetes

Patient _____ MR# _____ Reviewer _____

The record reflects:	YES	NO
1. Quarterly hemoglobin A1c (or glycosylated albumin if patient has Sickle Cell).	___	___
2. Blood sugar four times daily.	___	___
3. Insulin therapy at least twice daily.	___	___
4. Ophthalmologic or optometric exam at least annually.	___	___
5. Urine microalbumin at least annually.	___	___
6. Blood pressure monitoring on a regular basis.	___	___

Return this form to Quality Management immediately.

Xerox copy for Attending Physician for review ___Yes ___No

To be returned to Medical Director or designee following review.

Signature of Reviewer: _____ Date: _____

Appendix J

Pediatric Medicine Peer Review—Hypertension

TO BE COMPLETED BY PHYSICIAN REVIEWER

Patient _____ MR# _____ Reviewer _____

	YES	NO
1. Record reflects at least weekly blood pressure monitoring in the absence of acute hypertensive symptoms.	___	___
2. Treatment criteria have been identified.	___	___
3. Work-up includes:		
a. UA	___	___
b. Urine Culture	___	___
c. SMAC	___	___
d. Echocardiogram	___	___
e. Renal Ultrasound	___	___
f. Renin	___	___

Return this form to Quality Management immediately.

Xerox copy for Attending Physician for review Yes ___ No ___

To be returned to Medical Director or designee following review.

Signature of Reviewer: _____ Date: _____

Appendix K

Pediatric Medicine Peer Review—Asthma

TO BE COMPLETED BY PHYSICIAN REVIEWER

Patient _____ MR# _____ Reviewer _____

For chronic asthma maintenance management:	YES	NO

1. Twice daily peak flow (PEFR), particularly during seasons in which the patient has demonstrated previous difficulty.   ___   ___

2. If PEFR is below 80% of his baseline, or if symptoms (cough, wheeze, chest tightness or dyspnea), inhaled Albuterol 2 puffs every 4 h is used as needed or Abluterol Sulfate in nebulizer q 4 h.   ___   ___

3. Inhaled Beclomethasone or equivalent 2 puffs twice daily is used for recurrent symptoms or reduced peak flow below 80%.   ___   ___

4. Patient is scheduled to be seen by M.D. at next clinical visit or ASAP if PEFR below 50% or if continued symptoms.   ___   ___

Return this form to Quality Management immediately.

Xerox copy for Attending Physician for review ___Yes ___No

To be returned to Medical Director or designee following review.

Signature of Reviewer: _____ Date: _____

Appendix L

Pediatric Medicine Peer Review—Sinusitis

TO BE COMPLETED BY PHYSICIAN REVIEWER

Patient _____ MR# _____ Reviewer _____

	YES	NO
1. Symptoms include:		
a. Fever and facial pain and/or dental pain and/or purulent nasal discharge and/or nasal congestion and/or fetid breath and/or sore throat.	___	___
b. Facial tenderness, edema, erythema,and/or purulent nasal or oropharyngeal mucus or reduced sinus transillumination and/or abnormal Water's View x-ray.	___	___
2. Treatment with antibiotics should be appropriate to typical sinus pathogen within the limits of any patient allergy.	___	___
3. Follow up if not better in 2 days (earlier if worse).	___	___

Return this form to Quality Management immediately.

Xerox copy for Attending Physician for review. Yes ___ No ___

To be returned to Medical Director or designee following review.

Signature of Reviewer: _____ Date:_____

Appendix M

Psychiatrist Peer Review—Pemoline (Cylert)

TO BE COMPLETED BY PHYSICIAN REVIEWER

Patient _____ MR# _____ Reviewer _____

If the following medication was given, please indicate whether the following premedication and follow-up criteria were met.

PEMOLINE (Cylert)

PREMEDICATION:

MEDICAL	YES	NO	N/A
1. Evidence of normal physical exam within 12 months.	___	___	___
2. BP and PR, height and weight tracked.	___	___	___
3. Observe for tics (AIMS)	___	___	___

LABORATORY			
1. Liver profile	___	___	___
2. CBC with platelets and SMA-12	___	___	___

FOLLOW-UP:

MEDICAL			
1. Physical exam every year	___	___	___
2. Height and weight every 3–4 months	___	___	___
3. Observe for tics	___	___	___

(Continued)

Psychiatrist Peer Review—Pemoline (Cylert) *(Continued)*

LABORATORY	YES	NO	N/A
1. Liver profile every 6 months	___	___	___
2. SMA-12 annually	___	___	___

Comments:

Signature of Reviewer: _____ Date: _____

Appendix N

Psychiatrist Peer Review—Antipsychotics

TO BE COMPLETED BY PHYSICIAN REVIEWER

Patient _____ MR# _____ Reviewer _____ Unit _____

If the following medication was given, please indicate whether the following premedication and follow-up criteria were met.

ANTIPSYCHOTICS

PREMEDICATION:

	YES	NO	N/A
MEDICAL			
1. BP and pulse	___	___	___
2. Examine for abnormal involuntary movements	___	___	___
LABORATORY			
1. Complete CBC and SMA-12	___	___	___
2. Liver profile at admission and every 6 months	___	___	___
3. AIMs		___	___

FOLLOW-UP:

	YES	NO	N/A
MEDICAL			
1. Physical exam every year	___	___	___
2. BP and P with each dose increase	___	___	___
3. Examine for AIMs every 3 months	___	___	___
4. Orthostatics 72 hours after starting medication and then if patient complains of symptoms (MAR)	___	___	___

(Continued)

Psychiatrist Peer Review—Antipsychotics *(Continued)*

LABORATORY	YES	NO	N/A
1. Repeat CBC weekly with Clozaril	___	___	___
2. No specific indications with other medications	___	___	___
3. Liver profile within one month after initiation of medication, and at least every 3 months thereafter	___	___	___
4. CBC with diff within 3 months, then every 3 months	___	___	___

Comments:

Signature of Reviewer: _____ Date: _____

Appendix O

Psychiatrist Peer Review—Lithium, Lithobid

TO BE COMPLETED BY PHYSICIAN REVIEWER

Patient _____ MR# _____ Reviewer _____ Unit _____

If the following medication was given, please indicate whether the following premedication and follow-up criteria were met.

LITHIUM, LITHOBID

PREMEDICATION:

MEDICAL   YES   NO   N/A

  1. Evidence of normal physical exam within year.   ____   ____   ____

  2. BP, PR, height and weight.   ____   ____   ____

LABORATORY

  1. CBC and SMA-12.   ____   ____   ____

  2. Electrolytes, EKG, Thyroid Profile.   ____   ____   ____

FOLLOW-UP:

MEDICAL

  1. Physical exam every year.   ____   ____   ____

  2. BP every 3 months or with each dose increase.   ____   ____   ____

(Continued)

Psychiatrist Peer Review—Lithium, Lithobid *(Continued)*

LABORATORY	YES	NO	N/A
1. Level and electrolytes 1 week after dose increase. When stabilized, every 3 months and as clinically indicated.	___	___	___
2. Thyroid Profile and BUN/CR every year.	___	___	___

Comments:

Signature of Reviewer: _____   Date: _____

Appendix P

TO BE COMPLETED BY PHYSICIAN REVIEWER

Patient _____ MR# _____ Reviewer _____ Unit _____

If the following medication was given, please indicate whether the following premedication and follow-up criteria were met.

ALPHA-AGONISTS

PREMEDICATION:

MEDICAL	YES	NO	N/A
1. Evidence of normal physical exam within year	___	___	___
2. BP and pulse	___	___	___
3. Height and weight	___	___	___

LABORATORY			
1. No specific indications except as clinically indicated	___	___	___

FOLLOW-UP:

MEDICAL			
1. Physical exam every year	___	___	___
2. Monitor BP and pulse prior to each dose	___	___	___
3. Orders to hold dose if predosing BP is less than 80/50 or pulse is less than 60 beats per minute	___	___	___

(Continued)

235

Psychiatrist Peer Review—Alpha-Agonists (Continued)

LABORATORY	YES	NO	N/A
1. No specific indications	___	___	___

Comments:

Signature of Reviewer: _____ Date: _____

Appendix Q

Psychiatrist Peer Review—Anticonvulsants

TO BE COMPLETED BY PHYSICIAN REVIEWER

Patient _____ MR# _____ Reviewer _____ Unit _____

If the following medication was given, please indicate whether the following premedication and follow-up criteria were met.

ANTICONVULSANTS

PREMEDICATION:

MEDICAL   YES   NO   N/A

1. Evidence of normal physical exam within year   ___   ___   ___

LABORATORY

1. CBC, SMA-12   ___   ___   ___

FOLLOW-UP:

MEDICAL

1. Physical exam every year   ___   ___   ___

LABORATORY

1. Valproate & Tegretol   ___   ___   ___

2. For Tegretol, repeat CBC and for Valproate, repeat SMA-12   ___   ___   ___
   first month, then every 3 months

3. Serum level to assess therapeutic level achieved, and with each   ___   ___   ___
   dose change or change in clinical symptoms. If clinically stable,
   levels to be obtained every 6 months

Comments:

Signature of Reviewer: _____   Date: _____

Appendix R

Psychiatrist Peer Review—Anxiolytics

TO BE COMPLETED BY PHYSICIAN REVIEWER

Patient _____ MR# _____ Reviewer _____ Unit _____

If the following medication was given, please indicate whether the following premedication and follow-up criteria were met.

ANXIOLYTIC (Xanax, Valium, Ativan, Buspar, etc.)

PREMEDICATION:

MEDICAL	*YES*	*NO*	*N/A*
1. Evidence of normal physical exam within year	___	___	___

LABORATORY

1. No specific indications except as clinically indicated	___	___	___

FOLLOW-UP:

MEDICAL

1. Physical exam every year	___	___	___

LABORATORY

1. No specific indications	___	___	___

Comments:

Signature of Reviewer: _____ Date: _____

Appendix S

Psychiatrist Peer Review—Beta-Blockers

TO BE COMPLETED BY PHYSICIAN REVIEWER

Patient _____ MR# _____ Reviewer _____ Unit _____

If the following medication was given, please indicate whether the following premedication and follow-up criteria were met.

BETA-BLOCKERS

PREMEDICATION:

MEDICAL

	YES	NO	N/A
1. Evidence of normal physical exam within year	___	___	___
2. BP & pulse	___	___	___
3. Inquire regarding history of diabetes, cardiac disorder, or asthma	___	___	___

LABORATORY

1. No specific indications except as clinically indicated	___	___	___

FOLLOW-UP:

MEDICAL

1. Physical exam every year	___	___	___
2. BP or pulse with each dose increase	___	___	___

LABORATORY

1. No specific indications	___	___	___

Comments:

Signature of Reviewer: _____ Date: _____

Appendix T

Quality Indicator Report

Function: **Continuum of Care**

Goal: Define, shape, and sequence processes and activities to maximize coordination of care within the center's continuum of care. Continuum of care is defined as matching the individual's ongoing needs with the appropriate level of care and type of medical, health, or social service.

Indicator #1:   **Discharge placement will demonstrate discharge planning for individuals requiring continuing care.** *Definition: Discharge planning focuses on meeting individuals' health care needs after discharge. This includes appropriate level of care placement.*

Calculation:

     Data Elements:

         Total # discharges for month or quarter

         # discharges to each specified level of care for the month or quarter:

                 Greater level of care (e.g., day to residential; residential to inpatient, etc.)

                 Same level of care (e.g., move from one residential program to another)

                 Less restrictive level (e.g., residential to day; inpatient to residential; residential to independent living, etc.)

                 Home with planned services (e.g., family counseling, parent training, etc.)

                 Home (no other planned services)

                 AMA

                 AWOL

(Continued)

Quality Indicator Report (*Continued*)

Calculation (*continued*):

Formulas:

% of discharges to each specified level of care:

greater level of care / total # discharges for month or quarter = **x 100**

same level of care / total # of discharges for month or quarter = **x 100**

less restrictive level of care / total # of discharges for month or quarter = **x 100**

home with planned services / # total discharges for month or quarter = **x 100**

home (no other planned services) / # total discharges for month or quarter = **x 100**

AMA / # total discharges for month or quarter = **x 100**

AWOL / # total discharges for month or quarter = **x 100**

Note: The sum of the % of discharges to each level of care should equal 100%.

Sample size: All discharges

Population: Acute, residential/foster care/group home, partial/day (Respite not included)

Function: **Care of the Individual/Treatment**

Goal*:* Provide individualized care in settings responsive to specific individual needs.

Indicator #2: **Treatment effectiveness based on specific outcome measurement.** *Devereux Scales of Mental Disorders or the Devereux School Form. The scales are computerized and analyzed according to specified processes. Reassessment schedules are Center-specific. The positive zone responses are o—optimal, vf—very favorable, f—favorable.*

Calculation:

Data Elements:

Total # of individuals assessed at discharge (with comparable admission scores)

individuals assessed at discharge with O outcomes (compared to scores at admission)

individuals assessed at discharge with VF outcomes (compared to scores at admission)

individuals assessed at discharge with F outcomes (compared to scores at admission)

individuals assessed at discharge with E outcomes (compared to scores at admission)

individuals assessed at discharge with N outcomes (compared to scores at admission)

Formulas:

% of individuals with O, VF, F, E, N outcomes:

Total # of individuals assessed at discharge with O, VF, F, E, N outcomes = **x 100**
Total # of individuals assessed at discharge

Sample size: All DSMD or DSF assessments completed (sample need only be a sub-group, e.g., diagnosis type, program type, etc., and this can rotate)

Population: Residential/foster care/group home, partial/day

Function: **Care of the Individual/Treatment**

Indicator #3:   **The number of facility-administered medication errors.** *Definition of a medication error is any occurrence in which the medication actually reached the individual and should be counted as a medication error. Additionally, documentation errors are those that are detected by a subsequent shift after they are administered. The new definition includes: wrong medication, wrong route, wrong dose, dose omitted, wrong time and prescribing concern (i.e., medications prescribed by a physician that reach the individual that are questioned by other professional staff regarding their appropriateness and are subsequently modified). This excludes self-medication and ambulatory services; however, it is suggested that centers track this where applicable. In addition, medication refusals are not considered errors.*

Calculation:

Data elements:
Total # of errors for the month or quarter
# of medication errors by type for the month or quarter
# of Physician ordered doses for the month or quarter
(administered doses and omitted doses, less any that had to be destroyed)
Total # of individuals receiving meds during the month or quarter

Formula:
Ratio of medication errors:
# of errors for the month or quarter
# of Physician ordered doses for the month or quarter

Sample size: All errors submitted

Population: All programs (excludes self-administered and ambulatory services)

Indicator #4:   **Use of behavior management techniques / special treatment procedures.** *Special treatment procedures include seclusion, mechanical restraint and personal hold (exclusion of escorts). Seclusion should be defined according to individual state requirements for monitoring, i.e., a locked room or any area from which there is no egress, etc. PRNs will be a separate calculated category that includes only medications administered for behavioral control. Quarterly figures should be discrete regarding the number of individuals receiving STPs. (Each individual should only be counted once even if they received personal holds in each month of the quarter.)*

*Injuries are defined as those **requiring external medical attention (clinic or hospital remedies).***
(Continued)

Quality Indicator Report *(Continued)*

Calculation:

Data elements:

# of individuals receiving STPs

seclusions per policy definition for the month or quarter

mechanical restraints for the month or quarter

personal holds (excluding escorts) for the month or quarter

Average Daily Census for the month or quarter

# of client injuries secondary to STP for the month or quarter

# of staff injuries secondary to STP for the month or quarter

Formulas:

A. Ratio of STP occurrence:

$$\frac{\text{\# of seclusions + \# mechanical restraints + \# personal holds for the month or quarter}}{\text{Average Daily Census for the month or quarter}}$$

B. Average number of STPs per individual receiving STPs:

$$\frac{\text{\# of seclusions + \# mechanical restraints + \# personal holds for the month or quarter}}{\text{\# of individuals receiving STPs for the month or quarter}}$$

C. % of individuals receiving STPs:

$$\frac{\text{\# of individuals receiving STPs for the month or quarter}}{\text{Average Daily Census for the month or quarter}} = \text{\textbf{x 100}}$$

D. Rate of client injuries secondary to STP:

$$\frac{\text{\# of client injuries secondary to STP for the month or quarter}}{\text{Total number of STP occurrences for the month or quarter}}$$

E. Rate of staff injuries secondary to STP:

$$\frac{\text{\# of staff injuries related to STP for the month or quarter}}{\text{Total number of STP occurrences for the month or quarter}}$$

Average Daily Census:

$$\frac{\text{(Sum of the \# of residential clients listed per day of the month or quarter)} + \text{(Sum of the \# of day + partial clients listed per day of the month or quarter/3)}}{\text{Total \# of days in the month or quarter}}$$

Sample size: All occurrences

Population: All programs

Function:	**Management of Human Resources**

Indicator #5:	**Staff credentialing.** *Credentialing is defined as the review of staff credentials according to the process outlined in the Devereux Quality Site Visit.*
	
	Calculation:
	
	    Data Elements:
	        Total # staff for whom credentialing/recredentialing is applicable (at time of measure excluding those within the 90-day credentialing process)
	        # of staff that meet all credentialing/recredentialing requirements (at time of measure)
	
	    Formula:
	        % of staff credentialed according to defined Devereux procedure:
	        $\underline{\textit{\# of staff credentialed/recredentialed that meet all requirements}} = \textbf{x 100}$
	        Total number of staff for whom credentialed/recredentialed is applicable

	Sample size: All staff per requirement
	Population: All programs

Function:	**Surveillance Prevention and Control of Infection**
Goal:	Identify and reduce the risks of acquiring and transmitting communicable infections among clients, employees, physicians and other staff.
Indicator #6:	**Communicable Illness/Reportable Infectious Disease Rate.** *The definition of "reportable" is based on the requirements of the individual state in which the Center is located. The generally accepted definition of a communicable illness/infectious disease is an illness or disease that is due to a specific infectious agent or its toxic products which arise through transmission of that agent or its products from an infected person, animal, or inanimate reservoir to a susceptible host, either directly or indirectly through an intermediate plant or animal host, vector, or the inanimate environment.*

	Calculation:
	
	    Data Elements:
	        # of center communicable illness/reportable infections for the month or quarter
	        Average Daily Census for the month or quarter
	
	    Formula:
	        % of center communicable illnesses/reportable infections:
	        $\underline{\textit{\# of center communicable illnesses/reportable infections}} = \textbf{x 100}$
	        Average Daily Census for the quarter
	
	    Average Daily Census:
	    Sum of the # of acute + residential + group home + foster care clients listed
	    $\underline{\textit{per day of the month or quarter}}$
	    Total # of days in the month or quarter

	Sample size: All reported client infections
	Population: Acute, residential/group home/foster care <div align="right">*(Continued)*</div>

Quality Indicator Report *(Continued)*

Function:	**Management of the Environment of Care—Safety**
Goal:	Provide a safe, functional, and effective environment for individuals, staff members, and others.
Indicator #7:	**Risk Events.** Risk events are defined according to Corporate Policy. *Aggregate risk events are reported by category in the Quarterly Report for **ALL** risk events. Each risk event is reported and reviewed at the monthly Quality Management meeting. Formulas for reporting focus on the Major Risk category.*

Calculation:

Data Elements:
Total # of risk events
# of risk events in categories 1–5 for National QM review for the month or quarter
Average Daily Census for the month or quarter
# of Service Units for the month or quarter

Formulas:

A. Residential/Day
Ratio of risk events
Total # of risk events reported for the month or quarter
Average Daily Census for the month or quarter

B. Outpatient
Ratio of risk events
Total # of risk events reported for the month or quarter
# of Service Units for the month or quarter

C. % of risk events requiring follow-up:
# of risk events in categories 1–5 for the month or quarter
Total number of risk events reported for the month or quarter = **x 100**

Average Daily Census:
(Sum of the # of residential clients listed per day of the month or quarter)
+ (Sum of the # of day + partial clients listed per day of the month or quarter/3)
Total # of days in the month or quarter

Sample size: All incidents

Population: All programs

Glossary of Acronyms

ACMHA: American College of Mental Health Administration

ACYF: Administration for Children, Youth, and Families

AHCPR: Agency of Health Care Policy and Research

AMA: against medical advice

APA: American Psychiatric Association; American Psychological Association

CAMBHC: *Comprehensive Accreditation Manual for Behavioral Healthcare* (JCAHO)

CAMH: *Comprehensive Accreditation Manual for Hospitals*

CASSP: Child and Adolescent Service System Program

CCAM: Clinical Care Assessment Model

CE: continuing education

CEO: chief executive officer

CEU: continuing education unit

CMHS: Center for Mental Health Services

COA: Council on Accreditation

CPGs: clinical practice guidelines

CPR: cardiopulmonary resuscitation

CQI: continuous quality improvement

CRC: Children's Research Center

CS&O: Corporation for Standards and Outcomes

CV: curriculum vitae

CWLA: Child Welfare League of America

CYFC: Children, Youth and Family Council of the Delaware Valley

DCP: direct care provider

DEA: Drug Enforcement Agency

DHS: Department of Human Services

DRG: diagnostic referral group

DSM-IV: *Diagnostic and Statistical Manual of Mental Disorders* (Fourth Edition)

EIC: early intervention center

ES: effect size

FFTA: Family Focus and Treatment Association

FTE: full-time equivalent (amount of a manager's time devoted to QI management)

GAS: Goal Attainment Scale

GDP: gross domestic product

HCFA: Health Care Financing Administration

HIV-AIDS: human immunodeficiency virus–acquired immune deficiency syndrome

HR: human resources

ICTR: Institute of Clinical Training and Research

IS (or I-S): information systems

JCAHO: Joint Commission on Accreditation of Healthcare Organizations

LAN: local area network

MANOVA: multiple analysis of variance

MR/DD: mentally retarded/developmentally disabled

NAMI: National Alliance for the Mentally Ill

NAPTCC: National Association of Psychiatric Treatment Centers for Children

NASW: National Association of Social Workers

NCQA: National Committee on Quality Assurance

NGC: National Guidelines Clearinghouse

NIMH: National Institute of Mental Health

NMAC: National Medical Advisory Committee

OSHA: Office of Safety and Health Administration

Ph.D.: doctor of philosophy (academic degree)

PI: performance improvement

PEP: Positive Education Program

PPT: professional psychology trainee

PRN: *pro re nata* ("as needed"—written on medical prescriptions or orders)

QA: quality assurance

QI: quality improvement

QIC: quality improvement coordinator

QM: quality management

RTC: residential treatment center

SDM: structured decision making

SIDS: sudden infant death syndrome

SPSS: Statistical Program for Social Science

STP: special treatment procedure

TQM: total quality management

YSR: Youth Self-Report

References

Introduction

Abelson, S. (1998, Spring). Non-profits at the millennium: Facing change as opportunity. *Directions, 16,* 1–2. (Available from Philadelphia Health Management Corp., 260 South Broad Street, Philadelphia, PA 19102)

Braziel, D. J. (1996). *Family-focused practice in out-of-home care: A handbook and resource directory.* Washington, DC: CWLA Press.

Council on Accreditation of Services for Families and Children. (1996). *The Council on Accreditation 1997 standards for behavioral health care services and community support and education services* (U.S. ed.). New York: Author.

Gordon, A. L. (1999). *Outcome initiatives in child welfare.* Washington, DC: CWLA Press.

Health Care Financing Administration. (2000). *HCFA at a glance* [on-line]. http://www.hcfa.gov/about.htm.

Joint Commission on Accreditation of Healthcare Organizations. (1997, May). ORYX: The next evolution in accreditation. *Nursing Management, 28* (5), 49–52, 54.

Joint Commission on Accreditation of Healthcare Organizations. (1999a). *1999–2000 Comprehensive accreditation manual for behavioral health care.* Oakbrook Terrace, IL: Author.

Joint Commission on Accreditation of Healthcare Organizations. (1999b). *Who we are* [on-line]. Available Internet: http://www.jcaho.org/who_we_are.html.

McCullough, C., & Schmitt, B. (1998). *Outcomes in a managed care child welfare environment.* Washington, DC: Child Welfare League of America.

National Committee for Quality Assurance. (1999). *Standards and surveyor guidelines for the accreditation of MBHOs.* Washington, DC: Author.

SAMHSA grants will help states measure treatment effectiveness. (1998, October). *Alcoholism and Drug Abuse Weekly, 10* (40), 1, 6.

Spreat, S., & Jampol, R.C. (1997). Residential services for children and adolescents. In R. T. Ammerman & M. Hersen (Eds.), *Handbook of prevention and treatment with children and adolescents: Intervention in the real world context* (pp. 106–133). New York: Wiley.

Strupp, H. H. (1996). The tripartite model and the *Consumer Reports* study. *American Psychologist, 51,* 1017–1024.

Treatment outcomes performance pilot studies (TOPPS). Measuring the effectiveness of substance abuse treatment in Arizona (1999).[on-line]. Available Internet: http://www.hs.state.az.us/bhs/topps./htm.

Chapter One

Campbell, J. (1998). Consumerism, outcomes, and satisfaction: A review of the literature. In R. W. Manderscheid & M. J. Henderson (Eds.), *Mental health, United States* (pp. 11–28). Rockville, MD: U.S. Department of Health and Human Services, Public Health Service, Substance Abuse and Mental Health Services Administration, Center for Mental Health Services.

Carins, J. M., & Koch, J. R. (1997, October). *How to involve staff in developing an outcomes-oriented organizational culture.* Presented at the Institute for Behavioral Healthcare–How to Design and Implement Your Children's Services Outcomes Management Program, Pittsburgh, PA.

Deming, W. E. (1986). *Out of crisis.* Cambridge, MA: MIT Press.

Juran, J. M. (1979). *Quality control handbook* (3rd ed.). New York: McGraw-Hill.

Meadowcroft, P., & Mason, M. (1997, October). *Developing an outcomes-oriented organizational culture.* Presented at the Institute for Behavioral Healthcare–How to Design and Implement Your Children's Services Outcomes Management Program, Pittsburgh, PA.

Packard, T. (1995). TQM and organizational change and development. In B. Gummer & P. McCallion (Eds.), *Total quality management in the social services: Theory and practice* (pp. 209–227). Albany: Professional Development Program of Rockefeller College, State University of New York.

Townsend, P. L. (1990). *Commit to quality.* New York: Wiley.

Townsend, P. L., & Gebhardt, J. E. (1992). *Quality in action: 93 lessons in leadership, participation, and measurement.* New York: Wiley.

Chapter Two

American Association of State Social Work Boards. (1998). *Social work laws and board regulations: A comparison guide.* Culpepper, VA: Author.

American Medical Association. (1998). *U.S. medical licensure statistics and requirements by state, 1998–1999.* Chicago: Author.

Council on Accreditation of Services for Families and Children. (1996). *The Council on Accreditation 1997 standards for behavioral health care services and community support and education services* (U.S. ed.). New York: Author.

Flanagan, P. (1998, October). Credentialing committees, compliance and legal considerations. In *Corporate Compliance Forum: Physician credentialing and physician compliance issues* (pp. 1–3). (Available from the Corporate Compliance Forum, 13910 N. Frank Lloyd Wright Blvd., Suite 2A-336, Scottsdale, AZ 85260)

Joint Commission on Accreditation of Healthcare Organizations. (1999). *1999–2000 comprehensive accreditation manual for behavioral health care.* Oakbrook Terrace, IL: Author.

Lefkovitz, P. (1997, February). Implementing a behavioral health continuum: Issues of strategies for success in a multi-hospital setting (24 paragraphs). *Open Minds Newsletter* [on-line]. Available Internet: http://www.openminds.com/omlib2.htm

National Committee for Quality Assurance. (1998). *Standards for accreditation of managed behavioral healthcare organizations.* Washington, DC: Author.

National Committee for Quality Assurance. (1999a, November 17). *CVO certification list* [on-line]. Available Internet: http://www.ncqa.org/pages/policy/certification/cvo/cvostats.htm

National Committee for Quality Assurance. (1999b). *Standards and surveyor guidelines for the accreditation of MBHOs.* Washington, DC: Author.

Necessity for Licensure, 63 P.S. §1203 (West, 1999).

Practicing Psychology Licensing Act, N.J.S.A. 45:14B-6 (West, 1999).

Regulation of Professions and Occupations, 32 F.S. 491.14 (1999).

Strickland, M. D. (1997, June). *Best practices in quality-based purchasing of behavioral healthcare services.* Presented at the Fourth Annual Behavioral Healthcare Quality and Accountability Summit, Bloomington, MN.

Voelker, R. (1997, February 5). Quality standards intend to bring psychiatry, primary care into closer collaboration (22 paragraphs). *JAMA* [on-line], *277.* Available Internet: http://www.ama-assn.org/sci-pubs/journals/archive/jama/vol_277/no_5/mn7021.htm.

Chapter Three

American Psychiatric Association (1998). *The principles of medical ethics with annotations especially applicable to psychiatry.* Washington, DC: Author.

American Psychological Association (1992). Ethical principles of psychologists and code of conduct. *American Psychologist, 47*(12), 1597–1611.

Anfang, S. A., & Applebaum, P. S. (1996). Twenty years after Tarasoff: Reviewing the duty to protect. *Harvard Review of Psychiatry, 4*(2), 67–76.

Backlar, P., & McFarland, B. (1993). A national survey of ethics committees in state mental hospitals. *HEC Forum, 5,* 272–288.

Bersoff, D. (1976). Therapists as protectors and policemen: New roles as a result of Tarasoff. *Professional Psychology, 7,* 267–273.

Christensen, R. (1997). Ethical issues in community mental health: Cases and conflicts. *Community Mental Health Journal, 33*(1), 5–11.

Kagle, J. D., & Kopels, S. (1994). Confidentiality after Tarasoff. *Health and Social Work, 19,* 217–222.

Kaplan, H. (1988). *Synapses of psychiatry: Behavioral sciences/clinical psychiatry.* Baltimore: Williams & Wilkins.

Kemp, D. R. (1983). Assessing human rights committees: A mechanism for protecting the rights of institutionalized persons. *Mental Retardation, 21*(1), 13–16.

McCabe, M. A. (1996). Involving children and adolescents in medical decision making: Developmental clinical considerations. *Journal of Pediatric Psychology, 21*(4), 505–516.

National Association of Social Workers (1996). *Code of ethics of the National Association of Social Workers.* Washington, DC: Author.

National Committee for Quality Assurance (1998). *Standards for accreditation of managed healthcare organizations.* Washington, DC: Author.

Professional Risk Management Services, Inc. (1998). *The risk management quiz.* (Available from Professional Risk Management Services, Inc., 1000 Wilson Blvd., Suite 2500, Arlington, VA 22209.)

Ross, J. W., Glaser, J. W., Rasinski-Gregory, D., Gibson, J. M., & Bayley, C. (1993). *Health care ethics committees: The next generation.* Chicago: American Hospital Publishing.

Spratlen, L. P. (1997). Ombudsman: A new role for advanced practice nurses in psychiatric-mental health nursing. *Perspectives in Psychiatric Care, 33*(3), 5–13.

Thompson, H. M. (1996). Ethics committees: Their share in the advocacy role. *Seminars in Perioperative Nursing, 5,* 62–67.

Chapter Four

American Psychiatric Association. (1999). *Guidelines for psychiatric practice in community mental health centers* [on-line]. Available Internet: http://www.psych.org/psych/htdocs/pract_of_psych/com_cent.html

Bockar, J. A. (1976). *Primer for the nonmedical psychotherapist.* Laurel, MD: Spectrum Publications.

Commonwealth of Pennsylvania. (1990). 55 Pa. Code 5200.

Council on Accreditation of Services for Families and Children. (1996). *The Council on Accreditation 1997 standards for behavioral health care services and community support and education services* (U.S. ed.). New York: Author.

Grigsby, R. K. (1996). Consultation with youth shelters, group homes, foster care homes and Big Brothers/Big Sisters programs. In M. B. Lewis (Ed.), *Child and adolescent psychiatry: A comprehensive textbook* (2nd ed., pp. 908–912). Baltimore: Williams & Wilkins.

Guidelines for psychiatric practice in public sector psychiatric inpatient facilities. (1994). *American Journal of Psychiatry, 151*(5), 797–798.

Husain, S. A. (1995). Residential and inpatient treatment. In H. I. Kaplan & B. J. Sadock (Eds.), *Comprehensive textbook of psychiatry: Vol. 2.* (6th ed., pp. 2434–2439). Baltimore: Williams & Wilkins.

Joint Commission on Accreditation of Healthcare Organizations. (1999a). *1999–2000 comprehensive accreditation manual for behavioral health care.* Oakbrook Terrace, IL: Author.

Joint Commission on Accreditation of Healthcare Organizations. (1999b). *Comprehensive accreditation manual for hospitals: The official handbook.* Oakbrook Terrace, IL: Author.

Kelly, K. V. (1992). Parallel treatment: Therapy with one clinician and medication with another. *Hospital and Community Psychiatry, 43*(8), 778–780.

Lazarus, A. (1995). The role of primary care physicians in managed mental health care. *Psychiatric Services, 46,* 343–345.

Lewis, M. B., Summerville, J. W., & Graffagnino, P. N. (1996). Residential treatment. In M. B. Lewis (Ed.), *Child and adolescent psychiatry: A comprehensive textbook* (2nd ed., pp. 894–902). Baltimore: Williams & Wilkins.

Menninger, W. W. (1995). Role of the psychiatric hospital in the treatment of mental illness. In H. I. Kaplan & B. J. Sadock (Eds.), *Comprehensive textbook of psychiatry: Vol. 2.* (6th ed., pp. 2690–2696). Baltimore: Williams & Wilkins.

Pardes, H. (1995). Future of psychiatry. In H. I. Kaplan & B. J. Sadock (Eds.), *Comprehensive textbook of psychiatry: Vol. 2.* (6th ed., pp. 2801–2804). Baltimore: Williams & Wilkins.

Raney, D. F. (1994). Behavioral, psychosocial, and psychiatric pediatrics. In G. B. Merenstein, D. W. Kaplan, & A. A. Rosenberg (Eds.), *Handbooks of pediatrics* (17th ed., pp. 187–234). East Norwalk, CT: Appleton & Lange.

Schwab-Stone, M. E., & Henrich, C. (1996). School consultation. In M. B. Lewis (Ed.), *Child and adolescent psychiatry: A comprehensive textbook* (2nd ed., pp. 1085–1092). Baltimore: Williams & Wilkins.

Starr, P. (1982). *The social transformation of American medicine.* New York: Basic Books.

Chapter Five

American Psychiatric Association. (1993). Practice guidelines for major depressive disorders in adults. *American Journal of Psychiatry, 150,* 1–26.

American Psychological Association Task Force. (1995). *Template for developing guidelines: Interventions for mental disorders and psychosocial aspects of physical disorders.* Washington, DC: American Psychological Association.

Baird, S. C. (1997, August). Child abuse and neglect: Improving consistency in decision-making. *NCCD Focus,* 1–15. (Available from the National Council on Crime and Delinquency, 685 Market St., Suite 620, San Francisco, CA 94105)

Brown, J. B., Shye, D., & McFarland, B. (1997). The paradox of guideline implementation: How AHCPR's depression guideline was adapted at Kaiser Permanente Northwest. In K. M. Coughlin (Ed.), *Behavioral outcomes and guidelines sourcebook* (pp. 66–84). New York: Faulkner & Gray.

Children's Research Center. (1994). *A new approach to child protection: The CRC model.* San Francisco: National Council on Crime and Delinquency.

Cleo Wallace Centers. (1998). *The basics of solution-oriented treatment and the role of the clinician.* Denver: Author.

Crits-Christoph, P. (1996). The dissemination of efficacious psychological treatments. *Clinical Psychology: Science and Practice, 3,* 260–263.

Devereux. (1998). *Guidelines for support of children and adolescents with disruptive behavior disorders.* Villanova, PA: Author. (Available from Devereux, 444 Devereux Drive, Box 638, Villanova, PA 19085)

Garfield, S. L. (1996). Some problems associated with "validated" forms of psychotherapy. *Clinical Psychology: Science and Practice, 3,* 218–229.

Greengold, N. L., & Weingarten, S. R. (1996). Developing evidence-based practice guidelines and pathways: The experience at the local hospital level. *Journal on Quality Improvement, 22*(6), 391–402.

Hayes, S. (1998). *Outcomes management, practice guidelines, report cards, and other quality management and improvement methods.* Presented at the Quality and Accountability Summit, San Antonio, TX.

Institute of Medicine. (1992). Committee on clinical practice guidelines. In M. J. Field & K. N. Lohr (Eds.), *Guidelines for clinical practice: From development to use.* Washington, DC: National Academy Press.

Karon, B. P., & Teixeria, M. A. (1995). Guidelines for the treatment of depression in primary care and the APA response. *American Psychologist, 50,* 453–455.

Kramer, T. L. (1997). Outcomes and guidelines agenda moves forward: But troubling policy issues remain. In K. M. Coughlin (Ed.), *Behavioral Outcomes and Guidelines Sourcebook* (pp. xi–xv). New York: Faulkner & Gray.

Lewis, S. (1995). Paradox, process and perception: The role of organizations in clinical practice guidelines development. *Canadian Medical Association Journal, 153,* 1073–1077.

McIntyre, J. (1997). *Outcomes management, practice guidelines, report cards, and quality management and improvement tools.* Paper presented at the Quality & Accountability Summit, Bloomington, MN.

Meichenbaum, D. (in press). *Case conceptualization model.* Waterloo, Ontario: Institute Press.

Nathan, P. E. (1998). Practice guidelines: Not yet ideal. *American Psychologist, 53,* 290–299.

National Guideline Clearinghouse. (2000). [on-line]. Available Internet: http://www.guideline.gov/index.asp

Practice Guidelines Coalition. (1997). Practice Guidelines Coalition (PGC). In K. M. Coughlin (Ed.), *Behavioral outcomes and guidelines sourcebook* (pp. 9–13). New York: Faulkner & Gray.

Retsinas, J. (1998). Recent developments in behavioral guidelines: Creating order in Babel. In K. M. Coughlin (Ed.), *Behavioral outcomes and guidelines sourcebook* (pp. 1–8). New York: Faulkner & Gray.

U.S. Agency for Health Care Policy and Research. (1993). *AHCPR program note: Clinical practice guidelines development* (ACHPR Publication No. 93–0023). Rockville, MD: U. S. Department of Health and Human Services.

Chapter Six

Braukmann, C. J., Fixsen, D. L., Kirigin, K. A., Phillips, E. A., Phillips, E. L., & Wolf, M. M. (1975). Achievement place: The training and certification of teaching parents. In W. S. Wood (Ed.), *Issues in evaluating behavior modification* (pp. 131–152). Chicago: Research Press.

Demchak, M. (1987). A review of behavioral staff training in special education settings. *Education and Training in Mental Retardation, 22,* 205–217.

Ducharme, J. M., & Feldman, M. A. (1992). Comparison of staff training strategies to promote generalized teaching skills. *Journal of Applied Behavior Analysis, 25,* 165–179.

Gardner, J. F., & Chapman, M. S. (1993). *Developing staff competencies for supporting people with developmental disabilities: An orientation handbook* (2nd ed.). Baltimore: Brookes.

Hobbs, N. (1982). *The troubled and troubling child: Reeducation in mental health, education, and human services programs.* San Francisco: Jossey-Bass.

Kirkpatrick, D. L. (1996). *Evaluating training programs: The four levels.* San Francisco: Berrett-Koehler.

Mahoney, G. (1988). Enhancing the developmental competence of handicapped infants. In K. Marfo (Ed.), *Parent-child interaction and developmental disabilities: Theory, research, and intervention* (pp. 203–219). New York: Praeger.

Mahoney, G. (Ed.). (1996). *The Family/Child curriculum: A family/relationship focused approach to parent education/early intervention.* (Available from the Family Child Learning Center, Children's Hospital Medical Center of Akron, 142 Northwest Ave., Bldg. A, Tallmadge, OH 44278)

McCurdy, B. L., Ludwikowski, C., Serafin, C., & Maher, C. (1999). *Developing direct care professionals through skill-based training: An outcome study.* Manuscript submitted for publication.

McCurdy, B. L., Serafin, C., Nickerson, A., Maher, C., Weiss, J., & Duffy, J. (in press). *New directions: Essential skills for direct care providers.* Washington, DC: CWLA.

Munger, R. L. (1997). Ecological trajectories in child mental health. In S. W. Henggeler & A. B. Santos (Eds.), *Innovative approaches for difficult-to-treat populations* (pp. 3–25). Washington, DC: American Psychiatric Press.

Osher, D., & Hanley, T. (1996). Aiding our at-risk children. *Education SATLINK: Magazine and Program Guide, 4–8.*

Page, T. J., Iwata, B. A., & Reid, D. H. (1982). Pyramidal training: A large-scale application with institutional staff. *Journal of Applied Behavioral Analysis, 15,* 335–351.

Parsons, M. B., Reid, D. H., & Green, C. W. (1993). Preparing direct service staff to teach people with severe disabilities: A comprehensive evaluation of an effective and acceptable training program. *Behavioral Residential Treatment, 8,* 163–185.

Phillips, E. L., Phillips, E. A., Fixsen, D. L., & Wolf, M. M. (1971). Achievement Place: Modification of the behaviors of pre-delinquent boys within a token economy. *Journal of Applied Behavior Analysis, 4,* 45–59.

Reid, D. H., & Parsons, M. B. (Eds.). (1994). *The teaching-skills training program: Instructor's manual.* (Available from the Carolina Behavior Analysis and Support Center, Ltd., P.O. Box 425, Morganton, NC 28680)

Reid, D. H., Parsons, M. B., & Green, C. W. (1989). *Staff management in human services.* Springfield, IL: Thomas.

Silberman, M. L. (1990). *Active training: A handbook of techniques, designs, case examples, and tips.* San Francisco: New Lexington Press.

Timm, M. A., & Rule, S. (1981). RIP: A cost-effective parent-implemented program for young handicapped children. *Early Child Development and Care, 7,* 147–163.

Trieschman, A. E., Whittaker, J. K., & Brendtro, L. K. (1969). *The other 23 hours: Child-care work with emotionally disturbed children in a therapeutic milieu.* Chicago: Aldine.

Wolf, M. M. (1978). Social validity: The case of subjective measurement on how applied behavior analysis is finding its heart. *Journal of Applied Behavior Analysis, 11,* 203–214.

Chapter Seven

ACMHA summit moves closer to developing core measurement set. (1999, April). *Outcomes & Accountability Alert, 4*(4), 1, 9–11.

Atkinson, L. (1991). Three standard errors of measurement and the Wechsler Memory Scale–Revised. *Psychological Assessment, 3,* 136–138.

Bernstein, S. J., & Hilborne, L. H. (1993). Clinical indicators: The road to quality care? *Journal of Quality Improvement, 19*(11), 501–509.

Curtis, P. A., & Brockman, C. (1999). *Report #3: Progress on baseline statistics for the Odyssey Project.* Washington, DC: Child Welfare League of America.

Driggs, G. E. (1997). Outcomes based management. *Perspectives on Outcomes, 1,* 2.

Goldman, W., & Feldman, S. (Eds.). (1993). *Managed mental health care.* New Directions for Mental Health Services, no. 59. San Francisco: Jossey-Bass.

Hernandez, M. (2000). Using logic models and program theory to build outcome accountability. *Education and Treatment of Children, 23*(1).

Jacobson, N. S., & Truax, P. (1991). Clinical significance: A statistical approach to defining meaningful change in psychotherapy research. *Journal of Consulting and Clinical Psychology, 59,* 12–19.

Joint Commission on Accreditation of Healthcare Organizations. (1997, May). ORYX: The next evolution in accreditation. *Nursing Management, 28*(5), 49–52, 54.

Joint Commission on Accreditation of Healthcare Organizations. (1999). Program profile: Outcomes management, the Devereux Foundation. In *Preventing adverse events in behavioral healthcare: A systems approach to sentinel events* (pp. 90–99). Oakbrook Terrace, IL: Author.

Kazdin, A. E. (1989). Developmental psychopathology: Current research, issues, and directions. *American Psychologist, 4*(2), 180–187.

LeBuffe, P. A., Biggs, B., Hatch, K., Miller, J., & Roth, M. (1998, January). *How to prepare and present effective outcome reports.* Workshop presented at the Children's Services Outcomes Management Conference sponsored by the Institute for Behavioral Healthcare, Seattle.

LeBuffe, P. A., Naglieri, J. A., & Pfeiffer, S. I. (1996). *DSMD scoring assistant program.* San Antonio, TX: Psychological Corporation.

LeBuffe, P. A., & Pfeiffer, S. I. (1996). Measuring outcomes in residential treatment with the Devereux Scales of Mental Disorders. *Residential Treatment for Children and Youth, 13*(4), 83–91.

Lord, F. M., & Novick, M. R. (1968). *Statistical theories of mental test scores.* Reading, MA: Addison-Wesley.

Lyman, R. D., & Campbell, N. R. (1996). *Treating children and adolescents in residential and inpatient settings.* Thousand Oaks, CA: Sage.

Martin, D. W. (1991). *Doing psychology experiments* (3rd. ed.). Pacific Grove, CA: Brooks/Cole.

Naglieri, J. A., LeBuffe, P. A., & Pfeiffer, S. I. (1994). *Devereux SCALES OF MENTAL DISORDERS.* San Antonio, TX: Psychological Corporation.

National Alliance for the Mentally Ill. (1995). *Policy statement: Protection of human subjects in research.* [on-line]. Available Internet: http://www.nami.org/update/unitedprotect.html

Reddy, L. A., & Pfeiffer, S. I. (1997). Effectiveness of treatment foster care of children and adolescents: A review of outcome studies. *Journal of American Academy of Child and Adolescent Psychiatry, 36*(5), 581–588.

Rosenblatt, A., & Attkisson, C. C. (1993). Assessing outcomes for sufferers of severe mental disorders: A conceptual framework and review. *Evaluation and Program Planning, 16,* 347–364.

Sechrest, L. (1979). Some neglected problems in evaluation research: Strength and integrity of treatments. In L. Sechrest, S. G. West, M. A. Phillips, R. Redner, & W. Yeaton (Eds.), *Evaluation studies review annual* (Vol. 4). Thousand Oaks, CA: Sage.

Wholey, J. S. (1987). Evaluability assessment: Developing program theory. In L. Bickman (Ed.), *Using program theory in evaluation* (pp. 77–92). New Directions for Evaluation, no. 33. San Francisco: Jossey-Bass.

Yates, B. T. (1996). *Analyzing costs, procedures, processes, and outcomes in human services.* Thousand Oaks, CA: Sage.

Yeaton, W. H. (1985). Using measures of treatment strength and integrity in planning research. In D. S. Cordray (Ed.), *Utilizing prior research in evaluation planning* (pp. 49–61). New Directions for Testing and Measurement, no. 27. San Francisco: Jossey-Bass.

Chapter Eight

Achenbach, T. M. (1991). *Manual for the youth self-report and 1991 profile.* Burlington: University of Vermont, Department of Psychiatry.

Bengen-Seltzer, B. (1999). Nine tips for improving staff buy-in on outcomes. *Outcomes and Accountability Alert, 4*(3), 2–5.

Betters, J., Shea-Clauson, L., Daniel, M., & Varisco, A. (1998). *Alternative placement: The path of success.* Unpublished manuscript.

Busk, P. L., & Serlin, R. C. (1992). Meta-analysis for single-case research. In T. R. Kratochwill & J. R. Levin (Eds.), *Single-case research design and analysis* (pp. 187–212). Mahwah, NJ: Erlbaum.

Cohen, J. (1988). *Statistical power analyses for the behavioral sciences* (Rev. ed.). Mahwah, NJ: Erlbaum.

Davies, A. R., Doyle, M. A., Lansky, D., Rutt, W., Stevic, M. O., & Doyle, J. B. (1994). Outcomes assessment in clinical settings: A consensus statement on principles and best practices in project management. *Joint Commission Journal on Quality Improvement, 20,* 6–16.

Green, R. S., & Newman, F. L. (1996). Criteria for selecting instruments for treatment outcome assessment. *Residential Treatment for Children and Youth, 13*(4), 29–48.

Joint Commission on Accreditation of Healthcare Organizations. (1993). *The measurement mandate: On the road to performance improvement in health care.* Oakbrook Terrace, IL: Author.

Jurmain, M., & Jurmain, R. (1999). *Baby think it over.* Eau Claire, WI: Baby Think It Over, Inc.

Kiresuk, T. J. (1973). Goal attainment scaling at a county mental health service. *Evaluation, 1,* 12–18.

Newcomer, K. E. (1994). Using statistics appropriately. In J. S. Wholey, H. P. Hatry, & K. E. Newcomer (Eds.), *Handbook of practical program evaluation* (pp. 389–416). San Francisco: Jossey-Bass.

Norusis, M. J. (1988). *The SPSS guide to data analysis.* Chicago: SPSS.

Ogles, B. M., Lambert, M. J., & Masters, K. S. (1996). *Assessing outcome in clinical practice.* Needham Heights, MA: Allyn & Bacon.

Pfeiffer, S. I., Soldivera, S., & Norton, J. (1992). *A consumer's guide to mental health treatment outcome measures.* Villanova, PA: Devereux, Institute of Clinical Training and Research.

Reddy, L. A. (1995, October). *A practitioner's guide to developing and implementing treatment outcome evaluations.* Paper presented to the Pennsylvania Psychological Association, Harrisburg.

Reddy, L. A., & Pfeiffer, S. I. (1996, September-October). Treatment outcome assessment with adolescent substance abusers: Conceptual and practical considerations. *Counselor, 14*(5), 25–29.

Wilkinson, L., Blank, G., & Gruber, C. (1996). *Desktop data analysis with Systat.* Upper Saddle River, NJ: Prentice Hall.

Chapter Nine

Hernandez, M., & Hodges, S. (1996). *The ecology of outcomes.* Tampa: University of South Florida, Florida Mental Health Institute, Department of Child and Family Studies, System Accountability Project for Children's Mental Health.

Kaplan, H. (1988). *Synapses of psychiatry: Behavioral sciences/clinical psychiatry.* Baltimore: Williams & Wilkins.

McManus, C. (1999). Accountability is the future of managed behavioral health: The evolution of public sector managed care and its implications for providers. *Open Minds, 11*(6), 3–4.

Packard, T. (1995). TQM and organizational change and development. In B. Gummer & P. McCallion (Eds.), *Total quality management in the social services: Theory and practice* (pp. 209–228). Albany: Professional Development Program of Rockefeller College, State University of New York.

The Authors

HOWARD A. SAVIN is senior vice president and chief clinical officer of the Devereux Foundation—a nationwide, nonprofit network of treatment programs for individuals with emotional and developmental needs. He also directs Devereux's Institute of Clinical Training and Research (ICTR). Savin's office is located at Devereux's headquarters in Villanova, Pennsylvania. Savin received his bachelor's degree in psychology from the University of Vermont, a master's degree in general theoretical psychology from the University of Bridgeport, and his doctorate in psychology at the University of Georgia.

A clinical psychologist with twenty years of practice in the fields of child and adolescent and medical psychology, Savin is responsible for the overall quality and development of Devereux programs, coordination of research and demonstration activities throughout the national network, and leadership of the organization's doctoral internship program in psychology, which is accredited by the American Psychological Association.

A pioneer in the managed behavioral health care arena, Savin cofounded a multisite group practice in suburban Philadelphia that evolved to become Achievement and Guidance Centers of America (AGCA)—a managed behavioral health care company. Through several mergers and acquisitions, AGCA became a part of Merck and then Merit Behavioral Healthcare Corporation. During these transitions, Savin served in senior management positions. Prior to coming to Devereux, he was president and senior consultant for Behavior Healthcare Solutions, focusing on the development of clinical operating systems, product development, and marketing support.

Savin is married, has two sons, and resides in New Hope, Pennsylvania. He has written and presented in the areas of managed mental health care, quality and accountability, and clinical psychology. A member of numerous professional organizations such as the American Psychological Association, Pennsylvania Psychological Association, and the American College of Mental Health Administration, Savin is listed as a health service provider in psychology in the National Register of Health Care Providers in Psychology.

SUSAN SOLDIVERA KIESLING is the national quality improvement coordinator for Devereux. She is responsible for facilitating and monitoring Devereux's National Quality Improvement program. In her role, she was instrumental in developing and integrating a quality indicator measurement tool into the routine operation of all Devereux programs. This tool is featured in the *Institute of Behavioral Healthcare Sourcebook* and in "Preventing Adverse Events in Behavioral Health Care," a publication of the Joint Commission on the Accreditation of Healthcare Organizations. The tool is designed to enable programs to measure their performance in various functional areas such as medication errors, use of seclusion and restraints, incidence of restraint-related injury, and treatment outcome.

Kiesling leads the Best Practices Bureau—a program that serves as a vehicle to bring internally recognized experts together to develop practice guidelines for the treatment of specific populations based on the research base and experience. She has recently facilitated a Best Practices Workgroup for the treatment of children and adolescents with major depression and serves on the task forces for suicide prevention and intervention and for the revision of major risk event policy and procedures. She is also on the leadership committee for guiding Devereux's outcomes initiative, which is designed to support Devereux's movement to become a more data-driven organization.

Prior to assuming her position as QI coordinator, Kiesling worked as a research assistant on a federally funded, three-year research and demonstration grant to develop a training curriculum to teach mental health and education professionals the skills and knowledge essential to effective collaboration.

Kiesling is a graduate of Drew University and received her master's degree in education from the University of Pennsylvania. She has presented at numerous conferences, including the Albert E. Trieschman Clinical Technologies Conference, the Child Welfare League of America, the Institute for Behavioral Healthcare, the National Association for Healthcare Quality, and the American Psychological Association; she addressed such topics as treatment outcome, interagency collaboration, and quality improvement.

Kiesling lives in Pennsylvania with her husband.

Index

C

P

Q